Elbert County Georgia

Court *of* Ordinary

Record *of* Apprentices
- 1867-1903 -

(Volume #1)

Compiled by:
Michael A. Ports

Southern Historical Press, Inc.
Greenville, South Carolina

Copyright 2020
By: Michael A. Ports

All rights reserved. No part of this publication may be reproduced, stored in a retrieval system, transmitted in any form, posted on to the web in any form or by any means without the prior written permission of the publisher.

Please direct all correspondence and orders to:

www.southernhistoricalpress.com
or
SOUTHERN HISTORICAL PRESS, Inc.
PO BOX 1267
375 West Broad Street
Greenville, SC 29601
southernhistoricalpress@gmail.com

ISBN #0-89308-030-6

Printed in the United States of America

Introduction

On December 10, 1790, the Georgia General Assembly created Elbert County from a portion of Wilkes County, making Elberton the seat of its new Government. Portions of Elbert County were taken to establish Madison County in 1811 and Hart County in 1853. During the period covered by the following records, the powers of the Court of Ordinary were vested in an Ordinary, who was the ex officio clerk. The court had jurisdiction over all probate matters, including apprenticeships, subject to an appeal to the Superior Court.

The following transcription is taken from the microfilm photographed on March 16, 1960 at the courthouse in Elberton by the Genealogical Society of Salt Lake City, Utah, and available at the Georgia Archives in Morrow, Georgia. The heading on the microfilm reads

Elbert County
State of Georgia

Court of Ordinary
Record of Apprentices
1867 - 1903

Index

The records primarily consist of copies of the indentures of apprenticeship, essentially the contracts binding the apprentice to the master. The indentures provide the date and term of the apprenticeship, and the names of the apprentice, the master, the person authorizing the indenture, usually a parent, guardian, next of kin, the ordinary, or judge, as well as witnesses. The indentures also specify the duties and responsibilities of both the apprentice and master.

The original record volume contains an index arranged alphabetically only the name of the apprentice. A complete full-name index follows the transcription. The reader should know that a lone surname in the index indicates that no first name appears in the record, for example Mr. Smith, Smith & Company, or said Smith. An index entry such as Smith, ___ indicates that a first name was entered, but has been obscured by an ink blot, smear, tear, or other imperfection. Similarly, an index entry such as ___. Cynthia indicates that either no surname was entered, or the surname is obliterated. The pages of the original record volume are numbered. The numbers between brackets, for example [163], are the original page numbers and are placed in the upper right hand corner of each original page.

Due to the size of the original record book, the following transcription includes the first 266 pages of the original volume.

W. H. Edwards, E. B. Tate, Jr., James A. Andrew, George L. Almond, and James J. Burch served as ordinary during the period covered by the transcription. R. M. Willis, Clerk of the Superior Court, served as Acting Ordinary briefly in 1897. The records apparently contain no original signatures, except of course those of the ordinary.

For the most part, their handwriting is legible, and the quality of the microfilm is good, making the reading and transcription process straightforward and not too difficult, although several of the microfilm images are faint, blurred, or dark. The occasional ink blot, smear, or other imperfection is noted within brackets, for example [blot] or [faint]. The transcription follows Sperry's recommended guidelines for reading early American handwriting.[1] Generally, the transcription maintains the overall format of the minutes, but presents the case citations, jury panels, and other court proceedings in a standard and consistent format. No grammar or spelling errors are corrected in the transcription, although a few commas, semicolons, apostrophes, and periods are added for clarity. The clerks entered a vertical squiggly line to delineate case citations, affidavit and petition headings, and signature citations, replicated by the symbol } in the transcription.

Sometimes the clerk formed the letters "a" and "o" in a very similar manner, making abbreviations like Jas. and Jos. and surnames Bagg and Bogg or Shannan and Shannon difficult to distinguish. At other times, the letters "a" and "u" are too similar to differentiate such names as Barden and Burden or Barnett and Burnett. At still other times, the clerk failed to dot the letter "i," making the name Silman appear to be Selman. In a similar manner, the names Edmond and Edmund can be difficult to distinguish. The formation of the letters "n" and "r" at the end of surnames sometimes appear to be the same. Invariably, the formation of the capital letters "I" and "J" are identical. Determining which letter usually not difficult when the first letter of a name, but almost entirely a guess when an initial. The clerk often crossed the letter "t" by extending the horizontal line across the entire word, making it difficult to distinguish between such surnames as Watters and Walters. Compounding the problem, he sometimes neglected to cross any "t" in a word, making a "t" appear to be an "l," and making it difficult to distinguish Garrett from Garrell, Walter from Waller, or Motes from Moles. The letters "L" and "S" can be difficult to distinguish, confusing such names as Landers and

---

[1] Sperry, Kip, *Reading Early American Handwriting.* Genealogical Publishing Company, Baltimore, Maryland, Sixth Printing, 2008.

Sanders. Careful researchers will consult the original record or the microfilm copy to either confirm the transcription or formulate an alternative interpretation of the clerk's handwriting.

The book is dedicated to the memory of William Blake, John and Martha (Moon) Blake, Jacob and Caty Eberhart, David and Susannah (Griffith) Eberhart, James and Isabella (Rhea) McCleskey, William and Sarah Moon, William and Margaret (Harbin) Suttle, Isaac and Sarah Suttle, and Samuel and Elizabeth (Patton) Wood, all early residents of Elbert County and just a few of the author's numerous Georgia ancestors. Many thanks are offered to the kind, patient, and generous staff of the Georgia Archives, for their assistance and suggestions, not only in locating the original records, but in understanding their historical context. Thanks also are offered LaBruce Lucas of the Southern Historical Press for his sage professional advice and counsel. Special thanks are offered to the author's late mother, Ouida J. Ports, who inspired and encouraged her son's interest in history and genealogy.

Record of Apprentices

Indentures. Robert Daniel To Allen C. Daniel, 1867 [27]

State of Georgia }
Elbert County } This Indenture, made this 15th day of July 1867, between W. H. Edwards, Ordinary of Said County, And Robert Daniel, a colored Illegitimate boy, by the Consent of his mother Mary, former Slave of Allen C. Daniel, being of the age eleven years, all said State and County, of the one part, and Allen C. Daniel, of the same State and County, of the other part. Witnesseth: that the said Ordinary does bind out the above named Illegitimate boy to Said Allen C. Daniel, of said County, as an apprentice to him as a laborer on the farm, to be taught the art of Farming, and to live with, Continue, and Serve the Said Allen C. Daniel as an apprentice from the date hereof during and for the full Space and term of Ten years, during all of which time, the said W. H. Edwards, Ordinary, doth Covenant with with Said Daniel that the above named Robert Daniel Shall well and faithfully Demean himself as such apprentice, obeying and observing fully the Commands of said Allen C. Edwards, And in all things deporting and behaving himself as a faithful apprentice, neither revealing his Secrets, nor at any time leaving or neglecting his business. And for and in Consideration of the Service well and faithfully as aforesaid by said apprentice of the first part, Allen C. Daniel, of the Second part, doth covenant, promise, and agree to instruct his Said apprentice or otherwise cause him to be well and faithfully instructed in the art of farming, and also to read English, and Shall also allow, furnish, and provide his Said apprentice with meat, drink, and Clothing during the said Term, and all other necessaries meet and proper in Sickness and in health, and Shall also at the expiration of Said term allow to Said apprentice a common Horse, bridle, & saddle and Two suits of good Clothing, to be by him given and paid to said Robert Daniel by him, the Said Allen C. Daniel, of the second part.

Witness our hands and Seals the day and year above written in presence of

J. A. Trensard }	W. H. Edwards
Amos L. Vail, J. P. }	A. C. Daniel

The within filed in the Ordinary's office of Elbert County the 15th Jany 1867.

                                            W. H. Edwards, Ordinary

Revenue Stamp 5 Cents

Louisa Grogan (Col) To John H. Grogan, 1871 [28]

State of Georgia }
Elbert County } This Indenture, made this 17th day of May 1871, between E. B. Tate, Jr, Ordinary of said County, And Louisa Grogan, Colored, being of the age of nine years and nine months, all of said State and County, of the one part, and John H. Grogan, of the Same State and County, of the other part. Witnesseth: that the said Ordinary does bind out the above named Louisa Grogan (Col) to John H. Grogan, of Said County, as an apprentice to him as a house Servant and to live with, continue, and Serve the said John H. Grogan as an apprentice from the date hereof for and during the full Space and term of Eleven years & three months, during all of which time the Said E. B. Tate, Jnr, Ordinary, doth covenant with said John H. Grogan that the above named Louisa Grogan (Col) Shall well and faithfully demean herself as Said apprentice, obeying and observing fully the Commands of said John H. Grogan, and in all things deporting and behaving herself as a faithful apprentice, neither revealing his Secrets, nor at any time leaving or neglecting his business. And for and in consideration of the Service well and faithfully as aforesaid by said apprentice of the first part, John H. Grogan, of Second part, doth Covenant, promise, and agree to instruct his said apprentice, or otherwise cause her to be well and faithfully instructed, in the art of House Keeping, And also to read and write the English language an in the Common rules of arithmetic, and Shall also allow, furnish, and provide his Said apprentice with meat and drink and Clothing during the said Term, and all other necessaries meet and proper, in Sickness and in health, and Shall also, at the expiration of said term, allow to Said apprentice the sum of Fifty dollars and Two Suits of good Clothing to be by him given to Louisa [smear] Grogan (col) by him, the said John H. Grogan, of the Second part. Given in duplicate. Witness our hands and Seals the day and year above written, in presence of

Ezekiah Bailey }	E. B. Tate, Jr, Ordinary
H. J. Goss, J. P. }	John H. Grogan

Filed in the office of the Ordinary of Elbert County May 17th 1871.

E. B. Tate, Jr, Ordinary

Recorded August 18th 1876.

J. A. Andrew, Ordinary

Fill Dickerson (col) To David Roebuck, col, 1872 [29]

State of Georgia }
Elbert County } This Indenture, made this 31st day of October 1872, between E. B. Tate, Jr, Ordinary, and Fill Dickerson (col) being of the age of Fourteen years, all of said State and County, of the one part, David Roebuck (col), of the same State and County, of the other part. Witnesseth: that the said Ordinary does bind out the above named Fill Dickerson (Col) to David Roebuck (col), of Said County, as an apprentice to him as a laborer on the farm, to be taught the art of farming, and to live with, Continue, And Serve the Said David Roebuck (col) as an apprentice, from the date hereof for and during the full Space and term of Seven years, during all of which time the said E. B. Tate, Jr, Ordinary, doth covenant with Said David Roebuck (Col) that the above named Fill Dickerson (col) Shall well and faithfully demean himself as such apprentice, obeying and observing fully the Commands of said David Roebuck (col)m and in all things deporting and behaving himself as a faithful apprentice, neither revealing his Secrets, nor at any time leaving or neglecting his business. And for and in Consideration of the Service well and faithfully as aforesaid by said apprentice of the first part, David Roebuck (col0, of the second part, doth covenant, promise, and agree to instruct his Said apprentice, or otherwise cause him to be well and faithfully instructed, in the art of farming, and also to read and write the English language, and in the Common rules of arithmetic, and Shall also allow, furnish, and provide his Said apprentice with meat and Drink and Clothing during the said term, and all other necessaries meet and proper, in Sickness and in health, and Shall also, at the expiration of said term, allow to Said apprentice the sum of one hundred dollars and two Suits of good Clothing, to be by him given and paid to Fill Dickerson (Col) by him the said David Roebuck (Col) of the Second part.

Witness our hands and Seals the day and year above written, in the presence of

N. M. Brown } E. B. Tate, Jr, Ordinary
Thos M. Swift, Com Not } David X Roebuck, his mark
Pub & Ex off J. P. }

Recorded Aug 18th 1876.

J. A. Andrew, Ordinary

Wade Dickerson (col) To David Roebuck, 1872. [30]

State of Georgia }
Elbert County } This Indenture, made this 31st day of October 1872, between

E. B. Tate, J^r, Ordinary, and Wade Dickerson, (Col), being of the age of Twelve years, all of Said State and County, of the one part, and David Roebuck (col), of the Same State and County, of the other part. Witnesseth: that the said Ordinary does bind out the above named Wade Dickerson (col) to David Roebuck (Col), of Said County, as an apprentice to him as a laborer on the farm, to be taught the art of farming, and to live with, Continue, and Serve the said David Roebuck (col) as an apprentice from the date hereof for and during the full Space and term of Nine years, during all of which time, the Said E. B. Tate, J^r, Ordinary, doth Covenant with Said David Roebuck (col) that the above named Wade Dickerson (Col) Shall well and faithfully demean himself as such apprentice, obeying and observing fully the Commands of said David Dickerson (col), and in all things deporting and behaving himself as a faithful apprentice, neither revealing his Secrets, nor at any time leaving or neglecting his business. and for and in Consideration of the Service well and faithfully as aforesaid by said apprentice of the first part, David Roebuck (col) of the second part doth covenant, promise, and agree to instruct his said apprentice, or otherwise cause him to be well and faithfully instructed, in the art of farming, and also to read and write the English language, and in the Common rules of arithmetic, and Shall also allow, furnish, and provide his said apprentice with meat and drink and Clothing during the Said Term, and all other necessaries meet and proper, in Sickness and in health, and Shall also, at the expiration of Said term, allow to Said apprentice the Sum of One hundred dollars and two Suits of Good Clothing, to be by him given and paid to Wade Dickerson (col) by him the Said David Roebuck (col), of the Second part.

Witness our hands and Seals the day and year above written, in the presence of

N. M. Brown   }   E. B. Tate, J^r, Ordinary
Thos M. Swift, Com Not }   David X Roebuck, his mark
Pub & Ex off J. P.   }

Recorded Aug 18th 1876.

J. A. Andrew, Ordinary

Lucy Henry, Col To City Christian, col, 1872   [31]

State of Georgia }
Elbert County   } This Indenture, made this 2nd day of December 1872, between Martha Henry and Lucy Henry, col, her daughter, being of the age of Two years, both of Said County, of the one part, and City Christian, col, of the Same County, of the other part. Witnesseth: that the said Lucy Henry does by the consent of the said Martha Henry bind herself out to the Said City Christian to be taught the art

of House keeping and farming, And to live with, Continue, And Serve said City Christian as an apprentice from the date hereof for and during the full Space or term of Sixteen years, During all which time, the Said Martha Henry doth covenant with the Said City Christian that the Said Lucy Henry shall well and faithfully demean herself as such an apprentice, obeying and observing fully the commands of the said City Christian, and in all things deporting and behaving herself as a faithful apprentice to her, the said City Christian, neither revealing her Secrets, nor at any time leaving nor neglecting the business of the Said City Christian. And for and in consideration of the sum of one dollar to her, the said Martha Henry, in hand paid, the receipt whereof is hereby acknowledged, the said City Christian doth covenant, promise, and agree to teach and instruct her said apprentice, or otherwise cause her to be well and sufficiently instructed, in the said art of House Keeping and farming, and to read and write, and the common rules of Arithmetic, and shall also allow, furnish, and provide her said apprentice with meat and drink and Clothing during the said term, and all other necessaries meet and proper, in Sickness and in health, and also shall at the expiration of the said term allow to the said apprentice the sum of One hundred dollars to be by her to the said Lucy Henry paid in Cash.

Witness our hands and Seals the day and year above written, in presence of

W. B. Henry   }   Martha X Henry, col, her mark
E. B. Tate, J^r, Ordinary }   City X Christian, Col, her mark

Recorded Aug 18th 1876.

                                              J. A. Andrew, Ordinary

James Jones (Col) To Enoch W. Bell, 1873   [32]

State of Georgia }
Elbert County   } This Indenture, made this 18th day of October 1873, between James A. Andrew, Ordinary, and James Jones (col), being of the age Three years, all of said State and County, of the one part, and E. W. Bell, of the Same State and County, of the other part. Witnesseth: that the said Ordinary does bind out the above named James Jones to E. W. Bell, of Said County, as an apprentice to him as a laborer on the farm, to be taught the art of farming, and to live with, continue, and Serve the Said E. W. Bell as an apprentice from the date hereof for and during the full Space and term of Twelve years, during all of which time the said James A. Andrew, Ordinary, doth Covenant with said E. W. Bell that the above James Jones Shall well and faithfully demean himself as such apprentice in all things, deporting and behaving himself as a faithful apprentice, neither

revealing his Secrets, nor at any time leaving or neglecting his business. And for and in Consideration of the Service well and faithfully as aforesaid by said apprentice of the first part, E. W. Bell, of the Second part, doth covenant, promise, and agree to instruct his Said apprentice, or otherwise cause him to be well and faithfully instructed, in the art of farming, and also to read the English language, and shall also allow, furnish, and provide his said apprentice with meat and drink and Clothing during the said term, and all other necessaries meet and proper, in Sickness and in health, and shall also, at the expiration of said term, allow to said apprentice the sum of One hundred dollars and Two Suits of good Clothing, to be by him given and paid to James Jones, col, by him the said E. W. Bell, of the Second part.

Witness our hands and Seals the day and year above written, in presence of

J. A. Sanders }
Wm T. Vanduzer }
Judge c. c. E. C. }

James A. Andrew, Ordinary
E. W. Bell

Filed in office October 18th 1876.

James A. Andrew, Ordinary

Recorded August 21st 1876.

James A. Andrew, Ordinary

Henraetta Tenant (col) To Rolan J. Brown, 1873 [33]

State of Georgia }
Elbert County } This Indenture, made this 31st day of May 1873, between Jane Tenant, a Colored woman, and her child named Henraetta, Said Child being of the age of Five years, all of said State and County, of the one part, and Rolan J. Brown, of the same State and County, of the other part. Witnesseth: the said Jane Tenant does bind out the above named Henraetta, minor child, to Said Rolan J. Brown, of said County, as an apprentice to him as a laborer on the farm, to be taught the art of farming and House Service, and to live with, Continue, and Serve the Said Rolan J. Brown as an apprentice, from the date hereof for and during the full Space and term of Twelve years, during all of which time the Said Jane Tenant doth Covenant with said Rolan J. Brown that the above named Henraetta shall well and faithfully demean herself as such apprentice, obeying and observing fully the Commands of said Rolan J. Brown, and in all things deporting and behaving herself as a faithful apprentice, neither revealing his Secrets, nor at any time

leaving or neglecting his business. And for and in consideration of the Service well and faithfully as aforesaid by said apprentice of the first part, Rolan J. Brown, of the Second part, doth Covenant, promise, and agree to instruct his Said apprentice, or otherwise cause her to be well and faithfully instructed, in the art of farming & House Service, and also to read the English language, and Shall also allow, furnish, and provide his said apprentice with meat and drink and clothing during the Said term, and all necessaries meet and proper, in Sickness and in health, and Shall also, at the expiration of said term, allow to Said apprentice the sum of one hundred dollars and Two Suits of good Clothing to be by him given and paid to her by him, the said Rolan J. Brown, of the second part.

Witness our hands and Seals the day and year above written, in presence of

Jack X Gaines, his mark }   Jane X Tenant, her mark
J. O. Maxwell, N. P. Officio J. P. }   R. J. X Brown, his mark

Filed in office August 22nd 1873.

                                      James A. Andrew, Ordinary

Recorded August 21st 1876.

                                      James A. Andrew, Ordinary

Wilson Hulme, Col To William T. Davis, 1874   {34}

State of Georgia }
Elbert County } This Indenture, made this 23rd day of November 1874, between James A. Andrew, Ordinary, and Wilson Hulme (Col), being of the age of Sixteen years, all of said State and County, of the first part, and William T. Davis, of the same State and County, of the other part. Witnesseth: that the said Ordinary does bind out the above named Wilson Hulme to William T. Davis, of said County, as an apprentice to Serve him as a laborer on the farm, to be taught the art of farming, And to live with, Continue, and Serve the Said William T. Davis as an apprentice, from the date hereof for and during the full Space and term of Five years, during all of which time the said James A. Andrew, Ordinary, doth covenant with Said William T. Davis that the above named Wilson Hulme Shall well and faithfully demean himself as such apprentice, obeying and observing fully the Commands of said William T. Davis, and in all things deporting and behaving himself as a faithful apprentice, neither revealing his Secrets, nor at any time leaving or neglecting his business. And for and in Consideration of the Service well and faithfully as aforesaid by Said apprentice

of the first part, William T. Davis, of the Second part, doth Covenant, promise, and agree to instruct his said apprentice, or otherwise cause him to be well and faithfully instructed, in the art of farming, and also to read English, Shall also allow, furnish, and provide his said apprentice with meat and drink and Clothing during the Said term, and all other necessaries meet and proper, in Sickness and in health. And Shall also, at the expiration of Said Term, allow to said apprentice the sum of one hundred dollars and Two Suits of good Clothing to be by him given and paid to Wilson Hulme by him, the said William T. Davis, of the second part.

Witness our hands and Seals the day and year above written, in presence of

W. M. Haslett   }   James A. Andrew, Ordinary
H. A. Roebuck, J. P. }   W. T. Davis

Filed in office Nov 23rd 1874.

J. A. Andrew, Ordinary

Recorded August 21st 1876.

J. A. Andrew, Ordinary

Oliver Hulme (Col) To John M. Maxwell, 1874   [35]

State of Georgia }
Elbert County   } This Indenture, made this 23rd day of November 1874, between James A. Andrew, Ordinary, and Oliver Hulme (col), being of the age of Fourteen years, all of said State and County, of the one part, and John M. Maxwell, of the same State and County, of the other part. Witnesseth: that the said Ordinary does bind out the above named Oliver Hulme to John M. Maxwell, of said County, as an apprentice to him as a laborer on the farm, to be taught the art of farming, and to live with, Continue, and Serve the said John M. Maxwell as an apprentice, from the date hereof for and during the full Space and term of Seven years, during all of which time the said James A. Andrew, Ordinary, doth Covenant with said John M. Maxwell that the above named Oliver Hulme shall well and faithfully demean himself as such apprentice, obeying and observing fully the Commands of said John M. Maxwell, and in all things deporting and behaving himself as a faithful apprentice, neither revealing his Secrets, nor at any time leaving or neglecting his business. And for and in Consideration of the Service well and faithfully as aforesaid by said apprentice of the first part, John M. Maxwell, of the second part, doth Covenant, promise, and agree to instruct his said apprentice, or

otherwise cause him to be well and faithfully instructed, in the art of farming, and also to read English. And Shall also allow, furnish, and provide his said apprentice with meat and drink and clothing during the Said term, and all other necessaries meet and proper, in Sickness and in health, and Shall also, at the expiration of said term, allow to Said apprentice the sum of One hundred dollars and two Suits of good Clothing, to be by him given and paid to Oliver Hulme by him the said John M. Maxwell, of the Second part.

Witness our hands and Seals the day and year above written, in presence of

W. M. Haslett   }   J. A. Andrew, Ordinary E. C.
H. A. Roebuck, J. P. }   John M. X Maxwell, his mark

Filed in office Nov 23nd 1874.

J. A. Andrew, Ordinary

Recorded August 21st 1876.

J. A. Andrew, Ordinary

Ella Mattox, Col To William H. Mattox, 1874   [36]

State of Georgia }
Elbert County   } This Indenture, made this 10th day of August 1874, between James A. Andrew, Ordinary of said County, & Ella Mattox, Colored, being of the age of Five years, all of said State and County, of the one part, and William H. Mattox, of the Said State and County, of the other part. Witnesseth: that the said Ordinary does bind out the above named Ella Mattox to William H. Mattox, of said County, as an apprentice to him as a laborer on the farm to be taught the art of House Keeping or house Service, and to live with, continue, and Serve the said William H. Mattox as an apprentice, from the date hereof for and during the full Space and term of Sixteen years, during all of which time, the said James A. Andrew, Ordinary, does covenant with said William H. Mattox that the above named Ella Mattox Shall well and faithfully demean herself as such apprentice, obeying and observing the Commands of said Wm H. Mattox, and in all things deporting and behaving herself as a faithful apprentice, neither revealing his Secrets, nor at any time leaving or neglecting his business. And for and in Consideration of the Service well and faithfully as aforesaid by said apprentice of the first part, William H. Mattox, of the Second part, doth Covenant, promise and agree to instruct his said apprentice, or otherwise cause her to be well and faithfully instructed, in the art of house service and also to read the English

language, and Shall also allow, furnish, and provide his said apprentice with meat and drink and Clothing during the said Term, and all other necessaries meet and proper, in Sickness and in health, and Shall also, at the Expiration of said term, allow to Said apprentice the Sum of one hundred dollars and Two Suits of good Clothing to be by him given and paid to Ella Mattox by him, the said William H. Mattox, of the second part.

Witness our hands and Seals the day and year above written, in presence of

E. B. Tate, J^r }	Wm H. Mattox
Wm T. Vanduzer }	John M. X Maxwell, his mark
Judge, C. C. E. C. }	

Filed in office of Ordinary of Elbert County August 10th 1874.

J. A. Andrew, Ordinary

Recorded August 22nd 1876.

J. A. Andrew, Ordinary

Loucinda Hulme, Col To George Brown (Col), 1874 [37]

State of Georgia }
Elbert County } This Indenture, made this 22nd day of September 1874, between J. A. Andrew, Ordinary, and Loucinda Hulme (col), being of the age of Twelve years, all of said State and County, of the one part, and George Brown, Col, of the same State and County, of the other part. Witnesseth, that the said Ordinary does bind out the above named Loucinda Hulme (Col) to George Brown (col), of said County, as an apprentice to him as a laborer on the farm, to be taught the art of farming & house service, and to live with, continue, and Serve the said George Brown, Col, as an apprentice from the date hereof for and during the full space and term of Six years, during all of which time, the said J. A. Andrew, Ordinary, doth Covenant with Said George Brown (Col) that the above named Loucinda Hulme (Col) Shall well and faithfully demean herself as such apprentice, obeying and observing fully the Commands of Said George Brown (Col), and in all thing deporting and behaving herself as a faithful apprentice, neither revealing his Secrets, nor at any time leaving or neglecting his business. And for and in consideration of the Service well and faithfully as aforesaid by said apprentice of the first part, George Brown, Col, of the Second part, doth Covenant, promise, and agree to instruct his Said apprentice, or otherwise cause her to be well and faithfully instructed, in the art of farming & House Service, and also to

read English, and shall also allow, furnish, and provide his said apprentice with meat and drink and clothing during the said term, and all other necessaries meet and proper, in sickness and in health, and Shall also, at the Expiration of said term, allow to Said apprentice the sum of One hundred dollars and Two Suits of good Clothing to be by him given and paid to Loucinda Hulme, Col, by him, the said George W. Hulme, Col, of the Second part.

Witness our hands and Seals the day and year above written, in presence of

Wm T. Vanduzer }
Judge C. C. E. C. }
W. M. McIntosh }

J. A. Andrew, Ordinary
George X Brown, his mark

Recorded August 22nd 1876.

J. A. Andrew, Ordinary

Jefferson Davis (Col) To James M. Maxwell, 1874 [38]

State of Georgia }
Elbert County } This Indenture, made this 22nd day of July 1874, between James A. Andrew, Ordinary of said County, and Jefferson Davis (Col), being of the age of Ten years, all of said State and County of the one part, and James M. Maxwell, of the Same State and County, of the other part. Witnesseth: that the said Ordinary does bind out the above named Jefferson Davis (Col) to James M. Maxwell, of said County, as an apprentice to him as a laborer on the farm, to be taught the art of farming, and to live with, Continue, and serve the said James M. Maxwell as an apprentice from the date hereof for and during the full Space and term of Elven years, during all of which time, the said J. A. Andrew, Ordinary, doth covenant with said James M. Maxwell that the above named Jefferson Davis (col) Shall well and faithfully demean himself as such apprentice, obeying and observing fully the Commands of said James M. Maxwell, and in all things deporting and behaving himself as a faithful apprentice, neither revealing his Secrets, nor at any time leaving or neglecting his business. And for and in Consideration of the Service well and faithfully as aforesaid by said apprentice of the first part, James M. Maxwell of the second part doth Covenant, promise, and agree to instruct his Said apprentice, or otherwise cause him to be well and faithfully instructed, in the art of farming, and also to read the English language, and Shall also allow, furnish and provide his Said apprentice with meat and drink and clothing during the Said term, and all the necessaries meet and proper, in Sickness and in health, and Shall also, at the expiration of Said term, allow to Said apprentice the sum of One hundred dollars and two Suits of good clothing, to be

by him given and paid to Jefferson Davis (Col) by him the said James M. Maxwell, of the Second part.

Witness our hands and Seals the day and year above written, in presence of

E. B. Tate, J^r }	James A. Andrew, Ordinary
Wm T. Vanduzer }	James M. X Maxwell, his mark
Judge, C. C. E. C. }	

Filed in office of Ordinary of Elbert County July 22nd 1874.

J. A. Andrew, Ordinary

Recorded August 22nd 1876.

J. A. Andrew, Ordinary

Reubin Turman (col) To James J. Fuller, 1874   [39]

State of Georgia }
Elbert County } This Indenture, made this 23rd day of March 1874, between James A. Andrew, Ordinary of said County, and Reubin Turman, Colored, being of the age of seven years, all of the said State and County, of the one part, and James J. Fuller, of the Same State and County, of the other part. Witnesseth: that the said Ordinary does bind out the above named Reubin Turman to James J. Fuller, of Said County, as an apprentice to him as a laborer on the farm, to be taught the art of farming, and to live with, continue, and Serve the Said James J. Fuller as an apprentice from the date hereof for and during the full Space and term of Fourteen years, during all of which time the said James A. Andrew, Ordinary, doth covenant with Said James J. Fuller that the above named Reubin Turman shall well and faithfully demean himself as such apprentice, obeying and observing fully the Commands of said James J. Fuller, and in all things deporting and behaving himself as a faithful apprentice, neither revealing his Secrets, nor at any time leaving or neglecting his business. And for and in Consideration of the Service well and faithfully as aforesaid by said apprentice of the first part, James J. Fuller, of the second part, doth covenant, promise, and agree to instruct his said apprentice, or otherwise cause him to be well and faithfully instructed, in the art of farming, and also to read the English language, and Shall also allow, furnish, and provide his said apprentice with meat and drink and Clothing during the said term, and all other necessaries meet and proper, in Sickness and in health, and Shall also, at the Expiration of said term, allow to Said apprentice the sum of One

hundred dollars and Two Suits of good clothing to be by him given and paid To Reubin Turman by him, the said James J. Fuller, of the Second part.

Witness our hands and Seals the day and year above written, in presence of

H. A. Roebuck, J. C^t }   James A. Andrew, Ordinary
John W. Turner   }   J. J. Fuller

Filed in office of Ordinary of Elbert County March 22rd 1874.

                                           James A. Andrew, Ordinary

Recorded August 22nd 1876.

                                           J. A. Andrew, Ordinary

Bob Eberhart, col To D. P. Oglesby, 1874   [40]

State of Georgia }
Elbert County   } This Indenture, made this 30th day of March 1874, between James A. Andrew, Ordinary of said County, and Bob Eberhart, Colored, being of the age of Six years, all of said State and County, of the one part, and Drury P. Oglesby, of the same State and County, of the other part. Witnesseth: that the said Ordinary does bind out the above named Bob Eberhart to Drury P. Oglesby, of Said County, as an apprentice to him as a laborer on the farm, to be taught the art of farming, and to live with, continue, and serve the said Drury P. Oglesby as an apprentice from the date hereof for and during the full Space and term of Fifteen years, during all of which time the said James A. Andrew, Ordinary, doth Covenant with said Drury P. Oglesby that the above named Bob Eberhart shall well and faithfully demean himself as such apprentice, obeying and observing fully the Commands of said Drury P. Oglesby, and in all things deporting and behaving himself as a faithful apprentice, neither revealing his secrets, nor at any time leaving or neglecting his business. And for and in Consideration of the Service well and faithfully as aforesaid by said apprentice of the first part, Drury P. Oglesby, of the Second part, doth covenant, promise, and agree to instruct his said apprentice, or otherwise cause him to be well and faithfully instructed, in the art of farming, and also to read the English language, and Shall also allow, furnish, and provide his said apprentice with meat and drink and Clothing during the said term, and all other necessaries meet and proper, in Sickness and in health, and Shall also, at the Expiration of said term, allow to Said apprentice the sum of One hundred dollars and Two Suits of good clothing to be by him given and paid to Bob Eberhart, col by him, the said Drury P. Oglesby, of the Second part.

Witness our hands and Seals the day and year above written, in presence of

J. P. Shannon }	James A. Andrew, Ordinary
H. A. Roebuck, J. P. }	D. P. Oglesby

Filed in office of Ordinary of Elbert County March 30th 1874.

James A. Andrew, Ordinary

Recorded August 22nd 1876.

J. A. Andrew, Ordinary

Fannie Sophia Brown, col To George Dye, Col, 1872   [41]

State of Georgia }
Elbert County   } This Indenture, made this 7th day of October 1872, between E. B. Tate, J^r, Ordinary, and Fannie Sophia Brown, colored, being of the age Six years, all of said State and County, of the one part, and George Dye, colored, of the same State and County, of the other part. Witnesseth: that the said Ordinary does bind out the above named Fannie Sophia Brown, col to George Dye, Col, of said County, as an apprentice to him as a laborer on the farm, to be taught the art of farming and house Keeping, and to live with, continue, and Serve the said George Dye, Col as an apprentice from the date hereof for and during the full Space and term of Twelve years, during all of which time the said E. B. Tate, J^r, Ordinary, doth Covenant with Said George Dye, Col that the above named Fannie Sophia Brown, Col Shall well and faithfully demean herself as such apprentice, obeying and observing fully the Commands of said George Dye, Col, and in all things deporting and behaving herself as a faithful apprentice, neither revealing his Secrets, nor at any time leaving or neglecting his business. And for and in consideration of the service well and faithfully as aforesaid by said apprentice of the first part, George Dye, Col, of the Second part, doth covenant, promise, and agree to instruct his Said apprentice, or otherwise cause her to be well and faithfully instructed, in the art of farming & house Keeping, and also to read and write the English language, and in the Common rules of arithmetic, and Shall also allow, furnish, and provide his Said apprentice with meat and drink and Clothing during the said term, and all other necessaries meet and proper, in Sickness and in health, and Shall also, at the expiration of said term, allow to Said apprentice the sum of one hundred dollars and Two Suits of good Clothing to be by him given and paid to Fannie Sophia Brown, col by him, the said George Dye, Col, of the second part.

Witness our hands and Seals the day and year above written, in presence of

Robert Hester }
H. A. Roebuck, J. P. }

E. B. Tate, J{r}, Ordinary
George X Dye, Col, his mark

Recorded August 23${rd}$ 1876.

J. A. Andrew, Ordinary

Pleasant Mattox, Col To W${m}$ H. Mattox, 1874 [42]

State of Georgia }
Elbert County } This Indenture, made this 10${th}$ day of August 1874, between James A. Andrew, Ordinary of said County, and Pleasant Mattox, Colored, being of the age of Sixteen years, all of said State and County, of the one part, and William H. Mattox, of the same State and County, of the other part. Witnesseth: that the Said Ordinary does bind out the above named Pleasant Mattox, Col to William H. Mattox, of said County, as an apprentice to him as a laborer on the farm, to be taught the art of farming, and to live with, continue, and Serve the said William H. Mattox as an apprentice from the date hereof for and during the full Space and term of Five years, during all of which time the said James A. Andrew, Ordinary, doth Covenant with said William H. Mattox that the above named Pleasant Mattox shall well and faithfully demean himself as such apprentice, obeying and observing fully the Commands of said W${m}$ H. Mattox, and in all things deporting and behaving himself as a faithful apprentice, neither revealing his Secrets, nor at any time leaving or neglecting his business. And for and in Consideration of the service well and faithfully as aforesaid by said apprentice of the first part, William H. Mattox, of the second part, doth covenant, promise, and agree to instruct his Said apprentice, or otherwise cause him to be well and faithfully instructed, in the art of farming, and also to read the English language, and shall also allow, furnish, and provide his said apprentice with meat and drink and Clothing during the said term, and all other necessaries meet and proper, in Sickness and in health, and Shall also, at the Expiration of said term, allow to said apprentice the sum of One hundred dollars and Two Suits of good clothing to be by him given and paid to Pleasant Mattox by him, the said William H. Mattox, of the Second part.

Witness our hands and Seals the day and year above written, in presence of

E. B. Tate, J${r}$ }
W${m}$ T. Vanduzer }

W. H. Mattox
James A. Andrew, Ordinary

Duplicate filed in office of Ordinary of Elbert County August 10th 1874.

J. A. Andrew, Ordinary

Recorded August 23rd 1876.

J. A. Andrew, Ordinary

John Hulme (col) To Wm T. Davis, 1874 [43]

State of Georgia }
Elbert County } This Indenture, made this 23rd day of November 1874, between J. A. Andrew, Ordinary, and John Hulme, col, being of the age of Twelve years, all of said State and County, of the one part, and William T. Davis, of the same State and County, of the other part. Witnesseth: that the said Ordinary does bind out the above named John Hulme, col to Wm T. Davis, of Said County, as an apprentice to him as a laborer on the farm, to be taught the art of farming, and to live with, Continue, and Serve the said William T. Davis as an apprentice from the date hereof for and during the full Space and term of Nine years, during all of which time the said J. A. Andrew, Ordinary, doth Covenant with Said William T. Davis that the above named John Hulme, col Shall well and faithfully demean himself as such apprentice, obeying and observing fully the Commands of Said Wm T. Davis, and in all things deporting and behaving himself as a faithful apprentice, neither revealing his Secrets, nor at any time leaving or neglecting his business. And for and in Consideration of the service well and faithfully as aforesaid by said apprentice of the first, Wm T. Davis, of the Second part, doth covenant, promise, and agree to instruct his said apprentice, or otherwise cause him to be well and faithfully instructed, in the art of farming, and also to read English, and Shall also allow, furnish, and provide his said apprentice with meat and drink and Clothing during the said term, and all other necessaries meet and proper, in Sickness and in health, and shall also, at the Expiration of said term, allow to said apprentice the sum of one hundred dollars and Two Suits of good Clothing to be by him given and paid to John Hulme, col by him, the said William T. Davis, of the second part.

Witness our hands and Seals the day and year above written, in presence of

| W. M. Haslett } | James A. Andrew, Ordinary |
| H. A. Roebuck, J. P. } | W. T. Davis |

Filed in office Nov 23rd 1874.

J. A. Andrew, Ordinary

Recorded August 23rd 1876.

J. A. Andrew, Ordinary

Jacob Henry To John D. James, 1874 [44]

State of Georgia }
Elbert County } This Indenture, made this 30th day of December 1874, between Harriet Henry and her son, Jacob Henry, being of the age of Ten years, all of said State and County, of the one part, and John D. James, of the same State and County, of the other part. Witnesseth: that the said Harriet Henry does bind out the above named Jacob Henry to John D. James, of said County, as an apprentice to him as a laborer on the farm, to be taught the art of farming, and to live with, Continue, and Serve the said John D. James as an apprentice from the date hereof for and during the full Space and term of Eleven years, during all of which time the said Harriet Henry doth covenant with Said John D. James that the above named Jacob Henry Shall well and faithfully demean himself as such apprentice, obeying and observing fully the Commands of said John D. James, and in all things deporting and behaving himself as a faithful apprentice, neither revealing his Secrets, nor at any time leaving or neglecting his business. And for and in Consideration of the Service well and faithfully as aforesaid by said apprentice, of the first part, John D. James, of the second part, doth Covenant, promise, and agree to instruct his said apprentice, or otherwise cause him to be well and faithfully instructed, in the art of farming, and also to read English, and Shall also allow, furnish, and provide his said apprentice with meat and drink and Clothing during the said term, and all other necessaries meet and proper, in Sickness and in health, and Shall also, at the Expiration of said term, allow to Said apprentice the sum of One hundred dollars and Two Suits of good Clothing to be by him given and paid to Jacob Henry, by him, the said John D. James, of the Second part.

Witness our hands and Seals the day and year above written, in presence of

James A. Andrew }
H. A. Roebuck, J. P. }

John D. James
Harriet X Henry, her mark

Filed in office December 30th 1874.

J. A. Andrew, Ordinary

Recorded August 23rd 1876.

J. A. Andrew, Ordinary

James Brawner, col To Willis McGehee, 1875 [45]

State of Georgia }
Elbert County } This Indenture, made this 10th day of July 1875, between James A. Andrew, Ordinary of Said County, and James Brawner, a person of Color, who has no parents residing in Said County, being the age of Six years, all of said State and County of the one part, and Willis McGehee, of the same State and County, of the other part. Witnesseth: that the said Ordinary does bind out the above named James Brawner to Willis McGehee, of said County, as an apprentice to him as a laborer on the farm, to be taught the art of farming, and to live with, continue, and Serve the said Willis McGehee as an apprentice from the date hereof, for and during the full Space and term of Fifteen years, during all of which time the said James A. Andrew, Ordinary, doth Covenant with said Willis McGehee that the above named James Brawner Shall well and faithfully demean himself as such apprentice, obeying and observing fully the Commands of said Willis McGehee, and in all things deporting and behaving himself as a faithful apprentice, neither revealing his Secrets, nor at any time leaving or neglecting his business. And for and in consideration of the Service well and faithfully as aforesaid by said apprentice of the first part, & Willis McGehee, of the second part, doth Covenant, promise, and agree to instruct his Said apprentice, or otherwise cause him to be well and faithfully instructed, in the art of farming, and also to read English, and Shall also allow, furnish, and provide his Said apprentice with meat and drink and Clothing during the said term, and all other necessaries meet and proper, in Sickness and in health, and Shall also, at the Expiration of said term, allow to Said apprentice the sum of One hundred dollars and two Suits of good clothing to be by him given and paid to James Brawner by him, the said Willis McGehee, of the second part.

Witness our hands and Seals the day and year above written, in presence of

T. A. Chandler, clk S. C. E. C. }   James A. Andrew, Ordinary E. C.
S. N. Carpenter, N. P. & Ex off J. P. }   Willis X McGehee

Filed in office of Ordinary of Elbert County July 10th 1875.

J. A. Andrew, Ordinary

Recorded August 23rd 1876.

J. A. Andrew, Ordinary

Henry T. Gray To Asa C. Fortson, 1875 [46]

State of Georgia }
Elbert County } This Indenture, made this the 25th day of January 1875, between Rese Gray, of said County, and Henry T. Gray, who has no means and is unable to Support himself, being of the age of Five years, all of said State and County, of the one part, And Asa C. Fortson, of the same State and County, of the other part. Witnesseth: that the said Rese Gray, father of the Said Henry T. Gray, does bind out the above named Henry T. Gray apprentice to the said Asa C. Fortson, of Said County, as an apprentice to him as a laborer on the farm, to be taught the art of farming, and to live with, Continue, and Serve the said Fortson as an apprentice from the date hereof for and during the full Space and term of Sixteen years. during all of which time the said Rese Gray doth Covenant with said Fortson that the above named Henry T. Gray shall well and faithfully demean himself as such apprentice, obeying and observing fully the Commands of the said Asa C. Fortson, and in all things deporting and behaving himself as a faithful apprentice, neither revealing his Secrets, nor at any time leaving or neglecting his business. And for and in Consideration of the Service well and faithfully as aforesaid by said apprentice of the first part, Asa C. Fortson, of the Second part, doth Covenant, promise, and agree to instruct his said apprentice, or otherwise cause him to be well and faithfully instructed, in the art of farming, and also to read and write the English language, and in the Common rules of arithmetic, and Shall also allow, furnish, and provide his Said apprentice with meat and drink and clothing during the said term, and all other necessaries meet and proper, in Sickness and in health, and Shall also, at the Expiration of Said term, allow to Said apprentice the sum of One hundred and twenty five Two Suits of good Clothing to be by him given and paid to Said Henry T. Gray by him, the said Asa C. Fortson, of the Second part.

Witness our hands and Seals the day and year above written, in presence of

W. T. Davis   }   Rese X Gray, his mark
A. J. Bond, J. P. }   Asa C. Fortson

Filed in office April 6th 1875.

                                                 J. A. Andrew, Ordinary

Recorded August 24th 1876.

                                                 J. A. Andrew, Ordinary

Georgia Brawner, col To Jn° C. Hudgens, 1875 [47]

State of Georgia }
Elbert County } This Indenture, made this the 29th day of March 1875, between Eliza Brawner, col and Georgia Brawner, col, being of the age of Five years, All of said State and County, of the one part, and John C. Hudgins, of the same State and County, of the other part. Witnesseth: that the said Eliza Brawner, Mother of the said Georgia Brawner, does bind out the above named Georgia Brawner to the said John C. Hudgins, of said County, as an apprentice to him as a laborer on the farm, to be taught the art of farming and house business. And to live with, Continue, and serve the said John C. Hudgins as an apprentice from the date Hereof for and during the full Space and term of Sixteen years, during all of which time the said Eliza Brawner doth covenant with the said John C. Hudgins that the above named Georgia Brawner Shall well and faithfully demean herself as such apprentice, obeying and observing fully the Commands of said John C. Hudgins, and in all things deporting and behaving herself as a faithful apprentice, neither revealing his Secrets, nor at any time leaving or neglecting his business. And for and in Consideration of the services well and faithfully as aforesaid by said apprentice of the first part, John C. Hudgins, of the second part, doth Covenant, promise, and agree to instruct his Said apprentice, or otherwise cause her to be well and faithfully instructed, in the art of farming and house business, and also to read English, and Shall also allow, furnish, and provide his Said apprentice with meat and drink and clothing during the said term, and all other necessaries meet and proper, in Sickness and in health, and Shall also, at the Expiration of said term, allow to said apprentice the sum of One hundred dollars and two Suits of good Clothing to be by him given and paid to Georgia Brawner by him, the said John C. Hudgins, of the Second part.

Witness our hands and Seals the day and year above written. Signed & Sealed in presence of

Clark Mattox, N. P. & Ex off J. P. }   J. C. Hudgins
H. Mattox }   Eliza X Brawner, her mark

Filed in office of Ordinary of Elbert County April 3rd 1875.

James A. Andrew, Ordinary

Recorded Aug 24 1876.

J. A. Andrew, Ordinary

Lena Walton, Col & Luther Walton, Col To Z. H. C. Mattox, 1876 [48]

State of Georgia }
Elbert County } This Indenture, made and Entered into this the 6th day of March Eighteen hundred and Seventy Six, between James A. Andrew, Ordinary of said County, of the one part, and Z. H. C. Mattox, of Said County, of the other part. Witnesseth: that the said James A. Andrew, Judge as aforesaid, does hereby bind to the said Z. H. C. Mattox the following named children, Viz, Lena Walton, Nine years old, Luther Walton, Six years old, as apprentice to the Said Z. H. C. Mattox, Lena for Twelve years And Luther for the term of Fifteen years, or until they each obtained the age of Twenty one years, it having been made Satisfactorily to appear to the said James A. Andrew, Judge as aforesaid, that the said children above mentioned are orphans and children left without any provisions for their Support and maintenance, and likely to become a charge to Said County. And the said Z. H. C. Mattox hereby agrees to furnish the said Orphan children Suitable provisions, Clothing, and Medical attention during their term of Service as apprentice. And the said Z. H. C. Mattox further agrees that Lena Walton & Luther Walton shall be taught to read the English language. And the said Z. H. C. Mattox further agrees that the said Children shall be taught the business of farming as an occupation. And the Said Z. H. C. Mattox further agrees to Govern Lena Walton & Luther Walton with humanity and Kindness, using only the Same degree of force to compel their obedience as a father may use with his minor children. And to furnish Lena Walton & Luther Walton, at the Expiration of their apprenticeship, Such allowance in money as may be Commensurate with the length and of Kind of Service as apprentice, not less than one hundred dollars.

Witness our hands and Seals the day and year above written.
Test.

T. J. Bowman }   James A. Andrew, Ordinary
Wm T. Vanduzer }   Clark Mattox
Judge, C. C. E. C. }

Filed in office March 6th 1876.

J. A. Andrew, Ordinary

Recorded August 25th 1876.

J. A. Andrew, Ordinary

John Ellenburge To Elizabeth Dixon, 1876 [49]

Georgia }
Elbert County } This Indenture, made and entered into this the 2nd day of May Eighteen hundred and Seventy Six, between James A. Andrew, Ordinary of said County, on the one part, and Elizabeth Dixon. of said County, of the other part. Witnesseth: that the said James J. Andrew, Judge as aforesaid, does hereby bind to the said Elizabeth Dixon the following named child, Viz, John Ellenburge as apprentice to the said Elizabeth Dixon until he, the said John Ellenburge Shall have arrived or obtained the age of Twenty one years, it having been made satisfactorily to appear to the said James A. Andrew, Judge as aforesaid, that the said child above mentioned was an orphan and minor left without any provisions for his Support and maintenance, and likely to become a charge to Said County. And the said Elizabeth Dixon hereby agrees to furnish the said orphan child Suitable provisions, clothing, and medical attention during his term of Service as apprentice. And the said Elizabeth Dixon further agrees that John Ellenburge shall be taught to read the English language. And the said Elizabeth Dixon further agrees that the said child shall be taught the business of Farming as an occupation. And the Said Elizabeth Dixon further agrees to govern John Ellenburge with Humanity and Kindness, using only the same degree of force to compel his obedience as a parent may use with his or her minor child. And to furnish John Ellenburge, at the Expiration of his apprenticeship, Such allowance in money as may be Commensurate with the length and of Kind of Service as apprentice, not less than one hundred dollars.

Witness our hands and Seals the day and year above written.

Test.
J. M. Reynolds }   James A. Andrew, Ordinary
Wm T. Vanduzer }   Elizabeth X Dixon, her mark
Judge, C. C. E. C.}

Filed in office May 2nd 1876.

             J. A. Andrew, Ordinary

Recorded August 25th 1876.

             J. A. Andrew, Ordinary

Fannie & Laura Walton, col To Z. H. C. Mattox [50]

Georgia }
Elbert County } This Indenture, made and entered into this the 1st day of July Eighteen Hundred and Seventy Six, between James A. Andrew, Ordinary of Said County, of the one part, and Z. H. C. Mattox, of said County, of the other part. Witnesseth: that the said James A. Andrew, Judge as aforesaid, does hereby bind to the said Z. H. C. Mattox the following named children, Viz, Fannie Walton and Laura Walton as apprentice to the Said Z. H. C. Mattox until they each shall have arrived or obtained the age of Twenty one years, it having been made Satisfactorily to appear to the said James A. Andrew, Judge as aforesaid, that the said Children above mentioned are orphans and minors left without any provisions for their Support and maintenance, and likely to become a charge to Said County. And the said Z. H. C. Mattox hereby agrees to furnish the said Orphan Children Suitable provisions, Clothing, and medical attention during their term of Service as apprentice. And the said Z. H. C. Mattox further agrees that Fannie Walton and Laura Walton Shall be taught to read the English language. And the Said Z. H. C. Mattox further agrees that the Said Children shall be taught the business of farming & house service as an occupation. And the Said Z. H. C. Mattox further agrees to govern them with humanity and kindness, using only the same degree of force to compel their obedience as a parent may use with his or her minor Children. And to furnish Fannie Walton and Laura Walton, at the Expiration of their apprenticeship, Such allowance in money as may be Commensurate with the lenth and of kind of Service as apprentice.

Witness our hands and Seals the day and year above written.

Test.
S. N. Carpenter }   James A. Andrew
N. P. & Ex off J. P. }   Clark Mattox
Wm J. White }

Filed in office July 1st 1876.

     J. A. Andrew, Ordinary

Recorded August 25th 1876.

     J. A. Andrew, Ordinary

Mary A. A. E. Ashworth To William Hutchison [51]

State of Georgia }
Elbert County } This Indenture, made this 26th day of December 1874, between Sarah J. Ashworth and Mary A. A. E. Ashworth, being of the age of Four years, All of said State and County, of the one part, and William Hutchison, of the same State and County, of the other part. Witnesseth: that the said Sarah J. Ashworth does bind out the above named Mary A. A. E. A. Ashworth to William Hutchison, of said County, as an apprentice to him as a laborer, to be taught the art of house business, and to live with, continue, and Serve the said William Hutchison as an apprentice from the date hereof for and during the full Space and term of Fourteen years, during all of which time the said Sarah J. Ashworth doth covenant with said William Hutchison that the above named Mary A. A. E. A. Ashworth Shall well and faithfully demean herself as such apprentice, obeying and observing fully the Commands of said Wm Hutchison, and in all things deporting and behaving herself as a faithful apprentice, neither revealing his Secrets, nor at any time leaving or neglecting his business. And for and in Consideration of the Service well and faithfully as aforesaid by Said apprentice of the first part, Wm Hutchison, of the Second part, doth covenant, promise, and agree to instruct his Said apprentice, or otherwise cause her to be well and faithfully instructed, in the art of house business, and also to read English, And Shall also allow, furnish, and provide his Said apprentice with meat and drink and clothing during the said term, and all other necessaries meet and proper, in sickness and in health, and Shall also, at the Expiration of Said term, allow to Said apprentice the sum of One cow & calf & feather bed furnished and Two Suits of good Clothing to be by him given and paid to Mary A. A. E. A. Ashworth by him, the said Wm Hutchison, of the Second part.

Witness our hands and Seals the day and year above written, Signed & Sealed in presence of

H. J. Goss, N. P. & Ex off J. P. }   Sarah J. Ashworth
John W. Turner, witness   }   William Hutchison

Filed in office of Ordinary of Elbert County December 26th 1874.

                                                 J. A. Andrew, Ordinary

Recorded Aug 25th 1876.

                                                 J. A. Andrew, Ordinary

Francis Jones (Col) To Nathan Jones, 1876 [52]

Georgia }
Elbert County } This Indenture, made and entered into this 28th day of October Eighteen Hundred and seventy six, between James A. Andrew, Ordinary of said County, and Nathan Jones, of said County, of the other part. Witnesseth: that the said James A. Andrew, judge as aforesaid, does hereby bind to the said Nathan Jones the following named child, viz, Francis Jones as apprentice to the said Nathan Jones until he shall have arrived or obtained the age of Twenty one years, it having been made satisfactorily to appear to the said James A. Andrew, judge as aforesaid, that the said child above mentioned is an orphan and is left without any provisions for his support and maintenance, and likely to become a charge to said county. And the said Nathan Jones hereby agrees to furnish the said orphan child suitable provisions, clothing, and medical attention during his term of service as apprentice. And the said Nathan Jones further agrees that Francis Jones shall be taught to read the English language. And the said Nathan Jones further agrees that the said child shall be taught the business of Farming as an occupation. And the Said Nathan Jones further agrees to govern said child with humanity and kindness, using only the same degree of force to compel his obedience as a father may use with his or her minor child. And to furnish said Francis Jones, at the expiration of his apprenticeship, [blot] such allowance in money as may be commensurate with the length of his service as apprentice.

Witness our hands and Seals the day and year above written.

Test.
Robt Hester }
H. A. Robuck, J. P. }

J. A. Andrew, Ordinary
of Elbert County
Nathan Jones

Recorded Dec 23rd 1876.

J. A. Andrew, Ordinary

Sarah Carter (Col) To Miss Lizzie Clark, 1876 [53]

Georgia }
Elbert County } This Indenture, made and entered into this the 21st day of October Eighteen Hundred and Seventy six, between James A. Andrew, Ordinary of said County, of the one part, and Miss Lizzie Clerk, of said County, of the other part. Witnesseth: that the said James A. Andrew, judge as aforesaid, does hereby bind to the said Lizzie Clark the following named child, viz, Sarah Carter as

apprentice to the said Lizzie Clark until Sarah Carter shall have arrived or obtained the age of Twenty one years, it having been made satisfactorily to appear to the said James A. Andrew, judge as aforesaid, that the said child above mentioned was an orphan and Minor left without any provisions for her support and maintenance, and likely to become a charge to said County. And the said Lizzie Clark hereby agrees to furnish the said orphan child suitable provisions, clothing, and medical attention during her term of service as apprentice. And the said Lizzie Clark further agrees that Sarah Carter shall be taught to read the English language. And the said Lizzie Clark further agrees that the said child shall be taught the business of house Keeping as an occupation. And the Said Lizzie Clark further agrees to govern Sarah Carter with humanity and kindness, using only the same degree of force to compel her obedience as a Parent may use with his or her minor child. And to furnish said Sarah Carter, at the expiration of Sarah Carter's apprenticeship, such allowance in money as may be commensurate with the lenth of kind of service as apprentice.

Witness our hands and seals the day and year above written.

Test.
William T. Vanduzer, judge E. C. C. C. }   Miss Lizzie Clark
Henry A. Roebuck   }   James A. Andrew
                                            Ordinary E. C.

Recorded Dec 23rd 1876.

          J. A. Andrew, Ordinary

John Ham (Col) & Harrison & Wesley Ham To Thos J. Fortson [54]

Georgia }
Elbert County } This Indenture, made and entered into this the 19th day of December Eighteen Hundred and Seventy seven, between John Ham (col), of said County, of the one part, and Thomas J. Fortson, of said County, of the other part. Witnesseth: that the said John Ham (col) as aforesaid does hereby bind to the Said Thomas J. Fortson the following named children, viz, Harrison Ham, Eighteen years old, And Wesley Ham, Fifteen years old, as apprentices to the said Thomas J. Fortson until the 25th day of December Eighteen hundred and Seventy Eight or until Harrison shall have obtained Nineteen years of age and Wesley shall have obtained the age of Sixteen years. The consideration of the above is that the Said Thos J. Fortson has this day furnished & payed to me the sum of One hundred dollars.

And the said Thomas J. Fortson hereby agrees to furnish the said children Suitable provisions during their term of service as apprentices. And the said Thomas J. Fortson further agrees to govern Harrison Ham and Wesley Ham with Humanity, using only the same degree of force to compel their obedience as a parent may use with his minor children.

Witness our hands and Seals the day and year above written.

Test.
M. H. Jones   }   John X Ham, col, his mark
J. A. Andrew, Ordin }   Thomas J. Fortson

Filed in office December 19 1877.

                                              J. A. Andrew, Odny

Recorded Jany 8th 1878.

                                                J. A. Andrew, Ordny

Voges Daniel & John G. Daniel To W. R. Daniel   [55]

Georgia   }
Elbert County   } This Indenture, made and entered into this 24th day of September Eighteen hundred and Seventy Eight, between Voges Daniel, of Said County, of the one part, and W. R. Daniel, of said County, of the other part. Witnesseth: that the said Voges Daniel does hereby bind to the said W. R. Daniel the following named Child, viz, John G. Daniel as apprentice to the said W. R. Daniel until John G. Daniel Shall have arrived or obtained the age of Twenty one years. And the said W. R. Daniel hereby agrees to furnish the said Orphan child suitable provisions, clothing, and medical attention during his term of service as apprentice. And the said W. R. Daniel further agrees that John G. Daniel Shall be taught to read the English language. And the Said W. R. Daniel further agrees that the said Child Shall be taught the business of farming as an occupation. And the Said W. R. Daniel further agrees to govern John G. Daniel with humanity and Kindness, using only the same degree of force to compel his obedience as a Parent may use with his or her minor child. And to furnish said John G. Daniel, at the Expiration of his apprenticeship, such allowance in money as may be commensurate with the length and of faithfulness of Service as apprentice.

Witness our hands and Seals the day and yar above written.

Test.
J. R. E. Bond   }
J. W. Goss, J. P. }

Vorges X Daniel, her mark
W. R. Daniel

Filed in office December Tenth 1878.

James A. Andrew, Ordinary

Recorded December 10th 1878.

James A. Andrew, Ordinary

Voges Daniel & Allen Daniel, Jr To Allen Daniel, Sen   [56]

Georgia   }
Elbert County   } This Indenture, made and entered into this 24th day of September Eighteen hundred and Seventy Eight, between Voges Daniel, of Said County, of the one part, and Allen Daniel, Sen. of said County, of the other part. Witnesseth: that the said Voges Daniel does hereby bind to the said Allen Daniel, Sen. the following named Child, viz, Allen Daniel, Jr as apprentice to the said Allen Daniel, sen. until he shall have arrived or obtained the age of Twenty one years. And the said Allen Daniel, sen. hereby agrees to furnish the said orphan child suitable provisions, clothing, and medical attention during his term of Service as apprentice. And the said Allen Daniel, sen. further agrees that Allen Daniel, Jr Shall be taught to read the English language. And the Said Allen Daniel, Sen. further agrees that the said child shall be taught the business of farming as an occupation. And the Said Allen Daniel, Sen further agrees to govern Said child with humanity and Kindness, using only the same degree of force to compel his obedience as a father may use with his minor child. And to furnish said Allen Daniel, Jr, at the expiration of his apprenticeship, such allowance in money as may be commensurate with the length and of faithfulness of Service as apprentice.

Witness our hands and seals the day and year above written.

Test.
J. R. E. Bond   }
J. W. Goss, J. P. }

Vorges X Daniel, her mark
Allen X Daniel, his mark

Filed in office December Tenth 1878.

James A. Andrew, Ordinary

Recorded December 10th 1878.

J. A. Andrew, Ordinary

Dorcas A. Burch & Mary E. A. C. Harper, col To Susan R. Fortson [57]

Georgia }
Elbert County } This Indenture, made and entered into this the Seventeenth day of September Eighteen hundred and Seventy nine, between Dorcas A. Burch, the mother of Mary E. A. C. Harper, Colored, of said County, of the one part, and Susan R. Fortson, of Said County, of the other part. Witnesseth: that the said Dorcas A. Burch, mother as aforesaid, does hereby bind to the said Susan R. Fortson the following named Child, To wit, Mary [faint] Alice Cornelia Harper, Colored, as apprentice to the said Susan R. Fortson until the said Mary E. A. C. Harper shall have arrived at or obtained the age of Eighteen years, or for the space of Twelve years. And the said Susan R. Fortson hereby agrees to furnish the said Mary E. A. C. Harper suitable provisions, clothing, and medical attention during her term of Service as apprentice. And the said Susan R. Fortson further agrees that Mary E. A. C. Harper shall be taught to read the English language. And the Said Susan R. Fortson further agrees that the said child shall be taught the art of house business as an occupation. And the Said Susan R. Fortson further agrees to govern Mary E. A. C. Harper, col with humanity and kindness, using only the same degree of force to compel her obedience as a parent may use with his or her minor Child.

Witness our hands and seals the day and year above written.

Test.
D. B. Alexander }
James A. Andrew, Ordinary}
Elbert County, Ga. }

Susan R. Fortson
Dorcas A. X Burch, her mark

Recorded September 17th 1879.

J. A. Andrew, Ordinary

Anderson Gunter, Col To Wm M. Haslett [58]

Georgia }
Elbert County } This Indenture, made and entered into this the Sixth day of September Eighteen Hundred and Seventy Nine, between James A. Andrew, Ordinary of Elbert County, and Anderson Gunter, Col, a Minor of Said County, of the one part, and William M. Haslett, of said County, of the other part.

Witnesseth: that the said James A. Andrew, Judge as aforesaid, does hereby bind to the said William M. Haslett the following named child, viz, Anderson Gunter, Colored, as apprentice to the said William M. Haslett for the term of Seven years, or until he shall have arrived or obtained the age of Twenty one years, it having been made Satisfactorily to appear to the said James A. Andrew, Judge as aforesaid, that the said child above mentioned, an orphan and Minor left without any provision for his Support and maintenance, and likely to become a charge to Said County. And the said William M. Haslett hereby agrees to furnish the said orphan child Suitable provisions, clothing, and medical attention during his term of Service as apprentice. And the said William M. Haslett further agrees that Anderson Gunter shall be taught to read the English language. And the said William M. Haslett further agrees that the said child shall be taught the business of house Service and farming as an occupation. And the said William M. Haslett further agrees to govern Anderson Gunter with Humanity and Kindness, using only the same degree of force to compel his obedience as parents may use with their minor child. And to furnish said Anderson Gunter, at the expiration of his apprenticeship, Such allowance in money as may be commensurate with the length and faithfulness of Service as apprentice.

Witness our hands and Seals the day and year above written.

William M. Brown }
H. A. Roebuck, J. P. }

W. M. Haslett
James A. Andrew
Ordinary of Elbert County, Ga.

Recorded Sept 29th 1879.

J. A. Andrew, Ordinary
& Ex officio Clerk

Arther McDuffee To Andrew J. Cleveland [59]

Georgia }
Elbert County } This Indenture, made and entered into this 24th day of December Eighteen Hundred And Seventy nine, between A. J. Cleveland, of said County, of the one part, and Larra McDuffee, Col, of said County, of the other part. Witnesseth: that the said Larra McDuffee, Col Does hereby bind to the said A. J. Cleveland the following named child, to viz, Arthur McDuffee as apprentice to the said A. J. Cleveland until he Shall have obtained the age of Twenty one years.

And the said A. J. Cleveland hereby agrees to furnish the said Child Suitable provisions, clothing, and medical attention during the term of Service as apprentice Servant. And the said A. J. Cleveland further agrees that Arther shall be taught to read the english language. And the said A. J. Cleveland further agrees that the said child shall be taught the business of farming and general Services as an occupation. And the said A. J. Cleveland further agrees to govern the Child with humanity and Kindness, using only the same degree of force to Compel his obedience as a man may use with his minor child. And to furnish Arther, at the expiration of his Service, such allowance in money as may be Commensurate with the length and of service as apprentice.

Witness our hands and Seals the day and year above written.
Test.

F. B. Cleveland }
Ezekiah Bailey. }
N. P. Ex J. P. }

A. J. Cleveland
Larah X McDuffee, her mark

Filed in office May 17th 1880.

James A. Andrew, Ordinary

Recorded May 19th 1880.

J. A. Andrew, Ordinary

Louisa Gray & Toccoa Gray To Overton L. Henry [60]

Georgia }
Elbert County } This Indenture, made and entered into this the Twentieth day of July Eighteen hundred and Eighty, between Louisa Gray (Colored), Mother of Toccoa Gray, of said County, of the one part, and Overton L. Henry, of said County, of the other part. Witnesseth: that the said Louisa Gray, Mother as aforesaid, does hereby bind to Overton L. Henry the following named Child, viz: the said Toccoa Gray, as apprentice to the said Overton L. Henry Thirteen years or until he the said Toccoa Gray Shall have arrived or obtained the age of Twenty one years. And the said Overton L. Henry hereby agrees to furnish the said Toccoa Gray suitable provisions, clothing, and medical attention during his term of Service as apprentice. And the said Overton L. Gray further agrees that Toccoa Gray shall be taught to read the English language. And the said Overton L. Henry further agrees that the said child shall be taught the business of Farming as an occupation. And the said Overton L. Henry further agrees to govern the said

Toccoa Gray with humanity and Kindness, using only the same degree of force to Compel his obedience as parents may use with their minor children. And to furnish Toccoa Gray, at the Expiration of his apprenticeship, such allowance in money as may be Commensurate with the length and of quality of service as apprentice.

Witness our hands and Seals the day and year above written.
Test.

D. C. McCraskey }	O. L. Henry
James A. Andrew }	Louisa X Gray, her mark
Ordinary, Elbert Co., Ga. }	

Recorded July 20th 1880.

J. A. Andrew, Ordinary

Stephen Christian & Mary Christian, J^r To Mary Christian, Sen. [61]

Georgia }
Elbert County } This Indenture, made and entered into this the 31St day of August Eighteen Hundred and Eighty, between Stephen Christian, col, And father of Mary Christian, J^r, of said County, of the one part, and Mary Christian, Sen., of the same place, of the other part. witnesseth: that the said Stephen Christian, father as aforesaid, does hereby bind to said Mary Christian, S^r the following named child, viz, Mary Christian, J^r, as apprentice to the said Mary Christian, sen. thirteen years or until she the said child shall have arrived at or obtained the age of Twenty one years. And the said Mary Christian, s^r hereby agrees to furnish the said Mary Christian, J^r suitable provisions, clothing, and medical attention during her term of service as apprentice. And the said Mary Christian further agrees that the said minor child shall be taught to read the English language.

And She further agrees the Said child shall be taught such business and to do such work as will be for the best interest of her, the Said child. And the said Mary Christian, s^r further agrees to govern the said child with humanity and Kindness, using only the same degree of force to Compel her obedience as parents may use with their minor children. And to furnish to said child, at the expiration of said apprenticeship, such allowance in money as may be Commensurate with the length and quality of service as apprentice.

Witness our hands and Seals the day and year above written.

Test.
R. H. Jones   }
James A. Andrew }
Ordinary, E. C.   }

Stephen X Christian, his mark
Mary X Christian, her mark

Filed in office August 31st 1880.

J. A. Andrew, Ordinary

Recorded September 1st 1880.

J. A. Andrew, Ordinary

Stephen Christian & Georgia Christian To Georgia Harper   [62]

Georgia   }
Elbert County } This Indenture, made and entered into this the 31st day of August Eighteen hundred and Eighty, between Stephen Christian, col, And father of Georgia Christian, of said County, of the one part, and Georgia Harper, of the same place, of the other part. witnesseth: that the Stephen Christian, as aforesaid, does hereby bind to said Georgia Harper the following named child, viz, Georgia Christian, as apprentice to the said Georgia Harper Eleven years or until she shall have arrived at the age of Twenty one years. And the said Georgia Harper hereby agrees to furnish to the said Georgia Christian Suitable provisions, clothing, and medical attention during her term of Service as apprentice. And the said Georgia Harper further agrees that the said Georgia Christian Shall be taught to read the English language. And the said Georgia Harper further agrees the Said Child shall be taught such business as will be for best interest of her, the said Child.

And the Said Georgia Harper further agrees to govern the said Child with Humanity and Kindness, using only such means to Compel her obedience as parents may use with their minor children. And to furnish to said child, at the Expiration of her apprenticeship, such allowance in money as may be Commensurate with the length and of quality of service as apprentice.

Witness our hands and Seals the day and year above written.

Test.
R. H. Jones   }
James A. Andrew }
Ordinary, E. C.   }

Stephen X Christian, his mark
Georgia X Harper, her mark

Filed in office of Ordinary September 4th 1880.

J. A. Andrew, Ordinary

Recorded September 9th 1880.

J. A. Andrew, Ordinary

Caroline Greenway To M^r & Mrs A. R. Rucker [63]

Georgia }
Elbert County } This Indenture, made and entered into this the 20th day of May Eighteen hundred and Eighty one, between A. R. Rucker and Mrs A. R. Rucker, of said County, of the one part, and Caroline Greenway, of said County, of the other part. Witnesseth: that the said Caroline Greenway does hereby bind to the said A. R. Rucker and wife the following named child, viz, Mary Jane Greenway, the daughter of said Caroline, as apprentice to the said A. R. Rucker and wife until she shall have obtained the age of Twenty one years. And the said A. R. Rucker and wife hereby agrees to furnish the said child suitable provisions, clothing, and medical attention during the term of service as apprentice. And the said A. R. Rucker and wife further agrees that Mary Jane shall be taught to read the English language. And the said A. R. Rucker and wife further agrees that the said child shall be taught the business as general services in all household departments as an occupation. And the said A. R. Rucker and wife further agrees to govern the child with humanity and Kindness, using only the same degree of force to compel obedience as a man may use with his minor child. And to furnish Mary Jane, at the expiration of her service, such allowance in money as may be commensurate with the length and of her service as apprentice.

Witness our hands and seals the day and year above written.
Test.

J. W. Rucker   }   Mrs A. R. Rucker
Ezekiah Baily, N. P. & Exoff J. P. }   A. R. Rucker
                                                          Caroline X Greenway, her mark

Recorded May 24th 1881.

Ge° L. Almond, Ordinary

Caroline Greenway To M^r & Mrs A. R. Rucker [64]

Georgia }
Elbert County } This Indenture, made and entered into this the 20th day of May Eighteen hundred and Eighty one, between A. R. Rucker and Mrs A. R. Rucker, of said County, of the one part, and Caroline Greenway, of said County, of the other part. Witnesseth: that the said Caroline Greenway does hereby bind to the said A. R. Rucker and wife the following named child, viz, Wade Hampton Greenway, the son of said Caroline, as apprentice to the said A. R. Rucker and wife until he shall have obtained the age of Twenty one years. And the said A. R. Rucker and wife hereby agrees to furnish the said child suitable provisions, clothing, and medical attention during the term of service as apprentice. And the said A. R. Rucker and wife further agrees that Wade Hampton shall be taught to read the English language. And the said A. R. Rucker and wife further agrees that the said child shall be taught the business of Farming and general services as an occupation. And the said A. R. Rucker and wife further agrees to govern the child with humanity and Kindness, using only the same degree of force to compel obedience as a man may use with his minor child. And to furnish Wade Hampton, at the Expiration of his services, such allowance in money as may be commensurate with the length and of service as apprentice.

Witness our hands and seals the day and year above written.
Test.

J. W. Rucker }   Mrs A. R. Rucker
Ezekiah Baily, N. P. & Exoff J. P. }   A. R. Rucker
                        Caroline X Greenway, her mark

Recorded May 24th 1881.

Ge° L. Almond, Ordinary, E. C.

Dorcas Burch To Georgia A. Teasly [65]

Georgia }
Elbert County } This Indenture, made and entered into this the first day of June 1881, between Dorcas Burch (col), of Elbert County, Ga., of the one part, and Georgia A. Teasly, of Hart County, of the other part. Witnesseth: that the said Dorcas Burch does hereby bind to the said Georgia A. Teasly the following named child, to wit, Frank Harper, as apprentice to the said Georgia A. Teasly until the said Frank Harper shall have obtained the age of Eighteen years. And the said Georgia A. Teasly hereby agrees to furnish the said orphan child Suitable

provisions, clothing, and medical attention during his term of Service as apprentice. And the Said Georgia A. Teasly further agrees that said Orphan shall be taught to read the English language. And the said Georgia A. Teasly further agrees that the said Child shall be taught the business of Farming as an occupation. And the said Georgia A. Teasly further agrees to govern said Orphan with humanity and Kindness, using only the same degree of force to compel him to obedience as a mother may use with her minor child. And to furnish him, at the Expiration of his apprenticeship, such allowance in money as may be commensurate with the length and of service as apprentice.

Witness our hand and seals the day and year above written.
Test.

Ge⁰ L. Almond } Georgia A. Teasly
Ordinary, E. C. } Dorcas X Burch, her mark

Recorded June 1st 1881.

Ge⁰ L. Almond, Ordinary & Dpt
Clk Off

Leanna Christian To J. E. Campbell [66]

Georgia }
Elbert County } This Indenture, made and entered into this the 8th day of May 1882, between Leanna Christian, col, mother of Sam Fortson, col, of said County of the one part, and J. E. Campbell, of said County, of the other part. Witnesseth: that the said Leanna Christian, mother as aforesaid, does hereby bind to the said J. E. Campbell the following named child, viz, Sam Fortson (col), as apprentice to the said J. E. Campbell until the said Sam Fortson, col shall have arrived at or obtained the age of Eighteen years. The said Sam Fortson being now Eight years of age. And the said J. E. Campbell hereby agrees to furnish the said child suitable provisions, clothing, and medical attention during his term of Service as apprentice. And the said J. E. Campbell further agrees that said Sam Fortson shall be taught the business of Farming as an Occupation. And the said J. E. Campbell further agrees to govern Sam Fortson, col with humanity and Kindness, using only the same degree of force to compel his obedience as a parent with his or her minor child.

Witness our hands and seals the day and year above written.

Attest.
Abda Oglesby }
Ge° L. Almond, }
Ordinary, E. C.

J. E. Campbell
Leanna X Christian, her mark

Recorded May 8th 1882.

Ge° L. Almond, Ordinary

Julian Rucker To John P. Shannon, 1882 [67]

Georgia }
Elbert County } This Indenture, made this the 13th day of November 1882, between Ge° L. Almond, Ordinary for said County, and Julian Rucker, col, being of the age of Twelve years, All of said state and County, of the one part, and John P. Shannon, of the same State and County, of the other part. Witnesseth: that the said Ordinary does hereby bind the said Julian Rucker, col to John P. Shannon, of said County as apprentice to him as house servant and to live with, continue, and serve the said John P. Shannon as an apprentice from the date hereof for and during the full space and term of nine years, during all of which time, the said Ge° L. Almond, Ordinary, doth covenant with the said John P. Shannon that the above named Julian Rucker, col shall well and faithfully demean himself as such apprentice, obeying and observing the demands of said John P. Shannon in all things, deporting and behaving himself as a faithful Apprentice, neither revealing his secrets, nor at any time leaving or neglecting his business. And for and in consideration of the service well and faithfully as aforesaid by said Apprentice of the first part, John P. Shannon, of the second part, doth covenant, promise, and agree to instruct his said apprentice, or otherwise cause him to be well and faithfully instructed, in the art of house servant, and also to read and write the English language, and the common ruls of arithmetic. And shall also allow, furnish, and provide his apprentice with meat and drink and clothing during the said term, and all other necessaries meet and proper, in sickness and in health. And shall also, at the expiration of said term, allow said apprentice the sum of Fifty dollars and two suits of Clothes, to be by him paid to the said Julian Rucker by the said John P. Shannon, of the second part, unless otherwise directed by this Court.

Signed in presence of }
J. S. Barnett, Inf C. }
C. C. E. C. }

Ge° L. Almond, Ordinary
John P. Shannon

Recorded Nov 13 1882.

Ge° L. Almond, Ordny

Frank Humbles To Mrs Nery J. Penn [68]

Georgia }
Elbert County } This Indenture, made this July 19th 1883, between Frank Humbles (colored), of said County and State, of the one part, and Mrs Nary J. Penn, of the same place, of the other part. Witnesseth: That the said Frank Humbles is the sole surviving parent of Edwin Humbles, a minor child of said Frank Humbles and Scoot Humbles, his former wife, who is now deceased. That said minor child is six years old. And said Frank Humbles is the parent having the legal control of said minor male child.

That Said Frank Humbles is in feeble health, has no property of any Kind, is Unable to work, and therefore unable to furnish the necessaries of life for his aforesaid minor child and his other children. That for the Above Stated reasons, on account of his confidence in the aforesaid Mrs Nery J. Penn, taking into consideration the interest of said Edwin Humbles, and in consideration of the stipulations and contents herein agreed to be done and performed by the said Mrs Nary J. Penn, said Frank Humbles does hereby bind his said minor child, said Edwin Humbles, who is now Six years old, as an apprentice to the said Mrs Nary J. Penn until said Edwin Humbles, who is now six years old, shall attain the age of twenty one years, or for the Term of Fifteen years from the date of this Indenture.

Said Mrs Nary J. Penn agrees upon her part to teach said Edwin Humbles the business of house service, To furnish him with protection, wholesome food, Suitable Clothing, and necessary medicine and medical attention, to teach him habits of industry, honesty, and morality,

to cause him to be taught to read English, and to govern him with [69] humanity, using only the same degree of force to compel his obedience as a father may use with his minor child.

Witness our hands and seals this July 19th 1883.

Attested and approved by me }
this July 19 1883 } Frank X Humbles, his mark
W. P. Maxwell } N. J. Penn
Thos M. Smith }
Geo L. Almond, Ordinary E. C. }

Recorded July 20th 1883. Geo L. Almond, Ordiny

Nevada Moats To James T. Bohannan, 1883 [70]

Georgia }
Elbert County } This Indenture, made this 3rd day of September 1883, between Geo L. Almond, Ordinary for said County, and Nevada Moats, aged nine months, all of said State and County, of the one part, and James T. Bohanan, of the same place, of the other part.

Witnesseth: that the said Ordinary does bind the said Nevada Moats to James T. Bohannan, of said County, as apprentice to him as house servant, And to live with, continue, and serve the said James T. Bohannan as an apprentice from the date hereof for and during the full space of her minority. During all of which time, the said Geo L. Almond, Ordinary, doth covenant with the said James T. Bohannan that the above named Nevada Moats shall well and faithfully demean herself as such apprentice, obeying and observing the Demands of said James T. Bohannan in all things, deporting and behaving herself as apprentice, neither revealing his secrets, nor at any time leaving or neglecting his business. and for and in consideration of the service well and faithfully as aforesaid by said Apprentice of the first part, James T. Bohannan doth covenant, promise, and agree to instruct his said apprentice, or otherwise cause her to be well and faithfully instructed, in the art of house keeping, and also to read and write the English language, and the Common rules of Arithmetic. And shall also allow, furnish, and provide his apprentice with meat and drink and clothing during the said term of her minority, and all other necessaries meet and proper, in sickness and in health. And shall also, at the expiration of said term, allow to said apprentice the sum of One hundred dollars and sufficient Clothing. Provided Nevertheless, that if the said minor should choose to marry at the age of Eighteen years, then the [71] above obligation of the said Bohannan shall be and remain the same as if she remained with him for the full time of twenty one years.

Signed in presence of } Ge° L. Almond, Ordinary
R. M. Willis } Ja^s T. Bohannan
S. N. Carpenter, N. P. &c }

Recorded September 3rd 1883.

Ge° L. Almond, Ordinary

William McIntosh To America McIntosh [72]

Georgia }
Elbert County } This Indenture, this 3rd day of November 1883, between Ge° L. Almond, Ordinary for said County, and William McIntosh, col, aged 14 years 15th day of May last, all of said state and County, of the one part, and America McIntosh, col, of the same place, of the other part. Witnesseth: that the said Ordinary does bind the said William McIntosh to the said America McIntosh, of said County, as apprentice to her as house Servant, and to learn the several principals of farming. And to live with, continue, and serve the said America McIntosh as an apprentice from the date hereof for and during the full space of his minority. During all of which time, the said Ge° L. Almond, Ordinary, doth covenant with the said America McIntosh that the above named William McIntosh shall well and faithfully demean himself as such apprentice, obeying and observing the Demands of said America McIntosh in all things, deporting and behaving himself as apprentice, neither revealing his secrets, nor at any time leaving or neglecting her business. and for and in consideration of the service well and faithfully as aforesaid by said apprentice of the first part, America McIntosh doth covenant, promise, and agree to instruct her said apprentice, or otherwise cause him to be well and faithfully instructed, in the art of farming, and also to read and write the English language, and the Common rules of Arithmetic. And shall also allow, furnish, and provide her apprentice with meat, drink, and clothing during the said term of his minority, and all other necessaries meet and proper, in

sickness and in health. And shall also, at the Expiration of said term, allow [73] to said apprentice the sum of Two Hundred dollars and sufficient Clothing.

Signed in presence of } Ge° L. Almond, Ord
J. S. Barnett, Inf Clerk } America X McIntosh, her mark

Recorded Nov 21 1883.

Ge° L. Almond, Ordinary

Deadwyler, col To Davis, col, 1883 [74]

Georgia }
Elbert County } This Indenture, made this 21st day of November 1883, between Mitt Deadwyler, colored, of the one part, and J. W. Davis, of the other part, both of said State & County. witnesseth: That the said Mitt Deadwyler is the mother of Madison Marcus Deadwyler, minor child now nine years of age. That said Mitt Deadwyler is unable to raise the said Madison M. Deadwyler and to train him as he should be.

That for the above stated reasons, as well as for her confidence in said J. W. Davis, and taking into consideration the interest of said minor, the said Mitt Deadwyler does hereby bind her said son, Madison M. Deadwyler, as apprentice to the said J. W. Davis until said minor reaches the age of Twenty one years.

Said J. W. Davis on his part agrees to teach said minor the business of house servant and farming, To furnish him with Suitable meat, drink, and clothing. To furnish him with all necessary protection, in sickness and in health. To treat him Kindness, using only such means to compel obedience as a father would his son. To Teach him the rudiments of a common education. To furnish medicine and medical attention whenever necessary. And to compensate him when he reaches his majority as shall be equitable.

Attest. }   Mitt X Deadwyler, her mark
Ge° L. Almond }   J. W. Davis
Ordinary }

Recorded Nov 21 1883.

Ge° L. Almond, ordinary

Tate To Adams [75]

Georgia }
Elbert County } This Indenture, made and entered into this the 19th day of January 1884, between E. S. Adams, of said County, of the one part, and Ann Morrison, col, of said County, the other part. Witnesseth: that the said Ann Morrison, col does bind to the said E. S. Adams the following named child, viz, John Tate, the son of the said Ann Morrison, as apprentice to the said E. S. Adams

until he shall have attained the age of twenty one years. And the said E. S. Adams hereby agrees to furnish said child suitable provisions, clothing, and medical attention during the term of said apprenticeship. And the said Adams further agrees that the said John shall be taught to spell, read, and write the English language, and shall be taught the occupation of farming. And the said Adams further agrees to govern the said John with humanity. The said Ann Morrison agrees and covenants that said John shall remain with the said Adams during said term of service. And the said Adams agrees to give said John at the end of said term a horse, bridle, and saddle.

Witness our hands and seals.

Attest.   }   E. S. Adams
Geº L. Almond   }   Ann X Morrison, her mark
Ordinary   }

Recorded Jany 21st 1884.

                                                Geº L. Almond, Ordinary

Humbles To Campbell   [76]

Georgia   }
Elbert County   } This Indenture, made this 25th day of October 1882, between Frank Humbles (colored), of the one part, and Thomas Campbell, of the other part. witnesseth: That the said Frank Humbles is the only surviving parent of City and Dunston Humbles, minor children of said Frank Humbles and Scott Humbles, his former wife, who is now deceased. That said City is thirteen years old and the said Dunston is Seven years old. And said Frank Humbles is the parent having the legal control of said minor children. That Said Frank Humbles is in feeble health, has no property of any Kind, is Unable to work, and therefore unable to furnish the necessaries of life for his aforesaid minor children. That for the above stated reasons, on account of his confidence in the aforesaid Thomas Campbell, taking into consideration the interest of said minors, and in consideration and stipulations and contents herein agreed to be done and performed by the said Thomas Campbell, said Frank Humbles does hereby bind his said minor children, as apprentices to the said Thomas Campbell until said minors shall attain the age of Twenty one years. Said Thomas Campbell agrees upon his part to teach said minors the business of house servants and farming. To furnish them with protection, wholesome food, suitable clothing, and necessary medicine and medical attention. To teach them the habits of Industry and morality. To cause them to be taught to read and write the English language. To govern them with

humanity, using only parental force to compel obedience. And to compensate them when they reach their majority

As shall be equitable. [77]

Witness our hands and seals the day and year above written.

Attested by } Frank X Humbles, his mark
J. L. Mize, N. P. } Thomas X Campbell, his mark

Recorded Feb 29th 1884

                                      Geº L. Almond, Ordinary

Georgia }
Elbert County } These presents show that a contract made and entered into between Thom Campbell, of the one part, and Frank Humbles, of the other part. Witnesseth: that the said Frank has another boy child named Johnny, at this time down at Mary Hatter's. And by these presents, the said Frank binds him to the said Thom Campbell in the same way and manner as of the other two which is Shown in the above writing. This 25th day of Oct 1883

Attested by } Frank X Humbles, his mark
J. L. Mize, N. P. } Thomas X Campbell, his mark

Recorded Feb 29th 1884

                                      Geº L. Almond, Ordinary

Edwin Humbles To Thos Kimball [78]

Georgia }
Elbert County } This Indenture, made and entered into this first day of March Eighteen hundred and eighty four, between Thomas Kimble, of said County, of the One part, and Ordinary Almond, of said County, of the Other part. Witnesseth: that the said Geº L. Almond, Ordinary as aforesaid, does hereby bind to the said Thos Kimble the following named child, viz, Edwin Humble, a minor, as apprentice to the said Thomas Kimble until said Edwin Humble shall have obtained the age of twenty one years, it having been made satisfactorily to appear to the said Geº L. Almond, Ordinary as aforesaid, that the said child as above mentioned is an orphan and he is left without any provisions for his Support and maintenance and likely to become a charge to said County. And the said Thom Kimble hereby agrees to furnish the said Orphan child suitable provisions,

clothing, and medical Attention during his term of service as apprentice. And the said Thomas Kimble further agrees that said Edwin Humble shall be taught to read the English Language. And the said Thos Kimble further agrees that the said child shall taught the business of farming as an Occupation. And the said Thos Kimble further agrees to govern said minor with humanity and Kindness, using only such degree of force to compel his obedience as a father may use with his minor child. And to furnish him, at the Expiration of his apprenticeship, such Allowance in money as may be commensurate with the length of his service as apprentice.

Witness our hands and seals the day and year above written.

Test.   }
Jo^s N. Worly   }   Thomas X Kimball, his mark
R. A. Turner, N. P.   Ge° L. Almond, Ordinary

Recorded March 1st 1884.

                                        Ge° L. Almond, Ord

Jordan to Moss   [79]

Georgia   }
Elbert County   } This Indenture, made this 6th day of December 1884, between Rachel Jordan and John Moss, both colored, of the State and County aforesaid. Witnesseth: that the said Rachel has this day apprenticed to said John Moss her son Marshall until he is twenty one years old, on the Condition the said Moss aforesaid shall maintain, support, and give him, the said Marshall, such educational advantages as the said Moss is able to give.

The said Moss agrees to take said Marshall to feed, clothe, and give him such medical attention as he may require and also agrees to send him to school as much as his financial condition will allow. Said Marshall is now Eleven years old. In witness whereof, we set our hands and seals this 6th day of Dec 1884.

Signed in presence of   }   Rachel X Jordan, her mark
Jn° W. McCalla, N. P. & Eff J. P. }   John X Moss, his mark

Filed in office Dec 8th 1884.

                                        Ge° L. Almond, Ordinary

Recorded Dec 8th 1884.

Geo L. Almond, Ordinary

Wyley Clark To Wm H. Mattox [80]

State of Georgia }
Elbert County } This Indenture, made this the 7th day of April 1885, between Geo L. Almond, Ordinary of said County, and Wyley Clark, a minor, about the age of fifteen years, of the one part, and Wm H. Mattox, of the other part, all of said state and County. Witnesseth: That the Ordinary, in and upon the petition and representation of Moses Clark and Elizabeth Clark, nearest of kin of said minor, does bind minor Wyley Clark, of said County, as apprentice to Wm H. Mattox, of said County, to learn the general principals of farming and other such business therewith connected, to live with and to serve said Wm H. Mattox as said apprentice for and during the term of Twenty four months beginning from the date hereof. During all of which time, said Geo L. Almond, Ordinary, does covenant with said Wm H. Mattox that the said Wyley Clark shall well and faithfully demean himself as such apprentice, obeying and observing faithfully the instructions and commands of said Mattox, in all things deporting himself justly as such apprentice, neither revealing his secrets, nor leaving or neglecting his business. And for and in consideration of the services faithfully rendered as aforesaid by Wyley Clark as apprentice, Said Mattox does covenant, promise, and agree to instruct said apprentice in the Arts of farming, and also to read and write the English language, and the Common rules of Arithmetic, and Shall also furnish and provide his said apprentice with meat, drink, and clothing, and all necessary medical attention, in sickness as well as in health. The further consideration hereof however been paid heretofore to

Moses Clark and Elizabeth Clark and by them appropriated to the charges [81] against said Wiley for services rendered during the infancy of said Wyley and from then up to the date hereof, which charges were reasonable, proper, and just from them, As it Appears the said Moses Clark and Elizabeth Clark were by paral on the death bed constituted and accepted from the mother of said Wyley the great Kinnship and care of said minor.

Signed in presence of }   Geo L. Almond, Ordinary
Thos C. Carlton }   Wm H. Mattox
Judge, C. C. E. C. }

Recorded April 9th 1885.

Ge° L. Almond, Ordinary

Duplicate [82]

Henry Jones To P. M. Hawes

Georgia }
Elbert County } This Indenture, made this 1st day of January 1885.

P. M. Hawes and Henry Jones, father of Lindsy, Mary, Rebecca, and Henry Jones, aged Lindsy 18 years, Mary 15 years, Rebecca 12 years, and Henry Jones 7 years, of said County. witnesseth: that the said Henry hereby binds and apprentices to the said P. M. Hawes the said Lindsy, Mary, Rebecca, and Henry until they are Twenty one years of age.

Said Hawes agreeing to take into his Custody the said Lindsey, Mary, Rebecca, and Henry, teach them such business as is done on a plantation, and furnish them ~~protection~~, wholesome food, and provision, clothing, necessary medicine, & medical attention, teach them the habits of industry, and teach, or cause them to be taught, in the public Schools of the County so much time as the said Hawes can spare them from their several occupations, and shall govern them with humanity, using only enough force to Compel obedience. And when they, the said children, become of age, the said Hawes agrees to give them such things as may Seem best to them. In consideration of all of which, the said Hawes is entitled to the Services of the said Lindsey, Mary, Rebecca, and Henry until they Arrive at Twenty one years of age.

Witness our hands & Seals this 1st January 1885.

Witnss. James M. McIntosh } Henry X Jones, his mark
Jn° W. McCalla, N. P. & eff J. P. } P. M. Hawes

Recorded 15th May 1885.

Ge° L. Almond, Ordinary

Campbell To Mathews, 1885 [83]

Georgia }
Elbert County } This agreement made and entered into between W. J. Mathews, of Grayson County, Texas, and Thomas Campbell, of Elbert County, Georgia.

Witnesseth: that the said Campbell, having had City Humbles legally bound to him as apprentice, by the father of said City before his death, viz, on the 20th day of Oct. 1883, and the said indenture recorded by the Ordinary of Elbert County, Georgia, Feby 24th 1884. Now the said Campbell, wishing to dissolve the relation of Master under said apprenticeship, And with the Consent of the Ordinary of said County of Elbert, for and in consideration of the agreement which is herein made by the said Mathews does hereby dissolve the said relationship to the said City as apprentice and release and surrender her to the said Mathews for the time and under the following stipulations on the part of the said Mathews.

The said Mathews hereby agrees and binds himself to take the said City Humbles, to feed and clothe her, furnish her with medical attention, and provide for her suitably, and have her taught to read and write, and to teach her the business of a house girl and cooking.

And the said Mathews hereby binds himself to treat the said City humanely and to provide for her as above Till she is Twenty one years of age. The said City now being Fourteen years old, and at the expiration of said time, when she has arrived at her majority, viz, at the age of Twenty one years, to give her two changes of good clothing and Fifty Dollars.

Witness our hands and seals this Sept 21st 1885.

Signed and sealed   }
in presence of and   }   Wm J. Mathews
approved by me   }   Thomas X Campbell, his mark
Ge^o L. Almond,   }
Ordinary, Elbert County }

Recorded Sep^t 21 1885.

Ge^o L. Almond, Ordny

Johnson and Johnson To White and White, 1885 [84]

Georgia   }
Elbert County } This Indenture, made this 24th day of December 1885, between Tinsley R. White & wife, of said County, of the one part, and Willis Johnson and Julia Johnson, of the same place of the other part. witnesseth: That the said Willis and Julia Johnson does hereby bind to the said T. R. White & wife the following named child, to wit, William Johnson as apprentice to the said T. R. White & wife

until he shall have attained the age of twenty one years. The said William being now ten years of age.

And the said T. R. White & wife hereby agrees to furnish the said William, suitable provisions, clothing, and medical attention during the said term of service as apprentice servant. And the said T. R. White & wife further agrees to cause the said apprentice to be taught the rudiments of an english education, and to use only such force to compel his obedience as a parent would use with his minor child, and to furnish said William, at the expiration of said term of service with a horse and saddle. (The words "& wife" added to the name T. R. White in this instrument before signing.)

Witness our hands and seals this Dec 24 1885.

Witnss	}	T. R. White & wife
Geº L. Almond,	}	Willis X Johnson, his mark
Ordinary	}	Julia X Johnson, her mark

Recorded Dec 24 1885.

Geº L. Almond, Ordny

Jones To Maley [85]

Georgia }
Elbert County } This agreement made and entered into between T. A. S. Maly, of the one part, and Henrietta Jones, col, of the other part. witnesseth: That the said Henrietta Jones binds to said T. A. S. Maley her son, John Wesley Jones, the father of said boy having no claim on said boy, until said John Wesley Jones arrives at the age of Twenty one years. And said T. A. S. Maley agrees to furnish said John Wesley Jones with suitable good clothing and medical attention during his term of service, and to cause the said John Wesly Jones to be taught the art of farming and the rudiments of an english education, and to use only such force to compel his obedience as a parent would his minor child. and to furnish said John W. Jones, at the expiration of his term of service, a horse and saddle. This agreement being read over to the parties before signing and they consenting thereto. said John Wesly Jones being now of the age of Sixteen months.

Witness our hands and seals this the 24 day of December 1885.

Witness	}	
Geº L. Almond,	}	Henrietta X Jones, her mark
Ordinary	}	T. A. S. Maley

Recorded Dec 24 1885.

Geº L. Almond, Ordny

Harvey Mattox To Jnº W. McCalla [86]

State of Georgia }
Elbert County } This Indenture, made Sept 14th 1886, between Jnº W. McCalla, of one part, and Harvey Mattox, col, of the other part witnesseth, that the said Harvey Mattox, of said County, has this day apprenticed to said Jnº W. McCalla, of said County, his children, to wit, his son Binx Mattox 16 years old, his son Henry Mattox 14 years old, his son Lewis Mattox 11 years old, and his son Doc Mattox 18 years old until they respectively become of age, twenty one years old. Said Jnº W. McCalla is to give said children such education as is provided by the public school system, allowing said children time to attend said school. Said McCalla agrees to take said children and feed, clothe, and give them such medical attention as they may require. Said McCalla is to have the full and complete Control and custody of said children, free from the control of their parents, or either of them, and to treat said children kindly and learn them the Skill and art of agriculture as is taught and practiced on the farm of said McCalla in said County. This Indenture being read over to us and in our presence, we have each voluntarily hereunto agreed and signed our names the day and year above written.

Signed in }
presence of }
Geº L. Almond, }
Ordinary E. C. }

Harvey X Mattox, his mark
Jnº W. McCalla

Recorded September 16th 1886.

Geº L. Almond, Ordinary

Eldridge To Jones [87]

Georgia }
Elbert County } This Indenture, made and entered into this Fourth day of December Eighteen Hundred and Eighty Six, between John J. Jones, of said County, of the one part, and Frances Eldridge, colored, of said County, of the other part. witnesseth: That the said Frances Eldridge (col) does hereby bind as apprentice to the said John J. Jones her following named child, viz, Henry Eldridge, col, the son of the said Frances Eldridge, col, until he, the said Henry,

shall become Twenty one years of age. The said Henry now being seven years of age. And the said John J. Jones hereby agrees to furnish said child suitable provisions, clothing, and medical attention during the term of said apprenticeship. And the said Jones further agrees that the said child shall be taught to spell, read, and write the English language, and shall be taught the occupation or business of farming. and the said Jones further agrees to govern and treat said child with humanity. The said Frances Eldridge, col, agrees and covenants that the said child shall remain with said Jones during said term of service.

Witness our hands and seals the day and year above written.

Attest.	John J. Jones
Ge° L. Almond	Frances X Eldridge, her mark
Ordinary	

Recorded Dec 4th 1886.

Ge° L. Almond, Ordny

Mary Frances Jones To Martin R. Jones [88]

Georgia }
Elbert County } This Indenture, made this 8th day of January 1887, between Ge° L. Almond, Ordinary for said County, and Mary Frances Jones, aged twelve years on the 8th day of April 1887, All of said state and County, of the one part, and Martin R. Jones, of the same place, of the other part. witnesseth: That the said Ordinary does bind the said Mary Frances Jones to the said Martin R. Jones, as apprentice to him as house servant and the general principals of house keeping &c, and to be with, continue, and serve the said Martin R. Jones as such apprentice from the date hereof for and during the full space of her minority.

During all of which time, said Mary F. Jones shall well and faithfully demean herself as such apprentice, obeying and observing fully the demands of said Martin R. Jones, neither revealing his secrets, nor at any time leaving or neglecting his business.

And for and in consideration of such services as apprentice, the said Martin R. Jones doth covenant, promise, and agree to instruct said Mary F. Jones in the art of house servant and house keeping thoroughly, and also to read & write the English language, and the common rules of arithmetic, and shall also furnish and provide said Mary F. Jones with wholesome meat, drink, and clothing, and all necessary medical attention during said term of apprenticeship. And shall also, at the expiration of said term, to allow said apprentice a sum which shall be commensurate with her services.

Witness our hands and seals Jany 8th 1887.

Witness } M. R. Jones
H. A. Roebuck, J. P. } Ge^o L. Almond
Ordinary

Recorded Jany 8th 1887.

Ge^o L. Almond, Ord

John Washington To Thos S. Jones [89]

Georgia }
Elbert County } This Indenture, made and entered into this thirteenth day of August in the year of our Lord One thousand Eight Hundred and Eighty Seven, between Ge^o L. Almond, Ordinary for said County, of the one part, and Thomas S. Jones, of said County, of the other part. Witnesseth: That the said Ordinary does hereby bind John Washington, a minor nine years of age, unto said Thomas S. Jones, as apprentice to him as house servant and farm laborer, and to learn the general principles of house servant and farmer, and to live with, Continue, and Serve said Thomas S. Jones as an Apprentice from the date hereof for and during the full space of his minority.

During all of which time, the said Ge^o L. Almond, Ordinary, doth covenant with the said Thomas S. Jones that the said John Washington shall well and faithfully demean himself as such Apprentice, obeying and observing fully the demands of said Thomas S. Jones, in all things deporting and behaving himself as apprentice, neither revealing his secrets, nor at any time leaving or neglecting his business.

and for and in consideration of the service well and faithfully as aforesaid by said apprentice of the first part, the said Thomas S. Jones doth covenant promise, and agree to instruct his said apprentice, or otherwise cause him to be well and faithfully instructed, in the Art of farming, and also to read and write the English language and the common rules of arithmetic, and shall also allow, furnish, and provide his apprentice with meat, drink, and clothing during the said term of his minority, and all other necessaries meet and proper, in sickness and in health, and shall also, at the expiration of said term, allow to said apprentice the Sum which shall be commensurate with his services.

Signed in }
presence of }
R. M. Willis, }
Clerk S. C. E. C. }

Ge° L. Almond,
Ordinary, Elbert Co., Ga.
Thomas S. Jones

Recorded August 16th 1887.

Ge° L. Almond,
Ordinary

Mit ~~Deadwyler~~ Roebuck To Henry Thornton [90]

Georgia }
Elbert County } Know All men by these presents that we, Mit Roebuck, of Elbert County, and Henry Thornton, of Oglethorpe County, do enter into the following contract.

The said Mit Roebuck hereby binds her son, Mat Deadwyler, to the said Henry Thornton for the space of three years from this date. And the said Henry agrees on his part to feed said minor and treat him just as he does or would his own children during said time, to allow him all the advantages in every way that he does or would his own children, and to take good and parental care of and control over him for the space of three years. At the end of which time, he is to be returned to the custody and control of the said Mit Roebuck by the said Henry Thornton. If either party to this contract should die before the end of the three years, then this contract to terminate immediately.

Witness
H. A. Roebuck

Mit X Roebuck, her mark
Henry Thornton

The said Henry Thornton hereby agrees to pay to said Mit Roebuck fifteen dollars for the year 1888, Twenty Dollars for the year 1889, and Thirty five dollars for the year 1890, for the time of her said son, Mat Deadwyler. Oct 12, 1887

Henry Thornton

Rec^d of Henry Thornton twenty dollars on above contract. Oct 12th 1887

Witness, D. B. Alexander

Mit X Roebuck, her mark

Filed in office Oct 12th 1887.

Geº L. Almond, Ordinary

Recorded October 12th 1887.

Geº L. Almond, Ordinary

Ann Morrison To Eliza Derrett, 1887 [91]

Georgia }
Elbert County } This Indenture, made and entered into this 9th day of November 1887, between Ann Morrison, of said state and county, of the one part, and Eliza Derrett, of the same place, of the other part. Witnesseth: that the said Ann Morrison does hereby bind to her mother, the said Eliza Derrett, the following named child (which is her, the said Ann's, own son) John Tate, as apprentice to the said Eliza Derrett until the said John Tate Shall arrive at the full age of twenty one years. and the said Ann covenants and agrees that the said John shall remain with said Eliza during all of said term.

The said Eliza agrees to treat the said John humanely, using such means of compulsion as a prudent parent would with a child to cause obedience, and to feed and clothe him during said term, and to give him such education as is furnished by the common public schools of the County. And to teach him the principles of farming as an occupation.

The said John Tate being Eight years of age on the 24th day of August last past.

Witness our hands and seals this 9th day of November 1887.

Witness:	Ann X Morrison, her mark
Geº L. Almond,	Eliza X Derrett, her mark
Ordinary	

Filed in office Nov 9th and recorded Nov 9th 1887.

Geº L. Almond, Ordinary

Harriett Jones To Walton and Laurah Oglesby [92]

Georgia }
Elbert County } This Indenture, made and entered into this 19th day of November 1887, between Harriett Jones, of said State and County, of the one part, and Walton and Laura Oglesby, of said state and county, of the other part.

Witnesseth: That the said Harriett Jones does hereby bind to said Walton and Laura Oglesby her, the said Harriett's, daughter, Fannie Jones, a minor child aged Twenty five months, as apprentice to said Walton and Laura Oglesby, until said minor arrives at the age of Eighteen years. And the said Harriett Jones agrees and covenants that Fannie Jones shall live and remain with the said Walton and Laura Oglesby during all of said term.

Said Walton and Laura Oglesby agree to treat said child humanely, using only such means of compulsion to force obedience as a prudent parent would with a child, and to well feed and clothe and educate said minor, and furnish all necessary medical attention during said term of service as apprentice.

Witness our hands and seals this 19th day of November 1887.

Witness.   Harriett X Jones, her mark
Geo L. Almond,   Walton X Oglesby, his mark
Ordinary   Laura X Oglesby, her mark

DM Ordinary 1.00

Recorded November 22nd 1887.

                                  Geo L. Almond,
                                  Ordinary

Sarah C. Lively To Mary E. Moore, 1888   [93]

Georgia }
Elbert County } This Indenture, made this Feby 13th 1888, between Sarah C. Lively, of the one part, and Mary E. Moore, wife of L. L. Moore, and daughter of said Sarah C. Lively, of the other part, both of said state and county. Witnesseth: That the said Sarah C. Lively, hereby binds her daughter, Ida Lively, a minor aged seven years on March 1st 1888, unto said Mary E. Moore as apprentice, until the said Ida shall arrive At the Age of Eighteen years of age.

The said Sarah C. Lively hereby agrees and covenants never to claim said minor person, nor any profits from her labor, but that said Ida shall remain with said Mary E. Moore during the full term of said service.

Said Mary E. Moore agrees and covenants to treat said minor with humanity, furnish her with suitable food and clothing, and give her the advantages of the Common public schools of said County, and to provide for her the necessary medicine and medical attention during said term of apprenticeship, and to teach her the general business of house keeping and house servant. Always using only such means of compliance to force obedience as a prudent parent would use with a child.

And said Mary E. Moore agrees to give said Ida Lively, at the expiration of said apprenticeship, such Compensation as her services may demand and the ability of said Mary E. Moore to pay shall appear.

Witness our hands and seals Feby 13th 1888.

Witness.	Sarah C. X Lively, her mark
Ge^o L. Almond,	Mary E. Moore
Ordinary	

Recorded Feby 29, 1888.

Ge^o L. Almond, Ordinary

Morrison and Morrison To J. W. McCalla [94]

Georgia }
Elbert County } This Indenture, made this 21st day of May 1888, between Lem and Julia Morrison, father and mother of Ed Morrison three years old and Gordon Two years old, John W. McCalla, All of said County. witnesseth: that the said Lem and Julia Morrison has this day apprenticed unto the said McCalla, until they are Twenty one years of age.

The Said McCalla to teach them [blot] husbandry or such other business as he may see best.

The Said McCalla, upon his part, agrees to take said Children and to treat them humanely, giving them every Attention as he would his own, and agrees to give them $50.00 each when they arrive at the age of (21) Twenty years.

In witness whereof, we hereunto set our hands and seals the day and year above written.

Signed in presence of }	Lem X Morrison, his mark
L. A. Bond }	Julia X Morrison, her mark
D. W. X Lewis, his mark }	John W. McCalla

Georgia }
Elbert County } Personally appeared before me, L. A. Bond, and makes oath

that he saw Lem Morrison, Julia Morrison, and John W. McCalla Sign the within Instrument at the time mentioned and for the purpose specified and that deponent, together with D. W. Lewis, did sign the same as witnesses.

Sworn to before me }
May 22 1888 }
R. M. Willis, Clerk }
Sup^r Court E. C. }

L. A. Bond

Recorded 22 May 1888.

Ge° L. Almond, Ordinary

Duplicate [95]

Goss To Thornton, 1888

Georgia }
Elbert County } This Indenture, made this the 18th July 1888, between Pauline Goss, of Said County, for an in behalf of her son, Junius Goss, being of the age of Eight years, of the one part, and Henry Thornton, of the County of Oglethorpe, of the Other part. Witnesseth: that the said Pauline Goss aforesaid does by these presents bind her son Junius Goss, of said County, as Apprentice to said Henry Thornton in the trade or craft of farmer or as Laborer upon the plantation of the said Henry Thornton, to be taught the said Craft or trade of Farming or laborer, and to live with, continue, and serve the said Henry Thornton as an Apprentice from the date hereof for and during the term of his minority or 13 years.

During All of which time, said Pauline Goss as aforesaid doth Covenant with the said Henry Thornton that the said Junius Goss shall well and faithfully demean himself as such faithful apprentice, observing fully the Commands of the said Henry Thornton, and in all things deporting and behaving himself as a faithful Apprentice to the said Henry Thornton, neither revealing his secrets, nor at any time neglecting or leaving the business of the said Henry Thornton.

And for and in Consideration of the service well and faithfully rendered by the said Junius Goss of the first part, said Henry Thornton, of the second part, doth covenant, promise, and agree to instruct him, said apprentice, or otherwise Cause him to be well and faithfully instructed, in the said trade or Craft of farming or laborer, and also to read the English language. And shall also allow, furnish, and provide him, said Apprentice, with meat and drink and clothing during the said term, and all other necessaries meet and proper, in sickness and in health. And shall also, at the expiration of said term, [96] allow and pay the said Apprentice what is now allowed by the statute in such case made and provided.

Witness our hands and seals the day and year above written.

Executed before me }
Ge⁰ L. Almond, }
Ordinary }

Henry Thornton
Pauline X Goss, her mark

Filed in office July 18th 1888.

Ge⁰ L. Almond, Ordinary

Recorded July 19th 1888.

Ge⁰ L. Almond, Ordinary

Duplicate [97]

George Haygood To T. R. and M. E. White

Georgia }
Elbert County } This Indenture, made this the Seventh day of August 1888, between George Haygood, Sr, of said County, for and in behalf of George Haygood, Jr, being of the age of thirteen years, of the one part, and T. R. White and Mrs M. E. White, of the County Aforesaid, of the other part. Witnesseth: that the said George Haygood, Sr, as aforesaid, does by these presents bind out George Haygood, Jr, of said County, as apprentice to said T. R. White & Mrs M. E. White in the trade or Craft of house servant or as laborer upon the plantation of the said T. R. and Mrs M. E. White, to be taught the said Craft or trade of house servant or laborer, and live with, continue, and serve the said T. R. and Mrs M. E. White as an Apprentice from the date hereof for and during the term of Eight years.

During all of which time, said George Haygood, Sr doth covenant with the said T. R. and M. E. White that the said George Haygood, Jr shall well and faithfully demean himself as such faithful Apprentice, observing fully the Commands of the said T. R. and M. E. White, and in all things deporting and behaving himself as a faithful apprentice to the said T. R. and M. E. White, neither revealing their secrets, nor at any time neglecting or leaving the business of the said T. R. and M. E. White.

And for and in consideration of the service well and faithfully rendered by the said George Haygood, J^r of the first part, Said T. R. and M. E. White, of the second part, doth covenant, promise, and agree to instruct him, said Apprentice, or otherwise cause him to be well and faithfully instructed, in the said trade or craft of house servant or laborer, and also to read the English language, and shall also allow, furnish, and provide him, said Apprentice, with meat and drink and clothing during the said term, and all other necessaries meet and proper, in sickness

And in health. And shall also, at the expiration of the said term, allow [98] and pay the said Apprentice A horse, bridle, and Saddle and ten dollars in cash.

Witness Our hands and seals the day and year first before written.

Executed before us }	George X Haygood, S^r
Ge° L. Almond, }	T. R. White
Ordinary }	M. E. White, by T. R. White gt

Recorded August 9th 1888.

Ge° L. Almond, Ordinary

Filed in office Aug 7 1888.

Ge° L. Almond, Ordinary

Duplicate [99]

Tom Harris To Jn° C. Hudgens

Georgia }
Elbert County } This Indenture, Made this 9th day of November 1888, between Tom Harris, of said County, for and in behalf of Felix and Betsey Harris, being of the ages of 12 and 11 years, of the one part, and John C. Hudgens, of the County aforesaid, of the other part. Witnesseth: that the said Tom Harris does by these presents bind out Felix and Betsey Harris, of said County, as Apprentices to said John C. Hudgens in the trade or Craft of Farmers or as Laborers upon the plantation of the said John C. Hudgens, to be taught the craft or trade of Farmers or laborers, and to live with, continue, and serve the said John C. Hudgens as an Apprentices from the date hereof for and during the term of 8 and 9 years.

During all of which time, said Tom Harris doth Covenant with the said John C. Hudgens that the said Felix and Betsy Harris shall well and faithfully demean themselves as such faithful apprentices, observing fully the Commands of the said John C. Hudgens, and in all things deporting and behaving themselves as faithful Apprentices to the said John C. Hudgens, neither revealing his secrets, nor at any time neglecting or leaving the business of the said John C. Hudgens.

And for and in consideration of the services well and faithfully rendered by the said Felix & Betsy Harrison of the first part, said J. C. Hudgens, of the second part, doth covenant, promise, and agree to instruct them, said Apprentices, or otherwise cause them to be well and faithfully instructed, in the said trade or craft of farmers or laborers, and also to read the English language, and shall also allow, furnish, and provide them, said Apprentices, with meat, drink, and clothing during the said term, and all other necessaries meet & proper, in sickness and in health.

Witness our hands & Seals the day and year above written.

Executed before us }
H. A. Roebuck   }   J. C. Hudgens
Geº L. Almond,   }   Tom X Harris, his mark
Ordinary   }

Filed in office and Recorded Nov 9 1888.

Geº L. Almond, Ordinary

Duplicate   [100]

Tom Harris To John C. Hudgens

Georgia   }
Elbert County } This Indenture, made this 26th day of November 1888, between Tom Harris, of said County, for and in behalf of John Henry Harris, being of the ages of Eight years, of the one part, and John C. Hudgens, of the County aforesaid, of the other part. Witnesseth: that the said Tom Harris aforesaid does by these presents bind out John Henry Harris, of said County, as Apprentice to said John C. Hudgens in the trade or Craft of Farmer or as Laborer upon the plantation of the said John C. Hudgens, to be taught the said Craft or trade of Farmer or laborer, and to live with, Continue, and serve the said John C. Hudgens as an Apprentice from the date hereof for and during the term of thirteen years.

During all of which time, said Tom Harris aforesaid doth Covenant with the said John C. Hudgens that the said John Henry Harris shall well and faithfully demean himself as such faithful apprentice, observing fully the Commands of the said John C. Hudgens, and in all things deporting and behaving himself as a faithful

Apprentice to the said John C. Hudgens, neither revealing his secrets, nor at any time neglecting or leaving the business of the said John C. Hudgens. And for and in consideration of the services well and faithfully rendered by the said John Henry Harris of the first part, Said John C. Hudgens, of the second part, doth Covenant, promise, and agree to instruct him, said apprentice, or otherwise cause him to be well and faithfully instructed, in the said trade or craft of farmer or laborer, and also to read the English language, and shall also allow, furnish, and provide him, said apprentice, with meat and drink and clothing during the said term, and all other necessaries meet & proper, in sickness and in health. Witness our hands & Seals the day and year first aforementioned.

Executed before us }
H. A. Roebuck }
Ge° L. Almond, }
Ordinary }

Tom X Harris, his mark
J. C. Hudgens

Filed in office 26 Nov 1888 and Recorded same day.

Ge° L. Almond, Ordinary

This Indenture is hereby made null and void March 5th 1889.

Ge° L. Almond, }
Ordinary }

Tom X Harris, his mark
J. C. Hudgens

Duplicate [101]

Jane Howard to Henry Blackwell

Georgia }
Elbert County } This Indenture, made and entered into between Henry Blackwell and Jane Howard, the mother of the three minor children hereinafter named, to wit, John Blackwell aged sixteen years, James Blackwell aged fourteen years, Dunston Blackwell aged twelve years, all of said County. Witnesseth: that the said Jane Howard, mother as aforesaid, hereby binds and apprentices to the said Henry Blackwell the said Minor Children until each of said children is twenty one years old, upon the following conditions. The Said Henry Blackwell agrees to take into his custody the said Minor Children, teach them the business of husbandry and house service according to the sex of said children, furnish them with protection, wholesome food, suitable clothing, necessary medicine, and medical attention, teach them habits of industry, honesty, and morality, Cause them to be taught the elementary principles of Mathematics and to read English,

and shall govern them with humanity, using only such degrees of force to Compel their obedience as a father may use with his minor children.

In consideration of which, said Henry Blackwell is to be entitled to the services and earnings of said minor children until each of them is Twenty one years of age.

Witness our hands and seals this 26 November 1888.

Signed, sealed, and acknowledged in presence of

Ja^s L. Worly }	Jane X Howard, her mark
Ge^o L. Almond, }	Henry X Blackwell, his mark
Ordinary }	

Filed in office and recorded Nov 26th 1888.

            Ge^o L. Almond, Ordinaey

      Duplicate   [102]

Sam Christian To D. W. Thornton

Georgia   }
Elbert County } This Indenture, made this 15th day of December 1888, between Dick Christian, col, of said County, for and in behalf of Sam Christian, col, being of the age of 14 years, of the one part, and D. W. Thornton, of the County aforesaid, of the other part. Witnesseth: that the said Dick Christian as aforesaid does by these presents bind out Sam Christian, of said County, as apprentice to said D. W. Thornton in the trade or craft of House Servant or as Laborer upon the plantation of the said D. W. Thornton, to be taught or trade the said craft or trade of House servant or laborer, and to live with, continue, and serve the said D. W. Thornton as an Apprentice from the date hereof for and during the term of twelve and one half months. During all of which time, said Dick Christian as aforesaid doth covenant with the said D. W. Thornton that the said Sam Christian shall well and faithfully demean himself as such faithful apprentice, observing fully the Commands of the said D. W. Thornton, and in all things deporting and behaving himself as a faithful Apprentice to the said D. W. Thornton, neither revealing his secrets, nor at any time neglecting or leaving the business of the said D. W. Thornton.

And for and in consideration of the services well and faithfully rendered by the said Sam Christian of the first part, said D. W. Thornton, of the second part, doth Covenant, promise, and agree to instruct him, said apprentice, or otherwise cause him to be well and faithfully instructed, in the said trade or craft of House servant or laborer, and also to allow, furnish, and provide him, said apprentice, with meat and drink.

Witness our hands & Seals the day and year first above written.

Executed before us }
Wm M. Grogan }
Ge° L. Almond, }
Ordinary }

D. W. Thornton
Dick X Christian, his mark

Filed in office & recorded Decr 15 1888..

Ge° L. Almond, Ordinary

Duplicate [103]

John Henry Christian To J. L. Wilhite

Georgia }
Elbert County } This Indenture, made this 15th Dec 1888, between Dick Christian, col, of said County, for and in behalf of John Henry Christian, col, being of the age of Twelve years, of the one part, and John L. Wilhite, of the County aforesaid, of the other part. Witnesseth: that the said Dick Christian, col as aforesaid, does by these presents bind out John Henry Christian, of said County, as apprentice to said John L. Wilhite in the trade or craft of House servant or as Laborer upon the plantation of the said Jn° L. Wilhite, to be taught the said Craft or trade of House servant or laborer, and to live with, continue, and serve the said John L. Wilhite as an apprentice from the date hereof for and during the term of Two years.

During all of which time, said Dick Christian doth covenant with the said John L. Wilhite that the said John Henry Christian shall well and faithfully demean himself as such faithful apprentice, observing fully the commands of the said John L. Wilhite, and in all things deporting and behaving himself as a faithful apprentice to the said John L. Wilhite, neither revealing his secrets, nor at any time neglecting or leaving the business of the said John L. Wilhite.

And for and in consideration of the services well and faithfully rendered by the said John Henry Christian of the first part, said John L. Wilhite, of the second part, doth Covenant, promise, and agree to instruct him, said Apprentice, or otherwise cause him to be well and faithfully instructed, in the said trade or craft of House Servant or laborer, and shall also allow, furnish, and provide him, said apprentice, with meat and drink and clothing during the said term, and all other necessaries meet and proper, in sickness and in health.

Witness our hands & Seals the day and year first above written.

Executed before us }
D. W. Thornton }
Ge° L. Almond, }
Ordinary }

J. L. Wilhite
Dick X Christian, his mark

Filed in office & recorded 15 Decr 1888..

Ge° L. Almond, Ordinary

Duplicate [104]

Georgia }
Elbert County } This Indenture, made this 28th day of January 1889, between Lewis Grimes, of said County, for and in behalf of Jack Grimes and Fannie Grimes, being of the age of 13 and 8 years, of the one part, and A. G. Webb, of the County aforesaid, of the other part. Witnesseth: that the said Lewis Grimes does by these presents bind out Jack Grimes and Fannie Grimes, of said County, as apprentices to said A. G. Webb in the trade or Craft of House Servant or as Laborer upon the plantation of the said A. G. Webb, to be taught the said Craft or trade of house servant or laborer, and to live with, continue, and serve the said A. G. Webb as an Apprentices from the date hereof for and during the term of one year.

During all of which time, said Lewis Grimes doth covenant with the said A. G. Webb that the said Jack and Fannie shall well and faithfully demean themselves as such faithful apprentices, observing fully the commands of the said A. G. Webb, and in all things deporting and behaving themselves as a faithful apprentices to the said A. G. Webb, neither revealing his secrets, nor at any time neglecting or leaving the business of the said A. G. Webb.

And for and in consideration of the services well and faithfully rendered by the said Jack and Fannie of the first part, said A. G. Webb, of the second part, doth covenant, promise, and agree to instruct them, said Apprentices, or otherwise cause them to be well and faithfully instructed, in the said trade or craft of House Servant or laborer, and also to read the English language, and shall also allow, furnish, and provide them, said apprentices, with meat and drink and clothing during the said term, and all other necessaries meet and proper, in sickness and in health, and

and shall also, at the expiration of said term, allow and pay the said [105] apprentice what is now allowed by the statute in Such Case made and provided.

Witness our hands & Seals the day and year above written.

Executed before us }
Thos J. Campbell }   A. G. Webb
Ge^o L. Almond, }   Lewis X Grimes, his mark
Ordinary }

Filed and recorded Jany 28 1889.

                                  Ge^o L. Almond, Ordinary

                              Duplicate [106]

Lewis Grimes To A. G. Webb

Georgia }
Elbert County } This Indenture, made this 17th day of February 1889, between Lewis Grimes, of said County, for and in behalf of Julia Grimes, being of the age of six years, of the one part, and A. G. Webb, of the County aforesaid, of the other part. Witnesseth: that the said Lewis Grimes does by these presents bind out Julia Grimes, of said County, as apprentice to said A. G. Webb in the trade or craft of house servant or as Laborer upon the plantation of the said A. G. Webb, to be taught the said craft or trade of house servant or laborer, and to live with, continue, and the said A. G. Webb as an Apprentice from the date hereof for and during the term of one year. During all of which time, said Lewis Grimes doth covenant with the said A. G. Webb that the said Julia Grimes shall well and faithfully demean herself as such faithful apprentice, observing fully the commands of the said A. G. Webb, and in all things deporting and behaving herself as a faithful apprentices to the said A. G. Webb, neither revealing his secrets, nor at any time neglecting or leaving the business of the said A. G. Webb. And for and in consideration of the services well and faithfully rendered by the said Julia Grimes of the first part, said A. G. Webb, of the second part, doth covenant, promise, and agree to instruct him, said apprentice, or otherwise cause her to be well and faithfully instructed, in the said trade or craft of house servant or laborer, and also to read the English language, and shall also allow, furnish, and provide her, said apprentice, with meat and drink and clothing during the said term, and all other

necessaries meet and proper, in sickness and in health, and shall also, at the expiration of said term, allow and pay the said apprentice what is now allowed by the Statute in such cases made and provided.

Witness our hands & Seals the day and year above written.

Executed before us }
J. E. Anderson }   Lewis X Grimes, his mark
Geº L. Almond, }   A. G. Webb
Ordinary }

Filed in office and recorded 17th Feb 1889.

Geº L. Almond, Ordinary

Duplicate [107]

Georgia }
Elbert County } This Indenture, made the 2nd day of March 1889, between Ann Morrison, for and in behalf of Addie Morrison, being of the age of one and one half years, of the one part, and Addie Hester, of the County aforesaid, of the other part. Witnesseth: that the said Ann Morrison does by these presents bind out Addie Morrison, of said County, as Apprentice to said Addie Hester in the trade or Craft of house servant or as Laborer upon the plantation of the said Addie Hester, to be taught the said Craft or trade of house servant or laborer, and to live with, continue, and serve the said Addie Hester as an Apprentice from the date hereof for and during the term of Sixteen years.

During All of which time, said Ann Morrison doth covenant with the said Addie Hester that the said Addie Morrison Shall well and faithfully demean herself as such faithful Apprentice, observing fully the commands of the said Addie Hester, and in all things deporting and behaving herself as a faithful Apprentice to the said Addie Hester, neither revealing her secrets, nor at any time neglecting or leaving the business of the said Addie Hester.

And for and in consideration of the services well and faithfully rendered by the said Addie Morrison of the first part, said Addie Hester, of the second part, doth Covenant, promise, and agree to instruct her said apprentice, or otherwise cause her to be well and faithfully instructed, in the said trade or craft of house servant or laborer, and also to read the English language, and shall also allow, furnish, and provide her said apprentice, with meat and drink and clothing during the said term, and all other necessaries meet and proper, in sickness and in health, and shall also, at the expiration of said term, allow and pay the said Apprentice what is now allowed by the Statute in such cases made and provided.

Witness our hands and seals.

Executed before us }
John M. Brewer }　　　　　　　　　Ann X Morrison, her mark
Geº L. Almond, }　　　　　　　　　Addie Hester
Ordinary }

Filed and recorded in office 2 March 1889.

　　　　　　　　　　　　　　　Geº L. Almond, Ordinary

　　　　　　　　　　　Duplicate　　　　　　　　　　　　[108]

Berry Almond to D. W. Thornton

Georgia　　　　}
Elbert County } This Indenture, made the 6th day of March 1889, between Berry Almond, of said County, for and in behalf of John and Cosby Almond, being of the ages of 19 and 17 years, of the one part, and D. W. Thornton, of the County aforesaid, of the other part. Witnesseth: that the said Berry Almond aforesaid does by these presents bind out John and Cosby Almond, of said County, as apprentices to said D. W. Thornton in the trade or craft of house servants or as laborers upon the plantation of the said D. W. Thornton, to be taught the said craft or trade of house servants or laborers, and to live with and continue & serve the said D. W. Thornton as apprentices from the date hereof for and during the term of Two years.

During all of which time, said Berry Almond doth covenant with the said D. W. Thornton that the said John and Cosby Almond Shall well and faithfully demean themselves as such faithful apprentice, observing fully the commands of the said D. W. Thornton, and in All things deporting and behaving themselves as faithful Apprentices to the said D. W. Thornton, neither revealing his secrets, nor at any time neglecting or leaving the business of the said D. W. Thornton.

And for and in consideration of the services well and faithfully rendered by the said John and Berry Almond of the first part, Said D. W. Thornton, of the second part, doth covenant, promise, and agree to instruct said apprentices, or otherwise cause them to be well and faithfully instructed, in the said trade or craft of house servants or laborers, and also furnish and provide them, said Apprentices, with meat and drink and two suits of clothes to Cosby during the said term.

Witness our hands and seals the day and year first above written.

Executed before us }
H. A. Roebuck, Judge S. C. E. C. } Berry X Almond, his mark
Geº L. Almond, } D. W. Thornton
Ordinary }

Filed in office and recorded 6 March 1889.

Geº L. Almond, Ordinary

Duplicate [109]

Georgia }
Elbert County } This Indenture, made this 14 day of March 1889, between Lewis Grimes, of said County, for and in behalf of Julia and Francis Grimes, being of the ages of 6 and 7 years, of the one part, and A. G. Webb, of the County aforesaid, of the other part. Witnesseth: that the said Lewis Grimes aforesaid does by these presents bind out Julia and Francis Grimes, of said County, as apprentices to said A. G. Webb in the trade or craft of house Servants or as laborers upon the plantation of the said A. G. Webb, to be taught the said craft or trade of house servants or laborers, and to live with, continue and serve the said A. G. Webb as apprentices from January 28th 1890 for and during the term of One years.

During all of which time, said Lewis Grimes doth covenant with the said A. G. Webb that the said Julia and Francis shall well and faithfully demean themselves as such faithful apprentices, observing fully the commands of the said A. G. Webb, and in All things deporting and behaving themselves as faithful apprentices to the said A. G. Webb, neither revealing his secrets, nor at any time neglecting or leaving the business of the said A. G. Webb. And for and in consideration of the services well and faithfully rendered by the said Julia and Francis of the first part, Said A. G. Webb, of the second part, doth covenant, promise, and agree to instruct them, said apprentices, or otherwise cause them to be well and faithfully instructed, in the said trade or craft of house servants or laborers, and also allow, furnish, and provide them, said apprentices, with meat and drink and clothing during the said term, and all other necessaries meet & proper, in sickness and in health, and shall also at the expiration of said term allow and pay the said apprentices what is now allowed by the statute in such case made and provided.

Witness our hands and seals the day and year first above written.

Executed before us }
W. B. Hendricks }   Lewis X Grimes, his mark
Ge⁰ L. Almond, }   A. G. Webb
Ordinary }

We hereby agree that this Indenture shall be and is hereby made null & void Feby 1890.

Attest. Ge⁰ L. Almond, Ordinary   Lewis X Grimes, his mark
                                    A. G. Webb

Duplicate   [110]

Georgia }
Elbert County } This Indenture, made this 6th day of March 1889, between John W. McCalla and Cornelia McIntosh, mother of Lou McIntosh, Luther McIntosh, Carry McIntosh, Jn⁰ McIntosh, and May McIntosh, minor children of said Cornelia McIntosh, Lou being 14 years, Luther 12 years, Carry 10 years, Jn⁰ 8 years, and May 5 years of age, all of said County. witnesseth: that the said Cornelia McIntosh binds and apprentices to the said McCalla the said children until they are Twenty one years of age. The said McCalla agrees to take into his custody the children aforesaid, teach them the business of husbandry, and furnish them with suitable food, clothing, medicine, and medical attention, to furnish them with protection and such educational advantages as the children of the neighborhood of Same condition have.

And Shall teach them habits of industry and morality, using no force except to compel obedience, and when said children shall arrive at the age of twenty one, the said McCalla agrees to pay them the sum of $50.00 each, provided the said children shall remain with the said McCalla until said majority is obtained. In consideration of all of which, the said McCalla is entitled to the services of Said children until they are twenty one years old. In witness, we hereunto set our hands and seals the day and year above written.

Henry X Williams, his mark   John W. McCalla
L. A. Bond   Cornelia X McIntosh, her mark

Georgia }
Elbert County } In person comes L. A. Bond who on oath says that he, together

with Henry Williams, did see the within named John W. McCalla and Cornelia McIntosh sign the within Instrument.

That they signed the same for the purpose therein Stated and that deponent and said Williams Attested the same as witnesses. [111]

Sworn to & Subscribed before me 15 April 1889.

Geº L. Almond, Ordinary   L. A. Bond

Recorded April 16th 1889.

Geº L. Almond, Ordinary

Duplicate [112]

Moriah Allen to W. T. Arnold

Georgia }
Elbert County } This Indenture, made this 1st day of June 1889, between Moriah Allen, of said County, for and in behalf of Calvin Blackwell, being of the age of 17 years, of the one part, and W. T. Arnold, of the County aforesaid, of the other part. Witnesseth: that the said Moriah Allen does by these presents bind out Calvin Blackwell, of said County, as apprentice to said W. T. Arnold in the trade or craft of house servant or as laborer upon the plantation of the said W. T. Arnold, to be taught the said craft or trade of house servant or laborer, and to live with, continue, and serve the said W. T. Arnold as an apprentice from Jany 1, 1890 for and during the term of two years.

During all of which time, said Moriah Allen doth covenant with the said W. T. Arnold that the said Calvin Blackwell shall well and faithfully demean himself as such faithful apprentice, observing fully the commands of the said W. T. Arnold, and in all things deporting and behaving himself as a faithful Apprentice to the said W. T. Arnold, neither revealing his secrets, nor at any time neglecting or leaving the business of the said W. T. Arnold.

And for and in consideration of the services well and faithfully rendered by the said Calvin Blackwell of the first part, said W. T. Arnold, of the second part, doth covenant, promise, and agree to instruct him, said Apprentice, or otherwise cause him to be well and faithfully instructed, in the said trade or craft of house servant or laborer, and shall also allow, furnish, and provide him, said Apprentice, with meat and drink & clothing during the said term, and all other necessaries meet and proper.

Witness our hands & Seals the day & year first above written.

Executed before us }
Thos J. Hester }
Ge^o L. Almond, }
Ordinary }

Moriah X Allen, her mark
W. T. Arnold

Recorded June 1st 1889.

Ge^o L. Almond, Ordinary

Duplicate [113]

Gipson Verdel to W. H. Mattox

Georgia }
Elbert County } This Indenture, made this 12th day of Febr^y 1889, between Gipson Verdel, of said County, for and in behalf of Ge^o Verdel and Addie Verdel, being of the ages of Eight and seven years, of the one part, and W. H. Mattox, of the County aforesaid, of the other part. Witnesseth: that the said Gipson Verdel as aforesaid does by these presents bind out Ge^o Verdel and Addie Verdel, of said County, as apprentices to said W. H. Mattox in the trade or craft of house servants or as Laborers upon the plantation of the said W. H. Mattox, to be taught the said Craft or trade of house servants or laborers, and to live with, continue and serve the said W. H. Mattox as Apprentices from the date hereof for and during the term of Ten years.

During all of which time, said Gipson Verdel, as aforesaid, doth covenant with the said W. H. Mattox that the said George and Addie shall well and faithfully demean themselves as such faithful apprentices, observing fully the Commands of the said W. H. Mattox, and in all things deporting and behaving themselves as faithful Apprentices to the said W. H. Mattox, neither revealing his secrets, nor at any time neglecting or leaving the business of the said W. H. Mattox. And for and in consideration of the service well & faithfully rendered by the said George & Addie of the first part, Said W. H. Mattox, of the second part, doth covenant, promise, & agree to instruct them, said apprentices, or otherwise cause them to be well & faithfully instructed, in the said Craft or trade of house servants or laborers, and also to read the English language, and also allow, furnish, and provide them, said apprentices, with meat and drink and clothing during the said term, and all other necessaries meet & proper, in sickness and in health, and shall also at the expiration of the said term allow and pay the said Apprentice what is now allowed by the statute in such case made and provided.

Witness our hands and seals the day and year first Above written.

Executed before us }
Annie J. Mattox }   Gipson Verdel
S. P. Mattox   }   W. H. Mattox

Recorded June the 4th 1889.

                                        Geo L. Almond, Ordinary

Robert Clark To Joseph N. Worly, 1889   [114]

Georgia   }
Elbert County } This Indenture, made this the 17th day of July 1889, between Sam Clark, of said County, for and in behalf of his son Robert Clark, being of the age of Twelve years, of the one part, and Joseph N. Worly, of the County aforesaid, of the other part.

Witnesseth: that the said Sam Clark, as aforesaid, does by these presents bind out his son Robt Clark, of said County, as apprentice to said Jos N. Worly in the trade or craft of house servant or as laborer upon the plantation of the said Jos N. Worly, to be taught the said craft or trade of house service or laborer, and to live with, continue, and serve the said Jos N. Worly as an apprentice from the date hereof for and during the term of one year and six months.

During all of which time, the said Sam Clark, as aforesaid, doth covenant with the said Jos N. Worly that the said Robert Clark shall well and faithfully demean himself as such faithful apprentice, observing fully the Commands of the said Jos N. Worly, and in all things deporting and behaving himself as a faithful apprentice to the said Jos N. Worly, neither revealing his secrets, nor at any time neglecting or leaving the business of the said Jos N. Worly.

And for and in consideration of the services well and faithfully rendered by the said Robert Clark of the first part, said Joseph N. Worly, of the second part, doth covenant, promise, and agree to instruct him, said apprentice, or otherwise cause him to be well and faithfully instructed, in the said trade or craft of house service or laborer, and also to read the English language, and Shall also furnish and provide his said Apprentice, with meat, drink, and clothing during the said term, and all other necessaries meet and proper, in sickness and in health, and shall also at the

expiration of the said term allow and pay the said Apprentice or Sam   [115]
Clark Ten dollars.

Witness our hands and seals the day and year first above written.

Executed before us }
J. P. Baily }
Ge⁰ L. Almond, }
Ordinary }

Sam X Clark, his mark
W. T. Arnold

Filed in office and recorded July 18, 1889.

Ge⁰ L. Almond, Ordinary

Duplicate [116]

Zanie Bell To T. R. White, 1889

Georgia }
Elbert County } This Indenture, made this the 5th day of September 1889, between Jane Hudson, col, of said County, for and in behalf of Zanie Bell, col, being of the age of 13 years, of the one part, and T. R. White, of the County aforesaid, of the other part. Witnesseth: that said Jane Hudson aforesaid does by these presents bind out Zanie Bell, of said County, as Apprentice to said T. R. White in the trade or craft of House Servant or as Laborer upon the plantation of the said T. R. White, to be taught the craft or trade of House service or laborer, and to live with, continue, and serve the said T. R. White as an Apprentice from the date hereof for and during the term of Eight years.

During all of which time, said Jane Hudson doth covenant with the said T. R. White that the said Zanie Bell shall well and faithfully demean herself as a faithful such faithful Apprentice, observing fully the Commands of the said T. R. White, and in All things deporting and behaving herself as a faithful Apprentice to the said T. R. White, neither revealing his secrets, nor at any time neglecting or leaving the business of the said T. R. White.

And for and in consideration of the services well and faithfully rendered by the said Zanie Bell of the first part, said T. R. White, of the second part, doth covenant, promise, and agree to instruct him, said Apprentice, or otherwise cause him to be well and faithfully instructed, in the said craft of house servant or laborer, and shall also furnish and provide him, said Apprentice, with meat and drink & clothing during the said term, and all other necessaries meet and proper, in sickness and in health.

Witness our hands & seals the day and year first before written. [117]

Executed Before us }
J. P. Baily } Jane X Hudson, her mark
Ge° L. Almond, } T. R. White
Ordinary }

Recorded Sep¹ 5, 1889.

Ge° L. Almond, Ordinary

We, the undersigned, do agree and consent that the above Indenture shall from this day hence shall be null and void. August 16th 1890

Attest. } Jane X Hudson, her mark
Ge° L. Almond, } Tinsly R. White
Ordinary }

Georgia } [118]
Elbert County } For and in consideration of good and sufficient reasons, as well as the fact of my wife, Mary L. Alexander, being better qualified and more Able to rear my children by her, to wit, William, John, and Roda Alexander, I do hereby relinquish all of my parental Authority, custody, and control of said three children unto her, the said Mary L. Alexander, and hereby obligate myself never to claim or attempt to claim any custody, control, or authority over said children.

Attest. }
Ge° L. Almond, } J. L. + Alexander, his mark
Ordinary }

Filed in office & recorded this 10th Sep¹ 1889.

Ge° L. Almond, Ordinary

Duplicate [119]

Victoria Bell To W. H. Mattox, 1889

Georgia }
Elbert County } This Indenture, made this the 23rd day of September 1889, between Victoria Bell, col, of said County, for and in behalf of Henry, Willie, Lucy, Catherine, Bessie, and an infant, all being her children, being of the ages of 13, 11, 9, 6, 3 years, and 3 months, of the one part, and W. H. Mattox, of the

County aforesaid, of the other part. Witnesseth: that the said Victoria Bell, as aforesaid, does by these presents bind out her said children, of said County, as Apprentices to said W. H. Mattox in the said craft or trade of house servants or laborers upon the plantation of the said W. H. Mattox, to be taught the craft or trade of house servants or laborers, and to live with, continue, and serve the said W. H. Mattox as an apprentices from the date hereof for and during their minority.

During all of which time, said Victoria Bell, as aforesaid, doth covenant with the said W. H. Mattox that the said children shall well and faithfully demean themselves as such faithful Apprentices, observing fully the commands of the said W. H. Mattox, and in all things deporting and behaving themselves as faithful Apprentices to the said W. H. Mattox, neither revealing his secrets, nor at any time neglecting or leaving the business of the said W. H. Mattox.

And for and in consideration of the services well and faithfully rendered by the said children of the first part, said W. H. Mattox, of the second part, doth covenant, promise, and agree to instruct them, said apprentices, or otherwise cause them to be well and faithfully instructed, in the said trade or craft of house servants or laborers, and also to read the English language, and shall also allow, furnish, and provide them, said apprentices, with meat, drink, & clothing during the said term, and all other

necessaries meet and proper, in sickness and in health. [120]

Witness our hands & Seals the day and year first before written.

Executed Before us }	
W. B. Adams }	Victor X Bell, her mark
Ge° L. Almond, }	W. H. Mattox
Ordinary }	

Filed in office and recorded Sep^t 23, 1889.

Ge° L. Almond, Ordinary

We, W. H. Mattox and Victoria Bell, do hereby agree that, with Consent, the above Indenture is Null and void this October 8th 1889.

Attest. }	W. H. Mattox
Ge° L. Almond, }	by his att^y H. J. Brown
Ordinary }	Victoria X Bell, her mark

Duplicate

Russell Christian To W. H. Mattox, 1889

Georgia }
Elbert County } This Indenture, made this 12th day of Sep^t 1889, between Russell Christian, of said County, for and in behalf of Georgia, Janie, and Jinnie Christian, being of the ages of 15, 13, and 7 years, of the one part, and W. H. Mattox, of the County aforesaid, of the other part. Witnesseth: that the said Russell Christian does by these presents bind out Georgia, Janie, & Jinnie, of said County, as apprentices to said W. H. Mattox in the craft or trade of house servants or laborers upon the plantation of the said W. H. Mattox, to be taught the said Craft or trade of house servants or laborers, and to live with, continue, and serve the said W. H. Mattox as apprentices from the date hereof for and during their minority.

During all of which time, said Russell Christian, as aforesaid, doth covenant with the said W. H. Mattox that the said Georgia, Janie, and Jinnie shall well and faithfully demean themselves as such

faithful Apprentices, observing fully the commands of the said W. H.   [121]

Mattox, and in all things deporting and behaving themselves as ~~such~~ faithful apprentices to the said W. H. Mattox, neither revealing his secrets, nor at any time neglecting or leaving the business of the said W. H. Mattox.

And for and in consideration of the services well and faithfully rendered by the said Georgia, Janie, and Jinnie Christian of the first part, said W. H. Mattox, of the second part, doth covenant, promise, and agree to instruct them, said apprentices, or otherwise cause them to be well and faithfully instructed, in the said trade or craft of house servants or laborers, and also to read the English language, and also furnish and provide them, said apprentices, with meat and drink and clothing during the said term, and all other necessaries meet and proper, in sickness and in health.

Witness our hands and seals the day and year first before written.

Executed Before us }
J. L. Deadwyler   }   Russell + Christian, his mark
Ge^o L. Almond,   }   W. H. Mattox
Ordinary   }

Filed in office Sep^t 12, 1889. and recorded Sep^t 23, 1889.

Ge^o L. Almond, Ordinary

We, W. H. Mattox and Russell Christian, do hereby Agree and consent that the above Indenture is hereby null and void.

Attest.   }
Ge^o L. Almond, }
Ordinary   }

Russell + Christian, his mark
W. H. Mattox

Duplicate   [122]

Allen Carter To Gairdner and Arnold, 1889

Georgia   }
Elbert County } This Indenture, made this 23rd day of Sep^t 1889, between Allen Carter, of said County, for and in behalf of Paul & Louise Carter, being of the ages of 10 and 7 years, of the one part, and McAlpin Arnold & H. K. Gairdner (Gairdner & Arnold), of the County aforesaid, of the other part. Witnesseth: that the said Allen Carter does by these presents bind out Paul & Louise, of said County, as apprentices to said Gairdner & Arnold in the trade or craft of house servants or laborers upon the plantation of the said Gairdner & Arnold, to be taught the said Craft or trade of house servants or laborers, and to live with, continue, & serve the said Gairdner & Arnold as apprentices from the date hereof for and during the term of their minority.

During all of which time, said Allen Carter, as aforesaid, doth covenant with the said Gairdner & Arnold that the said Paul and Louise shall well and faithfully demean themselves as such faithful apprentices, observing fully the commands of the said Gairdner & Arnold, and in all things deporting and behaving themselves as such faithful apprentices to the said Gairdner & Arnold, neither revealing their secrets, nor at any time neglecting or leaving the business of the said Gairdner & Arnold.

And for and in consideration of the services well and faithfully rendered by the said Paul and Louise, of the first part, said Gairdner & Arnold, of the second part, doth covenant, promise, & agree to instruct them, said apprentices, or otherwise cause them to be well and faithfully instructed, in the said trade or craft of house servants or laborers, and Also to read the english language, and shall also allow, furnish, and provide them, said apprentices, with meat and drink & clothing during the said term, and all other necessaries meet and proper, in sickness and in health. [123]

Witness our hands and seals the day and year first before written.

Executed Before us }
D. B. Alexander   }   Allen + Carter, his mark
Geº L. Almond,   }   Gairdner & Arnold
Ordinary   }

Filed in office and recorded Sep^t 23, 1889.

Geº L. Almond, Ordinary

Duplicate [124]

Russell Christian To W. H. Cary, 1889

Georgia   }
Elbert County   } This Indenture, made this the 8th day of October 1889, between Russell Christian, of said County, for and in behalf of his daughter Janie Christian, being of the age of 13 years, of the one part, and W. H. Cary, of the County aforesaid, of the other part. Witnesseth: that the said Russell Christian does by these presents bind out Janie Christian, of said County, as apprentice to said W. H. Cary in the trade or craft of house servant or laborer upon the plantation of the said W. H. Cary, to be taught the said craft or trade of House servant or laborer, and to live with, continue, and serve the said W. H. Cary as apprentice from the date hereof for and during the term of Two years.

During all of which time, said Russell aforesaid doth covenant with the said W. H. Cary that the said Janie shall well and faithfully demean herself as such faithful Apprentice, observing fully the Commands of the said W. H. Cary, and in all things deporting and behaving herself as a faithful apprentice to the said W. H. Cary, neither revealing his secrets, nor at any time neglecting or leaving the business of the said W. H. Cary.

And for and in consideration of the services well and faithfully rendered by the said Janie, of the first part, said W. H. Cary, of the second part, doth covenant, promise, and agree to instruct his said Apprentice, or otherwise cause her to be well and faithfully instructed, in the said trade or craft of house servant or laborer, and also to read the English language, and shall also allow, furnish, and provide her, said Apprentice, with meat and drink and clothing during the said term, and all other necessaries meet and proper, in sickness and in health, and to pay the following, one and $^{25}/_{100}$ Dollars per month.

Witness our hands & Seals the day and year first before written.

Executed Before us }
H. J. Brewer   }   Russell + Christian, his mark
Geº L. Almond,   }   W. H. Cary
Ordinary   }

Filed in office and recorded October 8, 1889.

Geº L. Almond, Ordinary

Duplicate   [125]

Georgia   }
Elbert County } This Indenture, made this the 8th day of October 1889, between Russell Christian, of said County, for and in behalf of his son Jimmie Christian, being of the age of seven years, of the one part, and R. F. Tate, of the County aforesaid, of the other part. Witnesseth: that the said Russell Christian as aforesaid does by these presents bind out his son Jimmie Christian, of said County, as apprentice to said R. F. Tate in the trade or Craft of house servant or laborer upon the plantation of the said R. F. Tate, to be taught the said Craft or trade of house servant or laborer, and to live with, continue, and serve the said R. F. Tate as an Apprentice from the date hereof for and during the term of his minority. During all of which time, said Russell Christian, as aforesaid, doth covenant with the said R. F. Tate that the said Jimmie shall well and faithfully demean himself as such faithful Apprentice, observing fully the commands of the said R. F. Tate, and in all things deporting and behaving himself as a faithful Apprentice to the said R. F. Tate, neither revealing his secrets, nor At any time neglecting or leaving the business of the said R. F. Tate. And for and in consideration of the services well and faithfully rendered by the said Jimmie, of the first part, said R. F. Tate, of the second part, doth covenant, promise, and agree to instruct his said apprentice, or otherwise cause him to be well and faithfully instructed, in the said trade or craft of house servant or laborer, and also to read the English language, and shall Also Allow, furnish, and provide him, said Apprentice, with meat and drink & clothing during the said term, And all other necessaries meet and proper, in sickness and in health. Witness our hands and seals the day and year first before written.

Executed Before us }
H. J. Brewer   }   Russell + Christian, his mark
Geº L. Almond,   }   R. F. Tate
Ordinary   }

Filed in office and recorded Oct 8, 1889.

Ge° L. Almond, Ordinary

Duplicate [126]

Russell Christian To Georgia Harper, 1889

Georgia }
Elbert County } This Indenture, made this the 8th day of Oct 1889, between Russell Christian, of said County, for and in behalf of his daughter Janie Christian, being of the age of 13 years, of the one part, and Georgia Harper, of the County aforesaid, of the other part. Witnesseth: that the said Russell Christian, as aforesaid, does by these presents bind out said Janie, of said County, as apprentice to said Georgia in the trade or Craft of house servant or laborer upon the plantation of the said Georgia, to be taught the said Craft or trade of house servant or laborer, and to live with, continue, and serve the said Georgia as an apprentice from the date hereof for and during the term of her minority, beginning October 8th 1891 and continuing until said Janie is twenty one years old. During all of which time, said Russell, as aforesaid, doth covenant with the said Georgia that the said Janie shall well and faithfully demean herself as such faithful apprentice, observing fully the Commands of the said Georgia, and in all things deporting and behaving herself as a faithful Apprentice to the said Georgia, neither revealing her secrets, nor at any time neglecting or leaving the business of the said Georgia.

And for and in consideration of the services well and faithfully rendered by the said Janie, of the first part, said Georgia, of the second part, doth covenant, promise, and agree to instruct her said Apprentice, or otherwise cause her to be well and faithfully instructed, in the said trade or craft of house servant or laborer, and also to read the English Language, and shall Also Allow, furnish, and provide her said Apprentice, with meat and drink and clothing during the said term, and all other necessaries meet and proper, in sickness and in health, and shall also at the expiration of said term allow & pay to said Apprentice what is now allowed by the statute in such cases made and provided. It is understood and agreed that the said Janie is Apprenticed to W. H. Cary until the above date Oct 8, 1891.

Witness our hands & Seals the day & year first above written.

Executed Before us }
H. J. Brewer }   Russell + Christian, his mark
Ge° L. Almond, }   Georgia + Harper, her mark
Ordinary }

Filed in office & recorded 8 Oct 1889.

Geº L. Almond, Ordinary

Duplicate [127]

Georgia }
Elbert County } This Indenture, made this the 19th day of Nov 1889, between Harriett Heard, col, of said County, for and in behalf of Susie Heard, col, being of the age of Eleven years, on the one part, and C. E. Earle, of the County aforesaid, of the other part. Witnesseth: that the said Harriett Heard, as aforesaid, does by these presents bind out said Susie, of said County, as Apprentice to said C. E. Earl in the trade or craft of house servant or laborer upon the plantation of the said C. E. Earle, to be taught the said craft or trade of house servant or laborer, and to live with, continue, & serve the said C. E. Earle as an Apprentice from the date hereof for and during the term of ten years.

During all of which time, said Harriett Heard, as aforesaid, doth covenant with the said C. E. Earle that the said Susie Heard shall well and faithfully demean herself as such faithful Apprentice, observing fully the Commands of the said C. E. Earle, and in All things deporting & behaving herself as a faithful Apprentice to the said C. E. Earle, neither revealing his secrets, nor at any time neglecting or leaving the business of the said C. E. Earle.

And for and in consideration of the services well and faithfully rendered by the said Susie Heard, of the first part, Said C. E. Earle, of the second part, doth covenant, promise, & agree to instruct her, said Apprentice, or otherwise Cause her to be well and faithfully instructed, in the said trade or Craft of house servant or laborer, And also to read the English language, and Shall Also Allow, furnish, & provide her, said Apprentice, with meat and drink and clothing during the said term, and all other necessaries meet & proper, in sickness and in health.

Witness our hand and seal the day & year first above written.

Executed Before us }
T. J. Cordell }
Geº L. Almond, }
Ordinary }

Harriett + Heard, her mark
C. E. Earle

Filed in office & recorded Nov 19, 1889.

Geº L. Almond, Ordinary

Hugh Verdel to Jn° W. McCalla

Georgia }
Elbert County } This Indenture, made this the 9th day of December 1889, between Hugh Verdel, of said County, for and in behalf of his children, Dock 15 years old, Jane Ann, & Mary Frances 9 years, being of the age of Eleven years, on the one part, and John W. McCalla, of the County aforesaid, of the other part. Witnesseth: that the said Hugh Verdell does by these presents bind out said children, of said County, as apprentice to said Jn° W. McCalla in the trade or craft of as laborer upon the plantation of the said [blank], to be taught the said Craft or trade of Husbandry or laborer, and to live with, continue, & serve the said McCalla as an Apprentice from the date hereof for and during the term of their minority years.

During all of which time, said Hugh Verdel doth covenant with the said McCalla that the said children shall well and faithfully demean themself as such faithful Apprentice, observing fully the commands of the said McCalla, and in all things deporting & behaving theirself as a faithful Apprentice to the said McCalla, neither revealing his secrets, nor at any time neglecting or leaving the business of the said McCalla.

And for & in consideration of the service well and faithfully rendered by the said Apprentices, of the first part, said McCalla, of the second part, doth covenant, promise, & agree to instruct them, said Apprentice, or otherwise Cause them to be well & faithfully instructed, in the said trade or craft of husbandry or laborer, & also to read the English Language, And shall also allow, furnish, & provide his said Apprentices with meat, drink, & clothing during said term, and all other necessaries meet & proper, in sickness and in health, and shall also at the expiration of said term allow & pay the said Apprentices what is now allowed by the statute in such case made & provided. Provided however, they do not the service of said McCalla before the age of Twenty one years.

Witness our hands & Seals the day & year first above written.

Executed Before us }
L. A. Bond } Hugh + Verdel, his mark
Z. B. Taylor } Jn° W. McCalla

Filed in office and recorded 10th Dec 1889.

Ge° L. Almond, Ordinary

York Clark to Jnº W. McCalla [129]

Georgia }
Elbert County } This Indenture, made this 9th day of January 1890, between York Clark, father of Gabe Clark, a boy 16 years old, and John W. McCalla. witnesseth: that I, York Clark, has this day apprenticed unto Jnº W. McCalla my son Gabe, a boy 16 years old, for the term of Four years for the consideration of $70.00 Seventy dollars per year ½ $35.00 to be paid to York Clark & ½ $35.00 to be paid to Gabe. I hereby relinquish all controls over the said Gabe & give it unto the said McCalla.

The said John W. McCalla hereby accepts the said trust and agrees to take said boy as set forth above & agrees to furnish him board & all things as required of him by the statutes made & provided for master and apprentice agreeable to the above. Both parties reside in Elbert County, Ga. This writing was fully read over before signing.

I witness we set our hands and seals.

Z. B. Taylor } York + Clark, his mark
Andy X Morrison, his mark } John W. McCalla

Filed in office and recorded Janʸ 10th 1890.

Geº L. Almond, Ordinary

Duplicate [130]

Georgia }
Elbert County } This Indenture, made this the 24th day of January 1890, between Della Cleveland, of said county, for and in behalf of her son, John Brawner, being of the age of sixteen years, on the one part, and William H. Mattox, of the County aforesaid, of the other part. Witnesseth: that the said Della Cleveland, as aforesaid, does by these presents bind out John Brawner, of said County as apprentice to said W. H. Mattox in the trade or craft of husbandry or as laborer upon the plantation of the said W. H. Mattox, to be taught the said trade or craft of husbandry or laborer, and to live with, continue, and serve the said W. H. Mattox as an Apprentice from the date hereof for and during the term of three years.

During all of which time, said Della Cleveland, as aforesaid, doth covenant with the said W. H. Mattox that the said John shall well and faithfully demean himself as such faithful Apprentice, observing fully the Commands of the said W. H.

Mattox, and in all things deporting and behaving himself as a faithful Apprentice to the said W. H. Mattox, neither revealing his secrets, nor at any time neglecting or leaving the business of the said W. H. Mattox.

And for and in consideration of the service well and faithfully rendered by the said John, of the first part, said W. H. Mattox, of the second part, doth covenant, promise, & agree to instruct his said Apprentice, or otherwise cause him to be well & faithfully instructed, in the said trade or craft of husbandry or laborer, and shall Also allow, furnish, & provide him, said Apprentice, with meat and drink and clothing during said term, and all other necessaries meet and proper, in sickness and in health, and shall also Said Mattox further agrees to pay said Della the sum of four Dollars and 16⅔ cents per month.

Witness our hands and seals the day and year above written.

Executed before us }   W. H. Mattox
H. J. Brewer   }   Della + Cleveland, her mark
Ge° L. Almond, }
Ordinary   }

Recorded on Jany 24th 1890.

Ge° L. Almond, Ordinary

Duplicate [131]

Georgia   }
Elbert County } This Indenture, made this 18th day of February 1890, between Lewis Grimes, of said county, for and in behalf of Fannie and Julia Grimes, being of the age of 7 and 8 years, on the one part, and S. J. Lovinggood, S^r and S. J. Lovinggood, J^r, of the County aforesaid, of the other part. Witnesseth: that the said Lewis Grimes does by these presents bind out Fannie and Julia, of said County as Apprentices to said S. J. Lovinggood, S^r and J^r in the trade or craft of house servants or as laborers upon the plantation of the said Lovinggoods, to be taught the said trade or craft of house servants or laborers, and to live with, continue, and serve the said Lovinggoods as Apprentices from the date hereof for and during the term of 18 Months. During all of which time, said Lewis Grimes doth Covenant with the said Lovinggoods that the said Fannie and Julia shall well and faithfully demean themselves as such faithful Apprentices, observing fully the Commands of the said Lovinggoods, and in all things deporting and behaving themselves as faithful Apprentices to the said Lovinggoods, neither revealing their secrets, nor at any time neglecting or leaving the business of the said

Lovinggoods. And for and in consideration of the services well and faithfully rendered by the said Fannie and Julia, of the first part, said Lovinggoods, of the second part, doth covenant, promise, & agree to instruct them, said Apprentices, or otherwise cause them to be well and faithfully instructed, in the said trade or craft of house servants or laborers, and shall also allow, furnish, and provide them, said Apprentices, with meat and drink during the said term, and all other necessaries meet and proper, in sickness and in health.

Witness our hands & Seals the day & year first before written.

Executed before us }	Lewis + Grimes, his mark
A. G. Webb }	S. J. Lovinggood, S^r
Ge° L. Almond, }	S. J. Lovinggood, J^r
Ordinary }	

Filed in office & recorded Feby 18, 1890.

Ge° L. Almond, Ordinary

Duplicate [132]

Georgia }
Elbert County } This Indenture, made this the 1st day of April 1890, between Dick Christian, of said county, for and in behalf of John H. Christian, being of the age of 12 years, on the one part, and John L. Wilhite, of the County aforesaid, of the other part. Witnesseth: that the said Dick Christian, of said County as Apprentice as aforesaid, does by these presents bind out John H. Christian, of said County as apprentice to said John L. Wilhite in the trade or craft of house servant or as laborer upon the plantation of the said John L. Wilhite, to be taught the said trade or craft of house servant or laborer, and to live with, continue, and serve the said J. L. Wilhite as an apprentice from January 1, 1891 for and during the term of one year.

During all of which time, said Dick Christian, aforesaid, doth covenant with the said J. L. Wilhite that the said John H. Christian shall well and faithfully demean himself as such faithful Apprentice, observing fully the Commands of the said John L. Wilhite, and in all things deporting and behaving himself as a faithful Apprentice to the said J. L. Wilhite, neither revealing his secrets, nor at any time neglecting or leaving the business of the said John L. Wilhite.

And for and in consideration of the service well and faithfully rendered by the said John H. Christian, of the first part, said J. L. Wilhite, of the second part, doth covenant, promise, & agree to instruct him, said Apprentice, or otherwise cause him to be well & faithfully instructed, in the said trade or craft of house servant or laborer, and shall Also allow, furnish, & provide him, said Apprentice, with meat & drink & clothing during the said term.

Witness our hands and seals the day and year above written.

Executed before us }
S. J. Land }
Geo L. Almond, }
Ordinary }

J. L. Wilhite
Dick + Christlan, his mark

Filed in office and recorded on 1st April 1890.

Geo L. Almond, Ordinary

Duplicate [133]

Georgia }
Elbert County } This Indenture, made the 26th day of April 1890, between Jane Eberhart, of said County, for and in behalf of Louisa and James Eberhart, being of the ages of 12 & 10 years, on the one part, and Thompson S. Janes, of the County Aforesaid, of the other part. Witnesseth: that the said Jane Eberhart Aforesaid does by these presents bind out Louisa and James, of said County as Apprentices to said T. S. Janes in the trade or craft of house servants or as laborers upon the plantation of the said T. S. Janes, to be taught the said craft or trade of house servants or laborers, and to live with, continue, & serve the said T. S. Janes as an Apprentices from the date hereof for and during the term of their minority. During all of which time, said Jane Eberhart aforesaid doth covenant with the said T. S. Janes that the said Louisa & James shall well and faithfully demean themselves as such faithful Apprentices, observing fully the commands of the said T. S. Janes, and in all things deporting and behaving themselves as a faithful Apprentices to the said T. S. Janes, neither revealing his secrets, nor at any time neglecting or leaving the business of the said T. S. Janes.

And for and in consideration of the service well and faithfully rendered by the said Louisa & James, of the first part, said T. S. Janes, of the second part, doth covenant, promise, & agree to instruct the said apprentices, or otherwise cause them to be well and faithfully instructed, in the said trade or craft of house servants or laborers, and Also to read the English language, And shall also allow, furnish, & provide them, said Apprentices, with meat & drink & clothing during the said term, and all other necessaries meet & proper, in sickness and in health. Witness our hands and seals the day and year above written.

Executed before us }
J. J. Dye }
Ge° L. Almond, }
Ordinary }

Jane + Eberhart, her mark
T. S. Janes

Filed in office May 6, 1890 and Recorded on May 7, 1890.

Ge° L. Almond, Ordinary

Duplicate [134]

Alexander Gray to Jasper Bryan

Georgia }
Elbert County } This Indenture, made this the 10th day of May 1890, between Alexander Gray, of said County, for and in behalf of Earnest Gray, his son, being of the age of sixteen years, on the one part, and Jasper Bryan, of the County aforesaid, of the other part. Witnesseth: that the said Alexander Gray, as aforesaid, does by these presents bind out his son Earnest Gray, of said County as apprentice to said Jasper Bryan in the trade or craft of husbandry or as laborer upon the plantation of the said Jasper Bryan, to be taught the said Craft or trade of husbandry or laborer, and to live with, continue, and serve the said Jasper Bryan as an apprentice from Jany 1, 1891 for and during the term of (3) three years. During all of which time, said Alexander Gray, as aforesaid, doth covenant with the said Jasper Bryan that the said Earnest Gray shall well and faithfully demean himself as such faithful Apprentice, observing fully the commands of the said Jasper Bryan, and in All things deporting & behaving himself as a faithful Apprentice to the said Jasper Bryan, neither revealing his secrets, nor at any time neglecting or leaving the business of the said Jasper Bryan.

And for and in consideration of service well and faithfully rendered by the said Earnest Gray, of the first part, said Jasper Bryan, of the second part, doth covenant and agree to instruct his said apprentice, or otherwise cause him to be well faithfully instructed, in the said trade or craft of husbandry or laborer, and also to read the English language, and shall also allow, furnish, and provide his said apprentice with meat and drink & clothing during the said term, and all other necessaries meet & proper, in sickness and in health. And shall also, at the expiration of said term, allow & pay the said Apprentice what is now allowed by the statute in such cases made & provided.

Witness our hands & Seals the day & year first Above written.

Executed Before us   }
Jo^s N. Worly   }   Alexander + Gray, his mark
R. M. Willis, Clk S. C. }   Jasper Bryan

Filed in office & Recorded on May 10th 1890.

Ge^o L. Almond, Ordinary

Duplicate [135]

Georgia   }
Elbert County } This Indenture, made this the 27th day of May 1890, between Mid Brawner, of said County, for and in behalf of John Brawner, being of the age of 11 years, on the one part, and John C. Hudgens, of the County aforesaid, of the other part. Witnesseth: that the said Mid Brawner does by these presents bind out John Brawner, of said County as Apprentice to said John C. Hudgens in the trade or craft of house servant or as laborer upon the plantation of the said John C. Hudgens, to be taught the said Craft or trade of house servant or laborer, and to live with, continue, and serve the said John C. Hudgens as an apprentice from Jany 1, 1891 for and during the term of Four years.

During all of which time, said Mid Brawner doth covenant with the said John C. Hudgens that the said John Brawner shall well and faithfully demean himself as such faithful Apprentice, observing fully the commands of the said John C. Hudgens, and in all things deporting and behaving himself as a faithful Apprentice to the said John C. Hudgens, neither revealing his secrets, nor at any time neglecting the business of the said John C. Hudgens.

And for and in consideration of service well and faithfully rendered by the said John Brawner, of the first part, said John C. Hudgens, of the second part, doth covenant, promise, & agree to instruct him, said apprentice, or otherwise Cause him to be well faithfully and instructed, in the said trade or craft of house servant or laborer, and also to read the English language, and shall also allow, furnish, and provide him, said Apprentice, with meat, drink and clothing during said term, and all other necessaries meet & proper, in sickness and in health, and to pay $30.00 first year, $5 Second year, $5 3rd year, & $5 4th year. The $30 for first year this day paid.

Witness our hands and seals the day and year first before written.

Executed Before us }
D. H. Warren   }   J. C. Hudgens
Ge⁰ L. Almond,   }   Mid + Brawner, his mark

Filed in office & recorded on 27 May 1890.

          Ge⁰ L. Almond, Ordinary

       Duplicate   [136]

Georgia   }
Elbert County } This Indenture, made this 31 day of May 1890, between Josie Tate, of said County, for and in behalf Lulah Tate, being of the age of Six years, on the one part, and J. C. Hudgens, of the County aforesaid, of the other part. Witnesseth: that the said Josie Tate, as aforesaid, does by these presents bind out Lulah Tate, of said County, as Apprentice to said J. C. Hudgens in the trade or Craft of house servant or as laborer upon the plantation of the said J. C. Hudgens, to be taught the said Craft or trade of house servant or laborer, and to live with and continue & serve the said J. C. Hudgens as an apprentice from the date hereof for and during the term of twelve years.

During all of which time, said Josie Tate, as Aforesaid, doth covenant with the said J. C. Hudgens that the said Lulah Tate shall well and faithfully demean herself as such faithful Apprentice, observing fully the commands of the said J. C. Hudgens, and in all things deporting and behaving herself as a faithful apprentice to the said J. C. Hudgens, neither revealing his secrets, nor at any time neglecting or leaving the business of the said J. C. Hudgens.

And for and in consideration of service well and faithfully rendered by the said Lula Tate, of the first part, said J. C. Hudgens, of the second part, doth covenant, promise, & agree to instruct his said apprentice, or otherwise cause her to be well faithfully and instructed, in the said trade or craft of house Servant or laborer, and also to read the English language, and shall also allow, furnish, & provide his said Apprentice, with meat & drink & clothing during the said term, and all other necessaries meet & proper, in sickness and in health, and shall also, at the expiration of said term, allow and pay the said Apprentice what is now Allowed by the Statute in such case made & provided.

Witness our hands & Seals the day & year first before written.

Executed Before us }
D. B. Alexander } J. C. Hudgens
R. M. Willis, Clk S. C. E. C. } Josie + Tate, her mark

Filed & recorded on June 2, 1890.

Ge° L. Almond, Ordinary

Duplicate [137]

Georgia }
Elbert County } This Indenture, made the 26th day of April 1890, between Jane Eberhart, of said County, for and in behalf of Gussie Eberhart, being of the age of Six years, on the one part, and J. B. Janes, S^r, of the County aforesaid, of the other part. Witnesseth: that the said Jane Eberhart does by these presents bind out Gussie, of said County as apprentice to said J. B. Janes, S^r in the trade or craft of house servant or as laborer upon the plantation of the said J. B. Janes, S^r, to be taught the said Craft or trade of house servant or laborer, and to live with, Continue, and serve the said J. B. Janes, S^r as an apprentice from the date hereof for and during the term of her minority.

During all of which time, said Jane Eberhart doth covenant with the said J. B. Janes, S^r that the said Gussie shall well and faithfully demean herself as such faithful Apprentice, observing fully the Commands of the said J. B. Janes, S^r, and in all things deporting and behaving herself as a faithful apprentice to the said J. B. Janes, S^r, neither revealing his secrets, nor at any time neglecting or leaving the business of the said J. B. Janes, S^r.

And for and in consideration of service well and faithfully rendered by the said Gussie, of the first part, said J. B. Janes, S^r, of the second part, doth covenant, promise, and agree to instruct his said apprentice, or otherwise cause her to be well faithfully and instructed, in the said trade or craft of house servant or laborer, and also to read the English language, and shall also allow, furnish, and provide said Apprentice, with meat and drink and clothing during the said term, and all other necessaries meet & proper, in sickness and in health.

Witness our hands and seals the day and year first before written.

Executed Before us }
J. J. Dye } Jane + Eberhart, her mark
Ge° T. Fortson, N. Panff J. P. } J. B. Janes, S^r

Filed in office and recorded on Aug 12, 1890.

Ge° L. Almond, Ordinary

Duplicate [138]

Georgia }
Elbert County } This Indenture, made this the 7th day of October 1890, between J. J. Dunbar, of said County, for and in behalf Ada Dunbar, being of the age of Six weeks, on the one part, and W. T. M. Brown, of the County aforesaid, of the other part. Witnesseth: that the said J. J. Dunbar does by these presents bind out Ada Dunbar, of said County as Apprentice to said W. T. M. Brown in the trade or Craft of house servant or as laborer upon the plantation of the said W. T. M. Brown, to be taught the said Craft or trade of house servant or laborer, & to live with, Continue, & serve the said W. T. M. Brown as an Apprentice from the date hereof for and during the term of Eighteen years.

During all of which time, said J. J. Dunbar doth Covenant with the said W. T. M. Brown that the said Ada Dunbar Shall well & faithfully demean herself as such faithful Apprentice, observing fully the commands of the said W. T. M. Brown, and in all things deporting and behaving herself as a faithful apprentice to the said W. T. M. Brown, neither revealing his secrets, nor at any time neglecting or leaving the business of the said W. T. M. Brown.

And for & in consideration of the service well and faithfully rendered by the said Ada Dunbar, of the first part, said W. T. M. Brown, of the second part, doth Covenant, promise, & agree to instruct his said Apprentice, or otherwise cause her to be well faithfully and instructed, in the said trade or craft of house servant or laborer, & also to read the English language, & shall also allow, furnish, & provide his said apprentice, with meat, drink, & clothing during the said term, and all other necessaries meet & proper, in sickness and in health. And shall also, at the expiration of said term, allow & pay to said Apprentice what is now allowed by the statute in such cases made & provided. Witness our hands & Seals the day and year first before written.

Executed Before us }
J. H. B. Brown }   J. J. Dunbar
T. C. Edwards }   W. T. M. Brown

Filed & recorded Oct 23rd 1890.

Ge° L. Almond, Ordinary

Duplicate [139]

Georgia }
Elbert County } This Indenture, made this the 29th day of October 1890, between Jane Duncan, of said County, for & in behalf Lony and Samantha Duncan, being of the ages of 13 and 11 years, on the one part, and Dillard Ray, of the County aforesaid, of the other part. Witnesseth: that the said Jane Duncan does by these presents bind out Lony and Samantha Duncan, of said County as Apprentices to said Dillard Ray in the trade or craft of house servants or as laborers upon the plantation of the said Dillard Ray, to be taught the said craft or trade of house servants or laborers, and to live with, continue, and serve the said Dillard Ray as apprentices from the date hereof for and during the term of their minority.

During all of which time, said Dillard Ray doth covenant with the said Jane Duncan that the said Lony & Samantha shall well and faithfully demean themselves as such faithful Apprentices, observing fully the Commands of the said Dillard Ray, and in All things deporting & behaving themselves as faithful Apprentices to the said Dillard Ray, neither revealing his secrets, nor at any time neglecting or leaving the business of the said Dillard Ray.

And for and in consideration of services well and faithfully rendered by the said Lony and Samantha, of the first part, said Dillard Ray, of the second part, doth Covenant, promise, & agree to instruct them, said Apprentices, or otherwise cause them to be well & faithfully instructed, in the said trade or craft of house servant or laborers, and to read the English language, and shall also allow, furnish, & provide them, said Apprentices, with meat and drink and clothing during the said term, and all other necessaries meet and proper, in sickness and in health, and shall also, at the expiration of said term, allow and pay the said Apprentices what is now Allowed by the statute in such case made and provided.

Witness our hands & Seals the day & year first before written.

Executed Before me }
H. J. Brewer }   Jane + Duncan, her mark
Geo L. Almond,. }   Dillard + Ray, his mark
Ordinary }r

Filed in office and recorded Octo 29, 1890.

Geo L. Almond, Ordinary

Duplicate [140]

Georgia }
Elbert County } This Indenture, made this 27th day of December 1890, between Washington Hill, Abbeville Co., So. Ca., for and in behalf of his son William Hill, being of the age of fifteen years, on the one part, and Wm H. Mattox, of the County aforesaid, of the other part. Witnesseth: that the said Washington Hill, as aforesaid, does by these presents bind out William Hill, of said County of Abbeville, S. C., as Apprentice to said Wm H. Mattox in the trade or craft of house servant or as laborer upon the plantation of the said Wm H. Mattox, to be taught the said Craft or trade of husbandry or laborer, and to live with, Continue, & serve the said Wm H. Mattox as an apprentice from the date hereof for and during the term of three years.

During all of which time, said Washington Hill, as aforesaid, doth covenant with the said Wm H. Mattox that the said William Hill shall well & faithfully demean himself as such faithful Apprentice, observing fully the Commands of the said Wm H. Mattox, and in All things deporting & behaving himself as a faithful apprentice to the said Wm H. Mattox, neither revealing his secrets, nor at any time neglecting or leaving the business of the said W. H. Mattox. And for and in consideration of his service well & faithfully rendered by the said Wm Hill, of the first part, said Wm H. Mattox, of the second part, doth covenant, promise, and agree to instruct his said Apprentice, or otherwise cause him to be well and faithfully instructed, in the said trade or craft of husbandry or laborer, and shall also allow, furnish, and provide him, said Apprentice, with meat & drink & clothing during the said term, and all other necessaries meet & proper, in sickness and in health.

Said W. H. Mattox agrees to pay said Washington Hill fifty Dollars per year.

Witness our hands and seals the day and year first above written. [141]

Executed Before us }
J. B. Janes, J^r }
D. Meriwether }   W. H. Mattox
                       Washington + Hill, his mark

Georgia }
Elbert County } Personally appeared be fore me J. B. Janes, J^r, one of the witnesses to the above Indenture, who after being sworn says that he saw the

parties sign their names and that the Instrument was read over and discussed before both the parties and agreed upon by each party. This Dec 29, 1890.

Sworn to & Subscribed }
before me Dec 29, 1890 }   J. B. Janes, J^r
Jno W. McCalla   }

Filed in office and recorded this Dec 29, 1890.

Ge^o L. Almond, Ordinary

Duplicate   [142]

Georgia   }
Elbert County } This Indenture, made this the 13 day of January 1891, between Wm Griffin, of said County, for and in behalf James Griffin, being of the age of 14 years, on the one part, and A. J. Brown, of the County aforesaid, of the other part. Witnesseth: that the said Wm Griffin, as of said date, does by these presents bind out James Griffin, of said County, as Apprentice to said A. J. Brown to be taught the said Craft or trade of hand servant or laborer, and to live with, Continue, and serve the said A. J. Brown as an Apprentice from the date hereof for and during the term of one year. During all of which time, said Wm Griffin, as aforesaid, doth covenant with the said A. J. Brown that the said James Griffin shall well and faithfully demean himself as such faithful Apprentice, observing fully the Commands of the said A. J. Brown, and in All things deporting and behaving himself as a faithful Apprentice to the said A. J. Brown, neither revealing his secrets, nor at any time neglecting or leaving the business of the said A. J. Brown.

And for and in consideration of the service well and faithfully rendered by the said James Griffin, of the first part, said A. J. Brown, of the second part, doth covenant, promise, and agree to instruct him, said apprentice, or otherwise cause him to be well and faithfully instructed, in the said trade or craft of house servant or laborer, and shall also allow, furnish, and provide him, said Apprentice, with meat & drink & clothing during the said term, and All other necessaries meet & proper, in sickness and in health, and to pay said Wm Griffin Thirty Dollars.

Witness our hands and seals the day and year first before written.

Executed Before us   }
J. A. Andrew   }   William Griffin
Ge^o L. Andrew, Ordinary }   A. J. Brown

Filed in office and Recorded Jany 13, 1891.

                                          Ge° L. Almond, Ordinary

                    Duplicate   [143]

Georgia   }
Elbert County } This Indenture, made this 14 day of January 1891, between Wm Griffin, of said County, for and in behalf of Wm Griffin, J^r, being of the age of 12 years, on the one part, and Asa J. Mewborn, of the County aforesaid, of the other part. Witnesseth: that the said Wm Griffin does by these presents bind out Wm Griffin, J^r, of said County as Apprentice to said A. J. Mewborn in the trade or Craft of house Servant or as laborer upon the plantation of the said A. J. Mewborn, to be taught the said Craft or trade of house servant or laborer, and to live with, Continue, and Serve the said A. J. Mewborn as an Apprentice from the date hereof for and during the term of one year.

During all of which time, said Wm Griffin doth Covenant with the said A. J. Mewborn that the said Wm Griffin, J^r shall well & faithfully demean himself as such faithful Apprentice, observing fully the Commands of the said A. J. Mewborn, and in all things deporting and behaving himself as a faithful Apprentice to the said A. J. Mewborn, neither revealing his secrets, nor at any time neglecting or leaving the business of the said A. J. Mewborn.

And for and in consideration of the service well and faithfully rendered by the said Wm Griffin, J^r, of the first part, said A. J. Mewborn, of the second part, doth covenant, promise, & Agree to instruct his said apprentice, or otherwise cause him to be well and faithfully instructed, in the said trade or craft of house servant or laborer, and shall also allow, furnish, and provide his said Apprentice, with meat and drink and clothing during the said term, and All other necessaries meet and proper, in sickness and in health, and to pay said Wm Griffin $45.00.

Witness our hands and seals the day and year first before written.

Executed Before us   }
D. R. Flemming   }   Wm Griffin
Ge° L. Andrew, Ordiny}   A. J. Mewborn

Filed in office & recorded 14 January 1891.

                                          Ge° L. Almond, Ordinary

Duplicate [144]

Georgia }
Elbert County } This Indenture, made this the first day of May 1891, Between Alexander and Nancy Gray, of said County, for and in behalf Ticorn Alexander, their grandson, being of the age of Seventeen years, on the one part, and Jasper Bryan, of the County aforesaid, of the other part. Witnesseth: that the said Alexander and Nancy Gray, as aforesaid, does by these presents bind out Ticorn Alexander, of said County, as apprentice to said Jasper Bryan in trade or craft of husbandry or as laborer upon the plantation of the said Jasper Bryan, to be taught the said craft or trade of husbandry or laborer, and to live with, Continue, & serve the said Jasper Bryan as an apprentice from the date hereof for & during the term of three (3) years. During all of which time, said Alexander & Nancy Gray, as aforesaid, doth Covenant with the said Jasper Bryan that the said Ticorn Alexander shall well and faithfully demean himself as such faithful Apprentice, observing fully the commands of the said Jasper Bryan, and in all things deporting and behaving himself as a faithful apprentice to the said Jasper Bryan, neither revealing his secrets, nor at any time neglecting or leaving the business of the said Jasper Bryan. And for and in consideration of service well & faithfully rendered by the said Ticorn Alexander, of the first part, said Jasper Bryan, of the second part, doth covenant, promise, & agree to instruct his said Apprentice, or otherwise Cause him to be well and faithfully instructed, in the said trade or craft as husbandry or laborer, and also to read the English language, and shall also allow, furnish, & provide his said Apprentice, with meat and drink & clothing during the said term, And all other necessaries meet & proper, in sickness and in health, and shall also, at expiration of said term, allow and pay the said Apprentice what is now allowed by the statute in such case made and provided.

Witness our hands and seals the day and year before written. [145]

Executed Before us }   Nancy + Gray, her mark
W. C. Bryan   }   Alexander + Gray, his mark
J. J. Booth   }   Jasper Bryan

Georgia }
Elbert County } Personally Appeared before me W. C. Bryan and being duly sworn says on oath that he saw Alexander Gray and Jasper Bryan sign & seal the above Instrument at the time therein specified and for the purpose mentioned and also saw Alexander Gray sign the name of Nancy Gray to said instrument and stated at the time that he was Authorized to do so by his wife, said Nancy Gray,

and that Deponent, together with J. J. Booth, did sign the same at the time as witnesses.

Sworn & Subscribed }
before me May 1, 1891 }   W. C. Bryan
R. M. Willis, Clk }
Super Court }

Filed in Office and Recorded on this first day May 1891.

                           Ge° L. Almond, Ordinary

                Duplicate   [146]

                Heardmont, Ga. May 12, 1891

Georgia }
Elbert County }   This Indenture, made the day and year above written. Winesseth, that I, Ammanda Mattox, of the County aforesaid, mother of Mary Margaret, a girl Seven years old, Do by these presents apprentice to J. W. McCalla, of the County & State aforesaid, the said Mary Margret until she shall arrive at the age of Twenty one years old, giving up my Entire Parental authority unto the said McCalla over said child, Completely and fully, as if one of his own children.

The said McCalla, upon his part, agrees to take said child and treat of as his own, providing, Maintangs, & using it in the trade of agriculture & Sending it to School as the law requires, and giving it Such sum of money when it arrives at its majority, provided it remains said McCalla until its Majority, as the said McCalla may see fit.

This writing is intended as a strict compliance of the law of apprenticeship and is so intended to apply fully to said laws in all of its provisions. Given under our hands & seals the day & year above written. This was fully read over & understood before signing.

Witnesses }
J. B. Janes, J^r }   Amanda + Mattox, her mark
Z. B. Taylor }   Jn° W. McCalla

Georgia }
Elbert County }   Personally appears before me Z. B. Taylor who on oath says that he, together with J. B. Janes, J^r, did see Amanda Mattox & John W. McCalla

sign the within Indenture, that they signed it on the day it purports to have been signed & for the purposes therein stated & that Deponent & J. B. Janes, J^r Attested the same as witnesses.

Sworn & Subscribed }
Before me 27 May 1891 }   Z. B. Taylor
Ge° L. Almond, Ordy }

Filed & Recorded May 29, 1891.

         Ge° L. Almond, Ordinary

     Duplicate   [147]

Georgia }
Elbert County } This Indenture, made and entered into this the 24th day of April 1891, between Lige Blackwell, father of the minors hereinafter mentioned, of said County, of the one part, and John W. McCalla, of said County, of the other part. Witnesseth: that the said Lige Blackwell, father as aforesaid, does hereby bind to the said Jn° W. McCalla the following named children, viz, Jessie Blackwell 16 years old, Lina Blackwell 14 years old, Annie Blackwell 7 years old, and Lena Blackwell 8 years old. as apprentices to the said Jn° W. McCalla until they shall have arrived at or obtained the age of Twenty one years.

Said McCalla hereby agrees to furnish the said Orphan children suitable provisions, clothing, and Medical Attention during their term of service as apprentices. And the said Jn° W. McCalla further agrees that said Children shall be taught to read the English Language. And the said J. W. McCalla further agrees that the said children shall be taught the business of a farm laborers as an occupation. And the said Jn° W. McCalla further agrees to govern said children with humanity and Kindness, using only the same degree of force to compel their obedience as a parent may use with his minor children. And to furnish them, at the expiration of the term of apprenticeship, such allowance in Money as may be commensurate with the length and of their services as apprentice, Provided they remain with said McCalla until they are 21 years old/

Witness our hands and seals the day and year above written.

Test. }
J. T. Speed }   Lige + Blackwell, his mark
Z. B. Taylor }   Jn° W. McCalla

Georgia }
Elbert County } In person appears before me Z. B. Taylor who on oath says that he, together with J. T. Speed, did see Lige Blackwell & J. W. McCalla sign the within Indenture, that they signed it on the day it purports to have been signed & for the purposes therein stated & that deponent & J. T. Speed Attested the same as witnesses.

Sworn & Subscribed }
Before me 27 May 1891 }   Z. B. Taylor
Ge° L. Almond, Ordiny }

Filed in office & recorded May 29, 1891.

Ge° L. Almond, Ordinary

Duplicate   [148]

Georgia }
Elbert County } This Indenture, made this the 24 day of June 1891, between Martha Jane Stark, of said County, for and in behalf Carrie Stark, being of the age of Five years old, on the one part, and A. O. Harper, of the County Aforesaid, of the other part. Witnesseth: that the said Martha Jane Stark does by these presents bind out Carrie Stark, of said County, as Apprentice to said A. O. Harper in the trade or craft of house servant or as Laborer upon the plantation of the said A. O. Harper, to be taught the said craft or trade of house servant or laborer, and to live with, Continue, & serve the said A. O. Harper as an Apprentice from the date hereof for and during the term of Sixteen years.

During all of which time, said Martha J. Stark doth Covenant with the said A. O. Harper that the said Carrie Stark shall well & faithfully demean herself as such faithful apprentice, observing fully the Commands of the said A. O. Harper, and in all things deporting & behaving herself as a faithful apprentice to the said A. O. Harper, neither revealing his secrets, nor at any time neglecting or leaving the business of the said A. O. Harper.

And for and in consideration of the service well and faithfully rendered by the said Carrie Stark, of the first part, said A. O. Harper, of the second part, doth covenant, promise, & agree to instruct his said apprentice, or otherwise cause her to be well and faithfully instructed, in the said trade or craft of house servant or laborer, & also to read the English language, and shall also allow, furnish, & provide his said Apprentice, with meat & drink & clothing during said term, and all other necessaries meet & proper, in sickness and in health, and shall also, at the expiration of said term, allow & pay the said Apprentice what is now allowed by the statute in such case made & provided.

Witness our hands & seals the day & year above first written.

Executed Before us }
Th⁰ J. Hester }
Ge⁰ L. Andrew, Ordiny }

Martha Jane + Stark, her mark
A. O. Harper

Filed in office June 24, 1891 and Recorded June 26, 1891.

Ge⁰ L. Almond, Ordinary

Duplicate [149]

Georgia }
Elbert County } This Indenture, made this 26 day of June 1891, between Indiana Morrison, of said County, for and in behalf Ge⁰ & Joe Morrison, being of the ages of 10 and 8 years, on the one part, and King Mattox, of the County aforesaid, of the other part. Witnesseth: that the said Indiana Morrison, as aforesaid, does by these presents bind out Ge⁰ and Joe Morrison, of said County as apprentices to said King ~~Morrison~~ Mattox in the trade or Craft of Husbandry or as Laborers upon the plantation of the said King Mattox, to be taught the said Craft or trade of husbandry or laborers, and to live with, continue, and serve the said King Mattox as apprentices from the date hereof for and during the term of their Minority. During all of which time, said Indiana Morrison doth covenant with the said King Mattox that the said George and Joe shall well and faithfully demean themselves as such faithful apprentices, observing fully the Commands of the said King Mattox, and in All things deporting and behaving themselves as faithful apprentices to the said King Mattox, neither revealing his secrets, nor at any time neglecting or leaving the business of the said King Mattox, with the privilege to hire either or both of said apprentices as he, the said King Mattox, may see proper.

And for and in consideration of services well and faithfully rendered by the said Indiana Morrison, of the first part, said King Mattox, of the second part, doth Covenant, promise, & agree to instruct his said apprentices, or otherwise cause them to be well & faithfully instructed, in the said trade or craft of husbandry or laborers, and shall also allow, furnish, and provide his said apprentices, with meat and drink and Clothing during the said term, and all other necessaries meet & proper, in sickness and in health.

Witness our hands and Seals the day & year first Above written.

Executed Before us }
Jnº W. McCalla, N. P. ex off J. P. }   Inda + Morrison, her mark
J. B. Janes, Jʳ }   King + Mattox, his mark

Filed in office and Recorded June 26, 1891.

Geº L. Almond, Ordinary

Georgia } [150]
Elbert County } This Indenture this day made by Beatrix McCalla, That the said Beatrix this day apprentices and binds to J. W. McCalla her son Mc Morrison of the age of 12 years and her daughter Alaney 8 years of the age of until they Arrive at the age of Twenty one (21) years old. The said Jnº W. McCalla is to treat them humanely and Kindly, furnishing them proper food and Clothing, and instruct them in the art of husbandry. The said McCalla is to send them to School, giving them such education as can be obtained at the Common Schools of the County. All the above has been read over in presence of and fully agreed to by both parties. and when they arrive at the age of maturity, are to receive such compensation as the Law gives them, Provided they remain until they become of age.

This June 19, 1891 }
Attest. J. B. Janes, Jʳ}   Jnº W. McCalla
Z. B. Taylor }   Beatrix + McCalla, her mark

In person Comes before me J. B. Janes, Jʳ who on oath says he saw Beatrix McCalla and John W. McCalla sign the within. That they signed it for the purpose therein stated and the day it purports to have been signed and that deponent, together with Z. B. Taylor Attested the same as witnesses.

Sworn to & Subscribed }
before me July 3, 1891 }   J. B. Janes, Jʳ
Geº L. Almond, Ordny }

Filed in Office & Recorded July 3, 1891.

Geº L. Almond, Ordiny

Duplicate [151]

Georgia }
Elbert County } This Indenture, made this 1ˢᵗ Janʸ 1890, between Sarah Gray,

Mother of Amanda Gray, Aged 6 years old, and John Price Gray, one year old. Witnesseth: That I, the said Sarah, do Apprentice to my Mother Mary Gray and my father George Gray My said Children Above, to have and to hold them As their own, Against myself and All others, having them in their possession as their own. They upon their part Agreeing to Care for them as their own, giving them food, Clothing, and such other things that may be required as if they were their own children.

These Indentures are intended as a full and complete requirement of the law of Apprenticeship.

Signed, sealed, and delivered the day & year Above written.

Jnº W. McCalla, N. P. }	Sarah + Gray, her mark
ex off J. P. }	Mary + Gray, her mark
Z. B. Taylor }	Geº + Gray, his mark

Filed in Office and Recorded this 24 July 1891.

                              Geº L. Almond, Ordiny

                    Duplicate   [152]

Fannie Bullard To E. B. Starke

Georgia }
Elbert County } This Indenture, made this 25th day of Sept 1891, between Fannie Bullard, of said County, for and in behalf of Jesse Bullard, being of the age of seven years, on the one part, and E. B. Starke, of the County Aforesaid, of the other part. Witnesseth: That the said Fannie Bullard does by these presents bind out Jesse Bullard, of said County as Apprentice to said E. B. Starke in the trade or Craft of house servant or as laborer upon the plantation of the said E. B. Starke, to be taught the said craft or trade of house servant or laborer, and to live with, continue, and serve the said E. B. Starke as an apprentice from the date hereof for and during the term of Eleven years.

During all of which time, said Fannie Bullard doth covenant with the said E. B. Starke that the said Jesse Bullard shall well and faithfully demean himself as such faithful apprentice, observing fully the Commands of the said E. B. Starke, and in all things deporting and behaving himself as a faithful Apprentice to the said E. B. Starke, neither revealing his secrets, nor at any time neglecting or leaving the business of the said E. B. Starke. And for and in consideration of services well and faithfully rendered by the said Jesse Bullard, of the first part, said E. B. Starke, of the second part, doth covenant, promise, and agree to instruct him, said apprentice, or otherwise cause him to be well and faithfully instructed, in the said trade or craft of house servant or laborer, and also to read the English language, and shall also allow, furnish, and provide him, said apprentice, with meat, drink, and clothing during said term, and All Other necessaries meet and proper, in sickness and in health.

Witness our hands and seals the day and year first Above written.

Executed Before us }
W. B. Henry }   Fannie + Bullard, her mark
Geº L. Almond, Ordny }   E. B. Starke

Filed in office & recorded Sept 25, 1891.

       Geº L. Almond, Ordinary

    Duplicate   [153]

Georgia }
Elbert County } This Indenture, this day made and entered into, between Julia Jordan, of the one part, and Jnº W. McCalla, of the other part, and witnesseth: that the said Julia Jordan this day apprentices herself to the said Jnº W. McCalla for the term of three years. The said Julia to work for the said McCalla Wherever and whenever the said McCalla May direct. At All times being obedient and faithful in the discharge of her work.

Now the said McCalla, in consideration of the Above (which is the part to be performed by Julia) agrees to treat her humanely and kindly, protecting her from all imposition and cause her to obtain such education as can be gotten at the common schools of the County and cause her to be instructed in the art or Craft of husbandry. And should the said Julia be and Continue faithful for and during the full term of this Indenture, then in consideration of said faithful service the said McCalla agrees to pay the said Julia, Aside from food and clothing and all necessary medical attention, the Sum of $25.00 per year. and it is further understood and agreed by both parties that the relation of Master and Apprentice shall exist between them from this date until the expiration of three years. This Oct 20, 1891

Signed in presence of

J. B. Janes, Jr }   Julia Jordan
Z. B. Taylor }   Jnº W. McCalla

Personally comes before me J. B. Janes, J^r who on oath says he saw Julia Jordan and Jn° W. McCalla sign the within Indenture for the purposes therein stated and he, together with Z. B. Taylor, signed as witnesses.

Sworn to & Subscribed }
before me Nov 2, 1891 }   J. B. Janes, J^r
Ge° L. Almond, Ordny }

Filed in Office and Recorded Nov 2, 1891.

                     Ge° L. Almond, Ordinary

             Duplicate   [154]

Georgia   }
Elbert County   } This Indenture, this day made and entered into, between Jn° W. McCalla and Eliza Morrison, both of the County and State Above written. Witnesseth: That the said Eliza Morrison firmly binds and apprentices unto the said Jn° W. McCalla his four children, names and ages as follows, one girl named Fannie 9 years old, one girl named Annie 8 years old, one girl named Sarah 6 years old, one girl named Rachel 7 years old. All the above named children I apprentice unto the said Jn° W. McCalla during their minority or until they arrive at the age of Twenty one years. And the said Eliza hereby renounces all claim to said children as parent or otherwise and delegates the same to the said Jn° W. McCalla. The said Jn° W. McCalla is to have full and complete possession and control of said children, treating humanely and kindly, giving them such education as can be obtained at the common schools of the County, and instructing them in the art or craft of husbandry. And when said children arrive at the age of Twenty one years, the said Jn° W. McCalla is to give to each one such amount as he may deem a suitable reward for fidelity and faithful service. Given under our hands and seals this [blank] day of [blank] 1891.

Witnesses
J. F. Kemper   Eliza + Morrison, her mark
J. B. Janes, J^r Jn° W. McCalla

In person comes before me J. B. Janes, J^r who on oath says that he, together with J. F. Kemper, did see J. W. McCalla and Eliza Morrison sign this instrument, that they signed the same on the day it purports to have been signed, and for the purposes therein stated, and that deponent and J. F. Kemper attended the same as witnesses.

Sworn to Subscribed before me Nov 2, 1891.

Ge⁰ L. Almond, Ordinary   J. B. Janes, J^r

Filed in office and Recorded Nov 2, 1891.

                              Ge⁰ L. Almond, Ordinary

                Duplicate   [155]

Georgia   }
Franklin County } This Indenture, this day made and entered into, between John Christian, of said County and State, of the one part, and Jn⁰ W. McCalla, of Elbert County and State. witnesseth: That the said John Christian does by these presents bind himself unto the said John W. McCalla for the full term of Three years from this date, Oct 13, 1891, until Oct 13, 1894. and hereby contracts and promises and bind himself by these presents to labor for and with the said McCalla and under his control and management at such place in this State as said McCalla may direct, as an apprentice, and at such Kind of labor and work as said McCalla may direct. Said John W. McCalla hereby contracts and promises by these presents to Maintain and protect said apprentice, to treat him humanely, furnish him with wholesome food, suitable clothing, necessary medicine, and medical attention, Shall cause him to be taught habits of industry and morality and the business of husbandry or farming. and to allow said apprentice the sum of seventy five dollars annually on his wages for his labor and services as such apprentice. All of which is the consideration of the Indenture. Both parties hereto agree that these articles of Indenture this day executed in duplicate shall be filed and recorded as the law required and that the relation of Master and apprentice shall exist under the laws of Georgia and these articles enforced in accordance with the laws of Georgia. Witness our hands and seals this Oct 13, 1891.

Signed and Sealed in Duplicate this Oct 13, 1891.

John P. Shannan }   Jn⁰ W. McCalla
J. B. Janes, J^r }   John Christian

Personally comes before me J. B. Janes, J^r who on oath says that he, together with Jn⁰ P. Shannan, saw Jn⁰ W. McCalla & Jn⁰ Christian sign the within Indenture, for the purpose therein stated, and he and John P. Shannan signed as witnesses.

Sworn to Subscribed before me Nov 2, 1891.

Ge⁰ L. Almond, Ordinary   J. B. Janes, J^r

Filed in office and Recorded Nov 2, 1891.

Geº L. Almond, Ordinary

Duplicate [156]

Georgia }
Elbert County } This Indenture, this day made and entered into, between Charles Morrison and Jnº W. McCalla, both of the County and State above written. witnesseth: That the said Charles Morrison this day binds and apprentices unto the said Jnº W. McCalla his six (6) minor children, viz, his son Jnº Henry 12 years old, his son George 7 years old, his son Louie 4 years old, His daughter Mary Lou 10 years old, Dunn 8 years old, and his youngest child 2 years old. All the above named children are hereby apprenticed unto the said McCalla until they arrive at the age of Twenty one years.

Now in consideration of the above part to be performed by Charles, the said Jnº W. McCalla agrees to take said children, treat them humanely & Kindly, giving them proper food and clothing, furnishing all necessary medical Attention, causing them to obtain such education as can be had at the common Schools of the County, and instructing them in the art or craft of husbandry or farming. And when each child shall arrive at the age of twenty one years years, the said McCalla is to pay to them Such Amounts as he may deem a suitable reward for fidelity and faithful service. And it is further agreed and understood by both parties that the relation of Master and Apprentice Shall exist between them to all purposes and intent from and after this date. These Articles of Indenture made and signed in duplicate this 26th day of Oct 1891.

Z. B. Taylor	Jnº W. McCalla
J. B. Janes, Jr	Chas + Morrison, his mark

Personally comes J. B. Janes, Jr who on oath says that he saw Jnº W. McCalla & Chas Morrison Sign the within Indenture, for the purpose therein stated, and that he together with Z. B. Taylor signed as witnesses.

Sworn to before me Nov 2, 1891.

Geº L. Almond, Ordny	J. B. Janes, Jr

Filed in office & recorded Nov 2, 1891.

Geº L. Almond, Ordinary

Duplicate [157]

Georgia }
Elbert County } This Indenture, entered into this Oct 13, 1891, between Jn° W. McCalla, of the County of Elbert said State, and Stephen Christian, of the County of Franklin. Witnesseth: That for in consideration of the sum of Seventy five dollars annually, to begin Jany 1st 1892, said Stephen Christian binds himself unto said McCalla for the full term of three years, from Jany 1, 1892, to work for said McCalla at such labor and at such place as said McCalla may direct. Said Jn° W. McCalla hereby promises to treat said Stephen Christian humanely, to furnish him with wholesome food, Suitable Clothing, and proper medicine and medical attention, to maintain and protect him, to cause him to be taught to read English, and taught habits of industry, honesty, and morality, and taught the business of farming, and to allow him Annually said sum of seventy five dollars. Both parties agree that these Articles of Indenture shall be filed, recorded, and enforced as Articles of Indenture between Master and apprentice are enforced.

Witness our hands and seals Oct 13, 1891.

Signed and sealed in duplicate Oct 13th 1891.

John P. Shannan }   Jn° W. McCalla
J. B. Janes, J^r }   S. M. F. Christian

Personally comes before me J. B. Janes, J^r who on oath says he saw Jn° W. McCalla and Stephen Christian sign the within Indenture for the purposes therein stated, and he, together with Jn° P. Shannan, signed as witnesses.

Sworn to & Subscribed before me Nov 2, 1891.

Ge° L. Almond, Ordny   J. B. Janes, J^r

Filed in office and Recorded Nov 2, 1891.

Ge° L. Almond, Ordny

Duplicate [158]

Georgia }
Elbert County } This Indenture, this day made and entered into, between Oss Bowman, col, of the one part, and Jn° W. McCalla, of the second part, both of the State and County above written. and witnesseth: That the said Oss Bowman this day binds and apprentices unto the said Jn° W. McCalla his six (6) minor children,

viz, his son Esau fifteen (15) years old, his son George Twelve (12) years old, his son John Seven (7) years old, His son Walton Six (6) years old, His twins Alice and Ida (girls) Ten years old. All the above named children are hereby apprenticed unto the said Jn° W. McCalla until they arrive at the age of Twenty one years. Now in consideration of the above part to be performed by Oss, the said Jn° W. McCalla agrees to take said children, treat them humanely and Kindly, giving them proper food and clothing, furnishing all necessary medical attention, causing them to have such education as can be obtained at the common schools of the County, and instructing them in the art or craft of husbandry or farming. And when each child arrives at the age of twenty one years, the said McCalla is to pay to them such amount as he may deem a suitable reward for fidelity and faithful service. And it is further agreed & understood by both parties that the relation of Master & apprentice shall exist between them to all intents & purposes from and after this date. These articles of Indenture made and signed in duplicate this 26 day of Oct 1891.

Z. B. Taylor } Jn° W. McCalla
J. B. Janes, J^r } Osborn + Bowman, his mark

Personally comes before me J. B. Janes, J^r who on oath says he saw Jn° W. McCalla and Osborn Bowman sign the within Indenture for the purposes therein stated, & he, together with Z. B. Taylor, signed as witnesses.

Sworn to & Subscribed before me Nov 2, 1891.

Ge° L. Almond, Ordny   J. B. Janes, J^r

Filed in office & Recorded Nov 2, 1891.

        Ge° L. Almond, Ordinary

     Duplicate   [159]

Georgia }
Elbert County } This Indenture, made this the 1st day of May 1891, Between Alexander and Nancy Gray, of said County, for and in behalf Ticorn Gray, their grandson, being of the age of Seventeen years, of the one part, and Jasper Bryan, of the County aforesaid, of the other part. Witnesseth: That the said Alexander and Nancy Gray aforesaid does by these presents bind out their grandson Ticorn Gray, of said County, as apprentice to said Jasper Bryan in the trade or craft of husbandry or laborer upon the plantation of the said Jasper Bryan, to be taught the said craft or trade of husbandry or laborer, and to live with, continue, & serve the

said Jasper Bryan as an apprentice from the date hereof for and during the term of Three (3) years.

During all of which time, said Alexander and Nancy Gray, as aforesaid, doth Covenant with the said Jasper Bryan that the said Ticorn Gray shall well and faithfully demean himself as such faithful apprentice, observing fully the Commands of the said Jasper Bryan, and in all things deporting and behaving himself as a faithful apprentice to the said Jasper Bryan, neither revealing his secrets, nor at any time neglecting or leaving the business of the said Jasper Bryan.

And for and in consideration of service well & faithfully rendered by the said Ticorn Gray, of the first part, said Jasper Bryan, of the second part, doth covenant, promise, and agree to instruct his said Apprentice, or otherwise Cause him to be well and faithfully instructed, in said trade or craft as husbandry or laborer, and also to read the English language, and shall also allow, furnish, and provide his said Apprentice, with meat and drink and clothing during the said term, And all other necessaries meet & proper, in sickness and in health. And shall also, at the expiration of said term, allow and pay the said Apprentice what is now allowed by the Statute in such cases made & provided.

Witness our hands and seals the day

(over)

and year before written. [160]

Executed Before us }	Alexander + Gray, his mark
J. J. Booth }	Nancy + Gray, her mark
W. C. Bryan }	Jasper Bryan

Georgia }
Elbert County } Personally comes before me J. J. Booth and being duly sworn says on oath that he saw Alexander Gray and Nancy Gray and Jasper Bryan sign the within Instrument at the time and for the purposes therein stated and set forth and specified, and that Deponent, together with W. C. Bryan, did sign the same at the time as witnesses.

Sworn & Subscribed }
before me Oct 17, 1891 }   J. J. + Booth, his mark
R. M. Willis, Clk }
Super Court }

Filed in Office and recorded Nov 10, 1891.

Geº L. Almond, Ordinary

Duplicate [161]

Georgia }
Elbert County } This Indenture, made this the 21st day of Nov 1891, between Dan Thornton, of said County, for and in behalf of Rona, Melie, Clark, and Ida Thornton, being of the age of 16, 15, 14, & 13 years, on the one part, and W. H. Upshaw, of the County aforesaid, of the other part. Witnesseth: That the said Dan Thornton does by these presents bind out said Minors, of said County, as Apprentices to said W. H. Upshaw in the trade or craft of house servants or laborers upon the plantation of the said W. H. Upshaw, to be taught the said craft or trade of house servants or laborers, and to live with, continue, & serve the said W. H. Upshaw as apprentices from the date hereof for and during the term of their minority.

During all of which time, said Dan Thornton doth Covenant with the said W. H. Upshaw that the said minors shall well and faithfully demean themselves as such faithful apprentices, observing fully the Commands of the said W. H. Upshaw, and in all things deporting and behaving themselves as faithful apprentices to the said W. H. Upshaw, neither revealing his secrets, nor at any time neglecting or leaving the business of the said W. H. Upshaw.

And for and in consideration of the services well and faithfully rendered by the said minors, of the first part, Said W. H. Upshaw, of the second part, doth covenant, promise, and agree to instruct them, said Apprentices, or otherwise Cause them to be well and faithfully instructed, in the said trade or craft of house servants or laborers, and also to read the English language. And shall also allow, furnish, and provide them, said Apprentices, with meat and drink and clothing during the said term, And all other necessaries meet & proper, in sickness and in health. Witness our hands and seals the day and year before written.

Executed Before us }   W. H. Upshaw
Jnº C. Brown }   Dan + Thornton, his mark
Geº L. Almond, Ordny }

Filed in Office and Recorded Nov 21, 1891.

Geº L. Almond, Ordinary

Duplicate [162]

Georgia }
Elbert County } This Indenture, this day made and entered into, between Jnº W. McCalla, of the one part, and Elisha McCalla, of the second part. and witnesseth: That the said Elisha McCalla this day binds and apprentices unto the said Jnº W. McCalla his one (1) minor children, viz, Peter McCalla Seventeen (17) years old. All the above named children the said Elisha McCalla binds and apprentices unto the said Jnº W. McCalla until they arrive at the age of Twenty one years. And now the said Jnº W. McCalla agrees to take said children, treat them humanely and Kindly, furnish proper food & clothing, all necessary medical attention, give them such education as can be had at the Common schools of the County, and instruct them in the art or craft of husbandry or farming. And when they shall arrive at the age of twenty one years, the said McCalla is to give them to each child such amount as he may deem a suitable reward for fidelity & faithful service. And it is further agreed & understood by both parties that the relation of Master and apprentice shall exist between them to all intents & purposes from and after this date. Made & Signed in duplicate this –[blank] day of [blank] 1891.

Z. B. Taylor }
J. B. Janes, Jʳ }

Elisha + McCalla, his mark
Jnº W. McCalla

Georgia }
Elbert County } In person comes before me Z. B. Taylor who on oath says he saw the above named Elisha McCalla & J. W. McCalla sign the above Indenture for the purposes therein Stated, and that deponent and J. B. Janes, Jʳ attended the same as witnesses.

Sworn to & Subscribed before me Dec 4, 1891.

Geº L. Almond, Ordny   Z. B. Taylor

Filed in office and Recorded Dec 4, 1891.

Geº L. Almond, Ordiny

Duplicate [163]

Georgia }
Elbert County } This Indenture, this day made and entered into, between Jnº W. McCalla and Elizabeth Blackwell, both of the County and State above written. and witnesseth: That the said Elizabeth this day binds and apprentices unto the said Jnº W. McCalla her two minor children, her son Tom Joe 5 years old and her

daughter Alice 3 years old. Both of said children are hereby bound and apprenticed unto the said McCalla until they arrive at the age of twenty one years. Now the said McCalla agrees to take said children, treat them humanely and Kindly, furnish proper food and clothing, and such medical attention as may be necessary, and such education as can be obtained at the Common Schools of the County, and Cause them to be instructed in the Art or Craft of husbandry or farming. And when they shall arrive at the age of Twenty one years, the said McCalla is to give to each such Amount as he may deem a suitable reward for fidelity and faithful service. and it is further agreed and understood by both parties that the relation of Master and apprentice shall exist between them from and after this date. Made and signed in duplicate this Nov 13, 1891.

Witnesses
J. B. Janes, J^r }
Z. B. Taylor }

Jno W. McCalla
Elizabeth + Blackwell, her mark

Personally comes before me J. B. Janes, J^r who on oath says he saw Elizabeth Blackwell & J. W. McCalla sign the within Indenture for the purposes therein stated.

Sworn to & Subscribed before me Dec 5, 1891.

Ge^o L. Almond, Ordinary   J. B. Janes, J^r

Filed in office and recorded Dec 5, 1891.

Ge^o L. Almond, Ordiny

Duplicate   [164]

Georgia }
Elbert County } This Indenture, this day made and entered into, between Jno W. McCalla and Oliver Mattox, both of the County and State above written. and witnesseth: That the said Oliver Mattox this day binds and apprentices unto the said Jno W. McCalla his 2 minor children, viz, Oscar a boy 2 years old and Georgia Ann a girl 3 years old, and all the above named children the said Oliver Mattox binds and apprentices to the said McCalla until they arrive at the age of twenty one years, or during their minority. The said McCalla agrees to treat said children humanely and Kindly, furnish proper food and clothing, all necessary medical attention, and give them such education as can be had at the common schools of the County, and instruct them in the art or craft of husbandry or farming. and when they shall arrive at the age of Twenty one years, the said McCalla is to give

to each such Amount as he may deem a suitable reward for fidelity and faithful service. and it is further agreed by both parties that the relation of Master and apprentice shall exist between them from and after this date. Made and signed in duplicate this day of 19 Dec, 1891.

Attest
J. B. Janes, J^r }
Z. B. Taylor }

Oliver + Mattox, his mark
Jn° W. McCalla

Personally comes before me J. B. Janes, J^r who on oath says that he, together with Z. B. Taylor, saw J. W. McCalla and Oliver Mattox sign the within for the purposes therein stated.

Ge° L. Almond, Ordinary

J. B. Janes, J^r

Filed in office and recorded Dec 29, 1891.

Ge° L. Almond, Ordiny

Duplicate [165]

Georgia }
Elbert County } This Indenture, made this day between Jn° W. McCalla and Sam Bourne, both of the County and State Above written. and witnesseth: that the said Sam Bowman this day binds and apprentices unto the said Jn° W. McCalla his two minor Children, George Bourne Eleven years old and Wesley Bourne Sixteen years old, both the above named children the said Sam binds and apprentices unto the said McCalla until they arrive at the age of twenty one years, or during their minority. Said McCalla agrees to treat said children humanely and Kindly, furnish proper food and clothing, all necessary medical attention, and such education as can be had at the Common Schools of the County, and instruct them in the art or craft of husbandry or farming. and when each child shall arrive at the age of twenty one years, the said McCalla is to give to each such amount as he may deem a suitable reward for fidelity and faithful service. And it is further agreed by both parties that the relation of Master and apprentice shall exist between them from and after this date. Made and signed in duplicate this Dec 21, 1891.

Attest
J. B. Janes, J^r }
Z. B. Taylor }

Sam + Bourne, his mark
Jn° W. McCalla

Personally comes before me J. B. Janes, J^r who on oath says that he, together with Z. B. Taylor, saw Jn° W. McCalla and Sam Bourne sign the within for the purposes therein stated and that he and Z. B. Taylor signed as witnesses.

Ge° L. Almond, Ordinary   J. B. Janes, J^r

Filed in office and recorded Dec 29, 1891.

Ge° L. Almond, Ordiny

Duplicate   [166]

Georgia   }
Elbert County   } This Indenture, this day made and entered into, between Jn° W. McCalla and Charlotte Fleming, both of the County and State above written. & witnesseth: That the said Charlotte this day binds & apprentices unto the said Jn° W. McCalla her Five minor children, viz, May Liza 17 years old, Russel 15 years old, Willis 12 years old, Missouri 9 years old, Josephine 5 years old. All the above named children the said Charlotte binds and apprentices unto the said McCalla until they arrive at the age of twenty one, or during their minority. The said McCalla agrees to treat said children humanely and Kindly, furnish proper food and clothing, all necessary medical attention, and give them such education as can be had at the Common schools of the County, and instruct them in the art or craft of husbandry or farming. and when they shall arrive at the age of Twenty one years, the said McCalla is to give to each such Amount as he may deem a suitable reward for fidelity and faithful service. and it is further agreed by both parties that the relation of Master and Apprentice shall exist between them from and after this date. Made and signed in duplicate this 22 day of Dec 1891.

Attest
J. B. Janes, J^r }   Charlotte + Fleming, her mark
John H. McCalla }   John W. McCalla

Personally comes before me J. B. Janes, J^r who on oath says that he, together with Jn° H. McCalla, saw Jn° W. McCalla and Charlotte Fleming sign the within for the purposes therein stated.

Ge° L. Almond, Ordinary   J. B. Janes, J^r

Filed in office & recorded Dec 29, 1891.

Ge° L. Almond, Ordiny

Duplicate [167]

Georgia }
Elbert County } This Indenture, made this the first day of January 1892, between Nathan and Charlotte Blackwell, of said County, for and in behalf of Dougherty, Lins, Lonhannah, and Lavinia Blackwell, being of the ages of 12, 10, 8, & 6 years, on the one part, and J. W. Rucker, of the County aforesaid, of the other part. Witnesseth: that the said Nathan and Charlotte does by these presents bind out said minors, of said County, as apprentices to said J. W. Rucker in the trade or craft of house servants or Laborers upon the plantation of the said J. W. Rucker, to be taught the said craft or trade of house servants or laborers, and to live with, continue, & serve the said J. W. Rucker as apprentices from the date hereof for and during the term of their minority.

During all of which time, said Nathan and Charlotte doth covenant with the said J. W. Rucker that the said minors shall well and faithfully demean themselves as such faithful apprentices, observing fully the Commands of the said J. W. Rucker, and in all things deporting and behaving themselves as faithful apprentices to the said J. W. Rucker, neither revealing his secrets, nor at any time neglecting or leaving the business of the said J. W. Rucker.

And for and in consideration of the services well and faithfully rendered by the said minors, of the first part, Said J. W. Rucker, of the second part, doth Covenant, promise, and agree to instruct them, said Apprentices, or otherwise Cause them to be well and faithfully instructed, in the said trade or craft of house servants or laborers, and also to read the English language, and shall also allow, furnish, & provide them, said apprentices, with meat & drink and clothing during the said term, and all other necessaries meet & proper, in sickness and in health, and shall also, at the expiration of said term, allow & pay the said apprentices what is now allowed by the statutes in such case made and provided. Witness our hands and seals the day and year first before written.

Executed Before us }   J. W. Rucker
J. J. Chandler }   Nathan + Blackwell, his mark
Ge^o L. Almond, Ordny }   Charlotte + Blackwell, her mark

Filed in office and recorded Jany 1, 1892.

                                         Ge^o L. Almond, Ordiny

Duplicate [168]

Georgia }
Elbert County } This Indenture, this day made and entered into, between Jn° W. McCalla and Gipson Verdel, both of the County and State Above written. and witnesseth: that the said Gipson Verdel this day binds and apprentices unto the said Jn° W. McCalla his Seven (7) minor children, to wit, his daughters Addie, Ala, Lucy, and Fannie, ages respectfully 12, 10, 8, and 6, His sons George, Cleveland, and Albert, ages respectfully 14, 11, and 2, all the above named children the said Gipson this day binds and apprentices unto the said Jn° W. McCalla until they arrive at the age of twenty one years. Said McCalla agrees to treat said children humanely and Kindly, using such means in their reproof as he would use with his own children, furnish them proper food and clothing, all necessary medical attention, give them such education as can be obtained at the common schools of the County, and instruct them in the art or Craft of husbandry or farming, and when they shall arrive at the age of Twenty one years, the said McCalla is to give to each such amounts as he may deem a suitable reward for fidelity and faithful services, and it is further understood by both parties that the relation of master and apprentice shall exist between them from and after this date. Made and signed in duplicate this [blank] day of [blank] 1892.

Attest
J. B. Janes, J^r }   Jn° W. McCalla
Z. B. Taylor }   Gipson Verdell

Personally comes before me J. B. Janes, J^r who on oath says that he, together with Z. B. Taylor, saw Jn° W. McCalla and Gipson Verdel sign the within Indenture and that he and Taylor signed as witnesses, and that there is a duplicate of Original.

Sworn to & Subscribed }
before me Jany 9, 1892 }
Ge° L. Almond, Ordinary }   J. B. Janes, J^r

Filed in office and Recorded Jany 9, 1892.

Ge° L. Almond, Ordinary

Duplicate [169]

Georgia }
Elbert County } This Indenture, made this 21 day Jany 1892, between Sam

White, of said County, for and in behalf of Henry, Ida, Lula, and Anna White, being of the ages of 18, 16, 14, & 12 years, on the one part, and J. M. Harper, of the County aforesaid, of the other part. Witnesseth: that the said Sam White does by these presents bind out Henry, Ida, Lula, and Anna White, of said County, as apprentices to said J. M. Harper in the trade or craft of house servants or laborers upon the plantation of the said J. M. Harper, to be taught the said craft or trade of house servants or laborers, and to live with, continue, and serve the said J. M. Harper as apprentices from the date hereof for and during the term of their minority.

During all of which time, said Sam White doth Covenant with the said J. M. Harper that the said Henry, Ida, Lula, and Anna White shall well and faithfully demean themselves as such faithful apprentices, observing fully the commands of the said J. M. Harper, and in all things deporting & behaving themselves as faithful apprentices to the said J. M. Harper, neither revealing his secrets, nor at any time neglecting or leaving the business of the said J. M. Harper.

And for and in consideration of the service well and faithfully rendered by the said Henry, Ida, Lula, and Anna White, of the first part, Said J. M. Harper, of the second part, doth covenant, promise, and agree to instruct them, said Apprentices, or otherwise cause them to be well and faithfully instructed, in the said trade or craft of house servants or laborers, and shall also allow, furnish, and provide them, said Apprentices, with meat & drink and clothing during the said term, and all other necessaries meet and proper, in sickness and in health.

Witness our hands and seals the day and year first before written.

Executed Before us }   J. M. Harper
J. J. Chandler }   Sam + White, his mark
Ge° L. Almond, Ordny }

Filed in office and Recorded Jany 21, 1892.

Ge° L. Almond, Ordiny

Duplicate [170]

Georgia }
Elbert County } This Indenture, made this the 3rd day February 1892, between Jacob Almond, of said County, for and in behalf of Elbert, Tom, and Alfred Almond, being of the ages of 17, 15, 14 years, on the one part, and A. S. Oliver, of the County aforesaid, of the other part. Witnesseth: that the said Jacob Almond

does by these presents bind out Elbert, Tom, & Alfred Almond, of said County, as apprentices to said A. S. Oliver in the trade or craft of house servants or Laborers upon the plantation of the said A. S. Oliver, to be taught the said craft or trade of house servants or laborers, and to live with, continue, and serve the said A. S. Oliver as apprentices from the date hereof for and during the term of their minority.

During all of which time, said Jacob Almond doth covenant with the said A. S. Oliver that the said Elbert, Tom, & Alfred Almond shall well & faithfully demean themselves as such faithful apprentices, observing fully the commands of the said A. S. Oliver, and in all things deporting and behaving themselves as faithful apprentices to the said A. S. Oliver, neither revealing his secrets, nor at any time neglecting or leaving the business of the said A. S. Oliver.

And for and in consideration of the service well and faithfully rendered by the said Elbert, Tom, and Alfred Almond, of the first part, Said A. S. Oliver, of the second part, doth covenant, promise, and agree to instruct them, said apprentices, or otherwise cause them to be well and faithfully instructed, in the said trade or craft of house servants or laborers, and shall also allow, furnish, and provide them, said apprentices, with meat and drink and clothing during the said term, and all other necessaries meet and proper, in sickness and in health. Witness our hands and seals the day & year first above written.

Executed Before us }   A. S. Oliver
S. L. Carter   }   Jacob + Almond, his mark
Geº L. Almond, Ordny }

Filed in office and Recorded Feby 3, 1892.

Geº L. Almond, Ordiny

Duplicate   [171]

Georgia   }
Elbert County   } This Indenture, this day made and entered into, between Jnº W. McCalla and Pat Carson, both of the County and State above written. and witnesseth: that the said Pat Carson this day binds and apprentices unto the said Jnº W. McCalla his Six minor children, to wit, Sallie 10 years old, Marie Lou 6 years old, Sindy 8 years old, Thoˢ 5 years old, Ruddie 5 years old, Leola 3 years old. All the above named children the said Pat Carson this day binds and Apprentices unto the said Jnº W. McCalla until they arrive at the age of Twenty one years. Said McCalla agrees to treat said children humanely and Kindly,

furnish proper food and clothing, all necessary medical attention, and such education as can be obtained at the Common Schools of the County, and instruct them in the art or Craft of husbandry or farming. And when each child Shall arrive at the age of Twenty one years, the said McCalla is to give to them such amounts as he may deem a suitable reward for fidelity and faithful service. And it is further agreed by both parties that the relation of master and apprentice Shall exist between them from and after this date. Made and signed in duplicate this 26 day of Januy 1892.

Attest
J. B. Janes, J^r }   Jn° W. McCalla
Z. B. Taylor }   Pat + Carson, his mark

Personally comes before me J. B. Janes, J^r who on oath says that he, together with Z. B. Taylor, signed the within Indenture as witnesses, and Saw Jn° W. McCalla & Pat Carson sign for the purposes therein stated.

Ge° L. Almond, Ordiny   J. B. Janes, J^r

Recorded Feby 8, 1892.

Ge° L. Almond, Ordinary

Duplicate   [172]

Georgia   }
Elbert County   } This Indenture, this day made and entered into, between Jn° W. McCalla and Charity Verdel. and witnesseth: that the said Charity Verdel this day binds and apprentices unto the said Jn° W. McCalla her two minor children, A girl 10 years old named Etta and a boy 8 years old named Willie. Both the above named children the said Charity binds & apprentices unto the said Jn° W. McCalla until they arrive at the age of Twenty one years. The said McCalla is to treat said children humanely and Kindly, furnish proper food & clothing, all necessary medical Attention, and to instruct them in the art & Craft of husbandry or farming, and also to give them such education as can be had at the Common Schools of the County, and when each child shall arrive at the age of twenty one years, the said McCalla is to give to each such amount as he may deem a suitable reward for fidelity and faithful [blot] service, and it is further agreed by both

parties that the relation of Master & apprentice shall exist between them from and after this date. Made & signed in duplicate this Feby 1 1892.

Attest
J. B. Janes, J^r }   Charity + Verdel, her mark
Z. B. Taylor }   Jn° W. McCalla

Personally comes before me J. B. Janes, J^r who on oath says that he saw Jn° W. McCalla & Charity Verdel sign the within Indenture for the purposes therein stated, and that he, together with Z. B. Taylor, signed as witnesses.

Ge° L. Almond, Ord }   J. B. Janes, J^r

Filed in office and recorded Feby 8, 1892.

Ge° L. Almond, Ordinary

Duplicate   [173]

Georgia }
Elbert County } This Indenture, Made this 11 day of Feby 1892, between Wilson Mattox, of said County, for and in behalf of Guss Mattox, being of the age of Six years, on the one part, and Ellen Hunter, of the County aforesaid, of the other part. Witnesseth: that the said Wilson Mattox aforesaid does by these presents bind out Guss Mattox, of said County, as Apprentice to said Ellen Hunter in the trade or Craft of house servant or as Laborer upon the plantation of the said Ellen Hunter, to be taught the said Craft or trade of house servant or laborer, and to live with, continue, and serve the said Ellen Hunter as an apprentice from the date hereof for and during the term of Fifteen years.

During all of which time, said Wilson Mattox doth covenant with the said Ellen Hunter that the said Guss Mattox shall well and faithfully demean himself as such faithful apprentice, observing fully the Commands of the said Ellen Hunter, and in all things deporting and behaving himself as a faithful apprentice to the said Ellen Hunter, neither revealing her secrets, nor at any time neglecting or leaving the business of the said Ellen Hunter.

And for and in consideration of the service well and faithfully rendered by the said Guss Mattox, of the first, said Ellen Hunter, of the second part, doth covenant, promise, and agree to instruct him, said apprentice, or otherwise cause him to be well and faithfully instructed, in the said trade or craft of house servant or laborer, and also to read the English language, and shall also allow, furnish, & provide him, said apprentice, with meat & drink and clothing during the said term, and all other necessaries meet and proper, in sickness and in health, and shall also, at the expiration of said term, allow & pay the said apprentice what is now allowed by the statute in such Case made and provided.

Witness our hands and seals the day & year first before written.

Executed Before us }   Ellen + Hunter, her mark
J. J. Chandler   }   Wilson + Mattox, his mark
Ge° L. Almond, Ordinary }

Filed in office and recorded Feby 11, 1892.

Ge° L. Almond, Ordinary

Duplicate [174]

Georgia }
Elbert County } This Indenture, made this 6 day of February 1892, between Wilson Mattox, of Said County, for and in behalf of Augustus Mattox, being of the age of five years, on the one part, and Levi Heard, of the County aforesaid, of the other part. Witnesseth: that the said Wilson Mattox, as aforesaid, does by these presents bind out Augustus Mattox, of said County, as Apprentice to said Levi Heard in the trade or Craft of Husbandry or as Laborer upon the plantation of the Said Levi Heard, to be taught the Said Craft or trade of husbandry or laborer, and to live with, Continue, and serve the said Levi Heard as an Apprentice from the date hereof for and during the term of until he is 21 years of age.

During all of which time, Said Wilson Mattox, as aforesaid, doth Covenant with the Said Levi Heard that the said Augustus Mattox Shall well and faithfully demean himself as Such faithful Apprentice, observing fully the Commands of the said Levi Heard, and in all things deporting and behaving himself as a faithful Apprentice to the Said Levi Heard, neither revealing his secrets, nor at any time neglecting or leaving the business of the said Levi Heard.

And for and in Consideration of the Service well and faithfully rendered by the said Augustus Mattox, of the first part, Said Levi Heard, of the second part, doth Covenant, promise, and agree to instruct him, said Apprentice, or otherwise cause him to be well and faithfully instructed, in the said trade or Craft of husbandry or laborer, and also to read the English language. And shall also allow, furnish, and provide him, said Apprentice, with meat and drink and Clothing during Said term, and all other necessaries meet and proper, in Sickness and in health, and Shall also, at the expiration of Said term, allow and pay the said Apprentice what is now allowed by the Statute in Such Case made and provided.

Witness our hands and seals the day and year first before written.

Executed Before us }   Wilson + Mattox, his mark
W. M. Jones   }   Levi + Heard, his mark
Jn⁰ W. McCalla   }

Filed in Office and recorded Feby 17, 1892.

          Ge⁰ L. Almond, Ordinary

        Duplicate   [175]

Georgia   }
Elbert County } This Indenture, Made this 16 day of March 1892, between Judge and Mollie Blackwell, of said County, for and in behalf of themselves, being of the ages of twenty one years, on the one part, and A. S. Oliver, of the County Aforesaid, of the other part. Witnesseth: that the said Judge and Mollie Blackwell, does by these presents bind out themselves, of said County, as Apprentices to said A. S. Oliver in the trade or Craft of house Servants or as laborers upon the plantation of the said A. S. Oliver, to be taught the said Craft of house servants or laborers, and to live with, continue, and serve the said A. S. Oliver as apprentices from the date hereof for and during the term of Five years.

During all of which time, said Judge and Mollie Blackwell doth Covenant with the said A. S. Oliver that they will well and faithfully demean themselves as such faithful apprentices, observing fully the Commands of the said A. S. Oliver, and in all things deporting & behaving themselves as faithful apprentices to the said A. S. Oliver, neither revealing his secrets, nor at any time neglecting or leaving the business of the said A. S. Oliver.

And for and in consideration of the service well & faithfully rendered by the said Judge and Mollie Blackwell, of the first, said A. S. Oliver, of the second part, doth covenant, promise, & agree to instruct them, said apprentices, or otherwise cause them to be well and faithfully instructed, in the said trade or craft of house servants or laborers, and shall also allow, furnish, and provide them, said apprentices, with meat & drink and clothing during the said term, and all other necessaries meet & proper, in sickness and in health.

Witness our hands & Seals the day & year first above written.

Executed Before us }   Judge + Blackwell, his mark
A. J. Little   }   Mollie + Blackwell, her mark
Geº L. Almond, Ordny }   A. S. Oliver

Filed in office and Recorded March 16, 1892.

Geº L. Almond, Ordinary

Duplicate   [176]

Georgia   }
Elbert County } This Indenture, Made this 16 day of March 1892, between Mollie Blackwell, of said County, for and in behalf of Chan and Mattie Blackwell, being of the ages of one & 2 years, on the one part, and A. S. Oliver, of the County Aforesaid, of the other part. Witnesseth: that the said Mollie Blackwell, does by these presents bind out Chan and Mattie, of said County, as apprentices to said A. S. Oliver in the trade or Craft of house servants or as laborers upon the plantation of the said A. S. Oliver, to be taught the said Craft or trade of house servants or laborers, and to live with, continue, & serve the said A. S. Oliver as apprentices from the date hereof for and during the term of their minority.

During all of which time, said Mollie Blackwell doth covenant with the said A. S. Oliver that the said Chan and Mattie will well and faithfully demean themselves as such faithful apprentices, observing fully the Commands of the said A. S. Oliver, and in all things deporting & behaving themselves as a faithful apprentices to the said A. S. Oliver, neither revealing his secrets, nor at any time neglecting or leaving the business of the said A. S. Oliver.

And for and in consideration of the service well & faithfully rendered by the said Chan & Mattie Blackwell, of the first part, said A. S. Oliver, of the second part, doth covenant, promise, & agree to instruct them, said apprentices, or otherwise cause them to be well and faithfully instructed, in the said trade or craft of house servants or laborers, and shall also allow, furnish, & provide them, said apprentices, with meat, drink, and clothing during the said term, and all other necessaries meet & proper, in sickness & in health.

Witness our hands & Seals the day & year first above written.

Executed Before us }
A. J. Little   }   Mollie + Blackwell, her mark
Geº L. Almond, Ordny }   A. S. Oliver

Filed in Office & Recorded March 16, 1892.

Ge° L. Almond, Ordinary

Duplicate [177]

Georgia }
Elbert County } This Indenture, made this the 23rd day of March 1892, between Lucy Blackwell, of said County, for and in behalf of herself, being of the age of 16 years, on the one part, and J. W. Rucker, of the County Aforesaid, of the other part. Witnesseth: that the said Lucy Blackwell, does by these presents bind out herself, of said County, as apprentice to said J. W. Rucker in the trade or Craft of house servant or as laborer upon the plantation of the said J. W. Rucker, to be taught the said Craft of house servant or laborer, and to live with, continue, and serve the said J. W. Rucker as apprentice from the date hereof for and during the term of two years.

During all of which time, said Lucy Blackwell doth Covenant with the said J. W. Rucker that she will well & faithfully demean herself as such faithful apprentice, observing fully the Commands of the said J. W. Rucker, and in all things deporting and behaving herself as a faithful Apprentice to the said J. W. Rucker, neither revealing his secrets, nor at any time neglecting or leaving the business of the said J. W. Rucker.

And for and in consideration of the service well and faithfully rendered by the said Lucy Blackwell, of the first part, said J. W. Rucker, of the second part, doth covenant, promise, and agree to instruct her, said Apprentice, or otherwise cause her to be well and faithfully instructed, in the said trade or craft of house servant or laborer, and shall also allow, furnish, and provide her, said apprentice, with meat and drink and clothing during the said term, and all other necessaries meet and proper, in sickness and in health.

Witness our hands and seals the day and year first before written.

Executed Before us }
J. J. Chandler }   Lucy Blackwell
Ge° L. Almond, Ordny }   J. W. Rucker

Filed in office and Recorded Mrch 23rd 1892.

Ge° L. Almond, Ordinary

Duplicate [178]

Georgia }
Elbert County } This Indenture, made this the 1st day of April 1892, between Alfred McIntosh, of said County, for and in behalf of himself, being of the age of about 37 years, on the one part, and J. S. White, of the County aforesaid, of the other part. Witnesseth: that the said Alfred McIntosh, does by these presents bind out himself, of said County, as apprentice to said J. S. White in the trade or craft of house servant or as laborer upon the plantation of the said J. S. White, to taught the said craft of house servant or laborer, and to live with, continue, & serve the said J. S. White as apprentice from the date hereof for and during the term of Five years.

During all of which time, said Alfred McIntosh doth covenant with the said J. S. White that he shall well and faithfully demean himself as such faithful apprentice, observing fully the commands of the said J. S. White, and in all things deporting and behaving himself as a faithful apprentice to the said J. S. White, neither revealing his secrets, nor at any time neglecting or leaving the business of the said J. S. White.

And for and in consideration of the service well and faithfully rendered by the said Alfred McIntosh, of the first part, said J. S. White, of the second part, doth promise & agree to instruct him, said apprentice, or otherwise cause him to be well & faithfully instructed, in the said trade or craft of house servant or laborer, and shall also allow, furnish, & provide him, said apprentice, with meat & drink & clothing during the said term, and all other necessaries meet & proper, in sickness and in health, and to pay Alfred $25.00 per year.

Witness our hands and seals the day and year first before written.

Executed Before us }
W. T. Duncan } Alfred McIntosh
Geº L. Almond, Ordny } J. S. White

Filed in office and recorded April 1, 1892.

Geº L. Almond, Ordiny

Duplicate [179]

Georgia }
Elbert County } This Indenture, made this 1st day of April 1892, between Alfred McIntosh, of said County, for and in behalf of Mary, Anna, William, George,

Thomas, Lace, and Peter McIntosh, aged 18, 16, 15, 13, 11, 9, & 8 years, on the one part, and J. S. White, of the County aforesaid, of the other part. Witnesseth: that the said Alfred McIntosh, does by these presents bind out his said children, of said County, as Apprentices to said J. S. White in the trade or craft of house servants or as laborers upon the plantation of the said J. S. White, to be taught the said craft of house servants or laborers, and to live with, Continue, and serve the said J. S. White as apprentices from the date hereof for and during the term of their minority. During all of which time, said Alfred McIntosh doth covenant with the said J. S. White that the said minors shall well and faithfully demean themselves as such faithful Apprentices, observing fully the Commands of the said J. S. White, and in all things deporting and behaving themselves as faithful apprentices to the said J. S. White, neither revealing his secrets, nor at any time neglecting or leaving the business of the said J. S. White. And for and in consideration of the service well and faithfully rendered by the said minors, of the first part, said J. S. White, of the second part, doth covenant, promise, and agree to instruct them, said Apprentices, or otherwise cause them to be well & faithfully instructed, in the said trade or craft of house servants or laborers, and shall also allow, furnish, & provide them, said apprentices, with meat and drink and clothing during the said term, and All other necessaries meet and proper, in sickness and in health, and to pay Alfred $25.00 per year.

Witness our hands & Seals the day and year first before written.

Executed Before us }
W. T. Duncan }
Ge⁰ L. Almond, Ordny }

Alfred + McIntosh, his mark
J. S. White

Filed in Office and recorded April 1, 1892.

Ge⁰ L. Almond, Ordy

Duplicate [180]

Georgia }
Elbert County } This Indenture, made this 13th day of April 1892, between William Pass, of said County, for and in behalf of Edward, Rebecca, Carl, Liza, Janie, Mary, and Edmund, Minors being of the ages of 10, 8, 18, 14, 11, 10, & 9 years, on the one part, and J. E. Herndon, of the County aforesaid, of the other part. Witnesseth: that the said William Pass does by these presents bind out Edward, Rebecca, Carl, Liza, Janie, Mary, & Edmund, of said County, as apprentice to said J. E. Herndon in the trade or craft of house servants or as laborers upon the plantation of the said J. E. Herndon, to be taught the said Craft

of house servants or laborers, and to live with, continue, and serve the said J. E. Herndon as apprentices from the date hereof for and during the term of two years.

During all of which time, said William Pass doth Covenant with the said J. E. Herndon that the said minors shall well and faithfully demean themselves as such faithful apprentices, observing fully the commands of the said J. E. Herndon, and in all things deporting & behaving themselves as faithful apprentices to the said J. E. Herndon, neither revealing his secrets, nor at any time neglecting or leaving the business of the said J. E. Herndon.

And for and in consideration of the service well and faithfully rendered by the said minors, of the first part, said J. E. Herndon, of the second part, doth covenant, promise, and agree to instruct them, said apprentices, or otherwise cause them to be well and faithfully, in the said trade or Craft of house Servants or laborers, and shall also allow, furnish, & provide them, said apprentices, with meat & drink & clothing during the said term, and all other necessaries meet and proper, in sickness and in health.

Witness our hands and seals the day and year first above written.

Executed Before us }
G. M. Herndon }   William + Pass, his mark
Geº L. Almond, Ordinary }   J. E. Herndon

Filed in Office and recorded April 13, 1892.

                        Geº L. Almond, Ordiny

            Duplicate   [181]

Georgia }
Elbert County } This Indenture, made this 16 day of April 1892, between Fred and Katie Brewer, Parents, of said County, for and in behalf of Sallie, Heilly, and Sherman Brewer, Minors being of the age of 13, 12, 10 years respectively, on the one part, and W. B. Adams, of the County aforesaid, of the other part. Witnesseth: that the said Fred & Katie Brewer, Parents as aforesaid, does by these presents bind out Sallie, Heilly, Sherman, of said County, as apprentices to said W. B. Adams in the trade or craft of Servant or farm laborer upon the plantation of the said W. B. Adams, to be taught the said craft or trade of Servant or Farm laborer, and to live with, continue, and Serve the said W. B. Adams as an apprentice from the date hereof for and during the term of their Minority years.

During all of which time, Said Fred & Katie Brewer, Parents as aforesaid, doth Covenant with the Said W. B. Adams that the said Sallie, Hilly, & Sherman shall well and faithfully demean themselves as Such faithful apprentices, observing fully the Commands of the said W. B. Adams, and in all things deporting and behaving themselves as a faithful apprentice to the said W. B. Adams, neither revealing his Secrets, nor at any time neglecting or leaving the business of the said W. B. Adams.

And for and in Consideration of the Service well and faithfully rendered by the Said Sallie, Hilly, & Sherman, of the first part, Said W. B. Adams, of the Second part, doth Covenant, promise, and agree to instruct Said Apprentices, or otherwise Cause them to be well and faithfully instructed, in the said trade or Craft of servant or Farm laborer, and shall also allow, furnish, & provide them, said Apprentice, with Meat and Drink and Clothing during the said term, and all other necessaries meet & proper, in Sickness and in health, and shall also, at the expiration of said term, allow and pay the said parents, Fred & Katie Brewer, One Hundred Dollars.

Witness our hands and Seals the day and year first before written.

Executed Before us }	Fred + Brewer, his mark
Steve White }	Katie + Brewer, her mark
R. M. Willis }	W. B. Adams
Clerk, Sup^r Court }	

Filed in Office April 16, 1892 and Recorded April 18, 1892.

Ge^o L. Almond, Ordiny

Duplicate [182]

Georgia }
Elbert County } This Indenture, made and entered into this day, between Mary Jane Cade and Anderson Morrison, both of the County and State above written, and witnesseth: That the said Mary Jane this day binds and apprentice to the said Anderson Morrison her minor son, Sing Cade, one year old, until he arrives at the age of Twenty one years. Now, the said Anderson is to treat said Minor humanely and kindly, furnish proper food and clothing, all necessary medical attention, and give him Such education as can be had at the Common schools of the County, and instruct him in the Art of husbandry, and when said child shall arrive at the age of Twenty one years, the said Anderson is to give to him such amounts as he may deem a suitable reward for fidelity and faithful service.

Made and signed in duplicate this 23rd day of April 1892.

Signed, sealed, & delivered }
in presence of } Anderson + Morrison, his mark
J. B. Janes, Jr } Mary Jane + Cade, her mark
Gipson Verdel }

Personally comes before me J. B. Janes, Jr who on oath says that he, together with Gip Verdel, saw Anderson Morrison, together with Mary Jane Cade, sign the within Indenture for the purposes therein stated, and the same was signed by all parties in duplicate.

Jnº W. McCalla }
N. P. ex off J. P. } J. B. Janes, Jr
April 26, 1892 }

Filed in office & Recorded April 29, 1892.

Geº L. Almond, Ordy

Duplicate [183]

Georgia }
Elbert County } This Indenture, made this the 21st day of May 1892, between Dora Richardson, of said County, for and in behalf of Asa Mattox, her son, being of the age of one and one half years, on the one part, and Claudia Fortson, of the County aforesaid, of the other part. Witnesseth: that the said Dora Richardson does by these presents bind out Asa Mattox, of said County, as Apprentice to said Claudia Fortson in the trade or craft of house servant or as laborer upon the plantation of the said Claudia Fortson, to be taught the said Craft or trade of house servant or laborer, and to live with, Continue, & serve the said Claudia Fortson as an apprentice from the date hereof for and during the term of his Minority.

During all of which time, said Dora Richardson doth covenant with the said Claudia Fortson that the said Asa Mattox shall well and faithfully demean himself as such faithful Apprentice, observing fully the Commands of the said Claudia Fortson, and in all things deporting and behaving himself as a faithful apprentice to the said Claudia Fortson, neither revealing her secrets, nor at any time neglecting or leaving the business of the said Claudia Fortson. And for and in Consideration of the service well and faithfully rendered by the said Asa Mattox, of the first part, said Claudia Fortson, of the second part, doth covenant, promise, and agree to instruct him, said apprentice, or otherwise Cause him to be well and faithfully instructed, in the said trade or craft of house servant or laborer, and also to read the English language, and shall also allow, furnish, & provide him, said Apprentice, with meat, drink, and clothing during the said term, and all other necessaries meet and proper, in sickness and in health. And shall also, at the expiration of said term, allow & pay to the said Apprentice what is now allowed by the Statute in such case made and provided.

Witness our hands & seals the day and year first before written.

Executed Before us }
Thos J. Hester   }   Dora + Richardson, her mark
Ge^o L. Almond, Ordny }   Claudia Fortson

Filed in office and recorded 21 May 1892.

Ge^o L. Almond, Ordinary

Duplicate   [184]

Georgia   }
Elbert County } This Indenture, made and entered into this August 30th 1892, between Elijah Blackwell and Charity Blackwell, both of said County & State, of the one part, and Bedford H. Heard, of the same place, of the other part. witnesseth, that the said Elijah Blackwell and Charity Blackwell, for the consideration herein expressed, and the obligations and consent of said Bedford H. Heard herein contained, do by these presents bind out and apprentice to the said Heard their four minor children, to wit, Jesse Blackwell aged Seventeen years, Lina Blackwell aged fifteen years, Anna Blackwell aged fif ten years, Lula Blackwell aged Eight years, until each of said minor Children Shall Attain the age of Twenty one years. and they, the said Elijah Blackwell and Charity Blackwell, do by this Indenture surrender all parental control and right to the service, control, and labor of said minor children to the said Bedford H. Heard until each of said minors reach the age of Twenty one years.

Said Bedford H. Heard upon his part agrees and promises to teach of said minors the business of husbandry or house service, to furnish each of them with protection, wholesome food, suitable clothing, necessary medicine & medical attention, and habits of industry, honesty, and morality, and shall cause each of said apprentices to be taught to read the English, and shall govern said apprentices with humanity, using only the same degree of force to compel obedience as a father may use with his minor child.

In witness whereof, the said Bedford H. Heard and said Elijah Blackwell and Charity Blackwell have set their hands and affixed their seals in duplicate to this Indenture this August 30th 1892.

Executed in duplicate And }
signed & Sealed in presence of }   Charity + Blackwell, her mark
A. M. Shumate }   B. H. Heard
J. W. Rucker }   Elijah + Blackwell, his mark

Charity and Elijah Blackwell }
W. B. Adams }
Geº L. Almond, Ordinary }

(over)

Georgia } Personally comes before me A. M. Shumate and   [185]
Elbert County } being duly sworn says on oath that he saw Charity Blackwell and Bedford H. Heard sign within Indenture for the purposes therein stated, and that deponent, together with J. W. Rucker, did sign at the same time as witnesses.

Sworn to & Subscribed }
before me 6 Sept 1892 }
Jnº W. McCalla }   A. M. Shumate
N. P. off J. P. }

Filed in office and recorded Sept 7, 1892.

                           Geº L. Almond, Ordinary

                           Duplicate

Georgia }
Elbert County } This Indenture, made this August 30th 1892, between Bedford H. Heard, of said County & State, of the one part, and Elijah Blackwell and Charity Blackwell, of the same place, of the other part. witnesseth: That the said Elijah Blackwell and Charity Blackwell, for and consideration of the sum of seventy Five dollars to be Annually paid to said Elijah and the sum of Forty dollars to be Annually paid to the said Charity by the said Bedford H. Heard and the performance of the conditions and stipulations herein contained, and also in the consideration of furnishing to each of said parties by said Bedford H. Heard of maintenance and protection, they severally by this Indenture do hereby bind themselves to said Bedford H. Heard for the space of five years from this date, each of said persons being now of full age. and do each hereby agree to labor

reasonably under the direction of the said Bedford H. Heard for and during said term of five years and to receive as consideration or compensation the sums herein specified. The said Bedford H. Heard agrees and promises upon his part to afford said Elijah Blackwell & Charity Blackwell maintenance, protection, and humane treatment and to pay said Elijah Blackwell annually the sum of seventy five Dollars

and to said Charity Blackwell annually the sum of Forty dollars, all lost [186] time to be deducted, and to feed both said parties a sufficiency of wholesome food, and to work them reasonably.

In witness whereof, the said Elijah Blackwell and Charity Blackwell and said Bedford H. Heard have have set their hands and affixed their seals in duplicate this August 30th 1892.

Done in duplicate, and Signed,   }
sealed, and delivered in presence of }   Charity + Blackwell, her mark
A. M. Shumate   }   B. H. Heard
J. W. Rucker   }   Elijah + Blackwell, his mark

Attest as to Elijah Blackwell }
W. B. Adams   }
Ge° L. Almond, Ordinary   }

Georgia   }
Elbert County   } Personally comes before me A. M. Shumate and being duly sworn says on oath that he saw B. H. Heard and Charity Blackwell sign within Indenture for the purposes therein stated, and that deponent, together with J. W. Rucker, signed at same time as witnesses.

Sworn to & subscribed }
before me 6 Sep^t 1892 }
Jn° W. McCalla   }   A. M. Shumate
N. P. off J. P.   }

Filed in office & recorded Sep^t 7, 1892.

                                                              Ge° L. Almond, Ordy

Duplicate [187]

This Indenture, made this the first day of Sep^t 1892, between Richard Hill, of said County, for and in behalf of Henry fourteen years old, George ten years old, Jackson twelve years old, and Janie seven years old, on the one part, and J. W. McCalla, of the County aforesaid, of the other part. Witnesseth: that the said Hill aforesaid does by these presents bind J. W. McCalla, of said County, in the trade or craft of aggriculture or as laborer upon the plantation of the said McCalla, to be taught the said Craft or trade of husbandry or laborer, and to live with, continue, and serve the said McCalla as an Apprentice from the date hereof for and during the term of until they are Twenty one years of age.

During all of which time, said Hill, father of said children aforesaid, doth Covenant with the said McCalla that the said Children shall well and faithfully demean themselves as such faithful apprentices, observing fully the Commands of the said McCalla, and in all things deporting and behaving themselves as a faithful apprentice to the said McCalla, neither revealing his secrets, nor at any time neglecting or leaving the business of the said McCalla.

And for and in Consideration of the services well and faithfully rendered by the said Apprentice, of the first part, said McCalla, of the second part, doth Covenant, promise, and agree to instruct them, said apprentices, or otherwise cause them to be well and faithfully instructed, in the said trade or craft of husbandry or laborer, and also to read the English language, and shall also allow, furnish, & provide them, said apprentice, with meat, drink, & clothing during the said term, and all other necessaries meet and proper, in sickness and in health. Witness our hands and seals the day & year first before written.

Executed before us }
C. M. Mattox }
Z. B. Taylor }

Jno W. McCalla
Richard + Hill, his mark

over

Filed in office and recorded 21 May 1892.

Ge^o L. Almond, Ordinary

Georgia } [188]
Elbert County } Personally comes before me Z. B. Taylor and being duly sworn says on oath that he saw Jno W. McCalla and Richard Hill sign the within

Indenture for purpose therein specified, and that deponent, together with C. M. Mattox, did sign at same time as witnesses.

Sworn to & Subscribed }
before me 10 day of Oct 1892 }
Ge° L. Almond, Ordiny }   Z. B. Taylor

Filed in office and Recorded oct 10, 1892.

Ge° L. Almond, Ordinary

McIntosh and McCalla

Duplicate

Georgia }
Elbert County } This Indenture, this day made and entered into, between Ben McIntosh, of the one part, and Jn° W. McCalla, of the second part, both of the County and State above written. and witnesseth: That the said Ben McIntosh does this day bind and apprentice to the said Jn° W. McCalla his four minor children, 2 Boys ages 17 & 12 years named Ben and William, 2 girls Sarie 7 years old Melis 2 years. All the above named children the said Ben McIntosh binds and apprentices to the said Jn° McCalla until they arrive at the age of twenty one years. Now the said McCalla, of the second part, agrees to take said children, treat them humanely and kindly, furnish proper food and clothing, all necessary medical Attention, and give them such education as can be obtained at the Common Schools of the County, and instruct them in the art of farm laborer. And when each child shall have arrived at the age of twenty one years, the said McCalla is to give it such amounts as he may deem a suitable reward for fidelity and faithful service.

Signed, sealed, and delivered in presence of   [189]

Witnessed by }
J. B. Janes, J^r }   Ben + McIntosh, his mark
Z. B. Taylor }   Jn° W. McCalla

Personally came before me J. B. Janes, J^r who on oath says that he, together with Z. B. Taylor, saw Jn° W. McCalla and Ben McIntosh sign the within Indenture for the purposes therein stated.

Sworn to & Subscribed }
before me Dec 1, 1892   }   J. B. Janes, J^r
Ge° L. Almond, Ordinary }

Recorded December 2nd 1892.

Ge° L. Almond, Ordy

Duplicate   [190]

Georgia   }
Elbert County   } This Indenture, made this the 5th day of Dec 1892, between Addie Fortson, of said County, for and in behalf of Jimmie Fortson, being of the age of three years, on the one part, and Henrietta Smith, of the County aforesaid, of the other part. Witnesseth: that the said Addie Fortson does by these presents bind out Jimmie Fortson, of said County, as apprentice to said Henrietta Smith in the trade or craft of house servant or as laborer upon the plantation of the said Smith, to be taught the said Craft or trade of house servant or laborer, and to live with, continue, & serve the said Henrietta Smith as an apprentice from the date hereof for and during the term of 18 years. During all of which time, said Addie Fortson doth covenant with the said Henrietta Smith that the said Jimmie Fortson shall well and faithfully demean himself as such faithful apprentice, observing fully the Commands of the said Henrietta Smith, and in all things deporting & behaving himself as a faithful Apprentice to the said Smith, neither revealing her secrets, nor at any time neglecting or leaving the business of the said Henrietta Smith. And for and in Consideration of the service well & faithfully rendered by the said Jimmie Fortson, of the first, Said Smith, of the second part, doth covenant, promise, and agree to instruct him, said apprentice, or otherwise cause him to be well and faithfully instructed, in the said trade or craft of house servant or laborer, and also to read the English language, and shall also allow, furnish, & provide him, said apprentice, with meat & drink & clothing during the said term, and all other necessaries meet & proper, in sickness and in health, and also, at the expiration of said term, allow & pay the said apprentice what is now allowed by the Statute in such case made and provided.

Witness our hands and seals the day & year first before written.

Executed before us }
Ge⁰ L. Almond, Ordinary } Addie + Fortson, her mark
J. J. Chandler } Henrietta + Smith, her mark

Filed in office and recorded Dec 5, 1892.

Ge⁰ L. Almond, Ordny

Duplicate [191]

Georgia }
Elbert County } This Indenture, made this the 8th day of Dec 1892, between Lizzie Bell, of said County, for and in behalf of Mary Bell, being of the age of Five years, on the one part, and Easter Bell, of the County aforesaid, of the other part. Witnesseth: that the said Lizzie Bell does by these presents bind out Mary Bell, of said County, as apprentice to said Easter Bell in the trade or craft of house servant or as laborer upon the plantation of the said Easter Bell, to be taught the said Craft or trade of house servant or laborer, and to live with, Continue, and serve the said Easter Bell as an Apprentice from the date hereof for and during the term of Sixteen years. During all of which time, said Lizzie Bell doth Covenant with the said Easter Bell that the said Mary Bell shall well and faithfully demean herself as such faithful Apprentice, observing fully the Commands of the said Easter Bell, and in all things deporting and behaving herself as a faithful apprentice to the said Easter Bell, neither revealing her secrets, nor at any time neglecting or leaving the business of the said Easter Bell. And for and in consideration of the service well & faithfully rendered by the said Mary Bell, of the first part, said Easter Bell, of the second part, doth covenant, promise, and agree to instruct her said apprentice, or otherwise cause her to be well and faithfully instructed, in the said trade or craft of house servant or laborer, and also to read the English language, And shall also allow, furnish, and provide her said Apprentice with meat & drink and clothing during the said term, and all other necessaries meet and proper, in sickness and in health, and also, at the expiration of said term, allow and pay to said Apprentice what is now allowed by Statute in such case made and provided.

Witness our hands and seals the day and year first before written.

Executed before us }
E. B. Tate }   Lizzie + Bell, her mark
Geº L. Almond, Ordinary }   Easter + Bell, her mark

Filed in office and recorded Dec 8, 1892.

> Geº L. Almond, Ordinary

Duplicate [192]

Georgia }
Elbert County } This Indenture, this day made and entered into between Jnº W. McCalla and Robert Mattox, Jʳ, both of the County and State above written. witnesseth, that the said Robert Mattox, Jʳ this day binds and apprentices himself to the said Jnº W. McCalla for a term of four (4) years. The said Robert Mattox, Jʳ is to work whenever & wherever the said McCalla may direct and at any and all times to be subject to the Commands and and requirements of said McCalla, and at all times and in all things to deport himself in a way that right and Justice will dictate, always guarding the interest of said McCalla with a jealous care.

Now the said McCalla is to treat said Robert Mattox, Jʳ humanely and Kindly, require of him such work as he can perform without detriment to his health or constitution, and pay the said Robert Mattox, Jʳ for the year 1893 the Sum of $75.00, for the year 1894 the Sum of $75.00, for the year 1895 $75.00, for the year 1896 the sum of $75.00. And in addition to the above money considerations, the said McCalla is to furnish the said Robᵗ Mattox, Jʳ with 1 Bu meal and 12# meat per month during the full term of four years.

Signed, sealed, and delivered }
in presence of }   Robert + Mattox, Jʳ, his mark
J. B. Janes, Jʳ }   Jnº W. McCalla
Z. B. Taylor }

Georgia }
Elbert County } Personally Comes before me J. B. Janes, Jʳ who on oath says that he saw Robᵗ Mattox, Jʳ & Jnº W. McCalla sign the within for the purposes therein Stated, and that he, together with Z. B. Taylor, signed as witnesses.

Sworn to & Subscribed }
before me Dec 17, 1892 }   J. B. Janes, Jʳ
Geº L. Almond, Ordinary }

Filed in office & Recorded December 17, 1892.

Ge° L. Almond, Ordiny

Duplicate [193]

Georgia }
Elbert County } This Indenture, this day made and entered into between Jn° W. McCalla and Louellen Bowman, both of county and State above written, and witnesseth: That the said Louellen Bowman this day binds and apprentices himself to the Said Jn° W. McCalla for a term of four (4) years. The Said Lewellen Bowman is to work whenever and wherever the said McCalla may direct and at any and all times to be Subject to the commands and requirements of the Said McCalla, and at all times and in all things to deport himself in a way that right and justice will dictate, always guarding the interest of Said McCalla with a jealous care.

Now the Said McCalla is to treat said Louellen Bowman humanely and kindly, and require of him Such work as he can perform without detriment to his health or constitution, and to pay the said Louellen Bowman for the year 1894 the Sum of $75.00, for the year 1895 the Sum of $75.00, for the year 1896 the Sum of $75.00, for the year 1897 the Sum of $75.00, and in addition to the above money consideration, the said McCalla is to furnish the Said Louellen Bowman 1 Bu Meal and 12 lbs meat per month during the full term of four (4) years.

Signed, Sealed }
in presence of }   Llewellyn Bowman
J. B. Janes, Jr }   J. W. McCalla
Z. B. Taylor }

Georgia }
Elbert County } Personally comes before me J. B. Janes, Jr who on oath Says that he saw Llewellyn Bowman and Jn° W. McCalla sign the within for the purposes therein Stated, and that he, together with Z. B. Taylor, Signed as witnesses.

Sworn to and Subscribed }
before me 17 Dec 1892 }   J. B. Janes, Jr
Ge° L. Almond, Ordinary }

Filed in Office & Recorded Dec 17, 1892.

Ge° L. Almond, Ordinary

Duplicate [194]

Georgia }
Elbert County } This Indenture made between Jn° W. McCalla, of one part, and Languire Verdel, Grand mother of the following minor children, Dane Morrison aged 13 years and Charlott aged Elven years. witnesseth: that the said ~~Dane and Charlott Morrison~~ Languire Verdel binds out said Dane and Charlott Morrison to Jn° W. McCalla, of said County, in the trade or craft of farm laborer upon the plantation of said Jn° W. McCalla, to live with and continue with said McCalla from this date for and during their age of Minority and until each becomes of the age of Twenty one years. Said McCalla is to furnish said Minors with meat, drink, clothing, and medical attention during said term, and teach them the Craft of farm labor. Said Minors are to faithfully demean themselves for said term, doing all things faithfully and well, when, where is as directed by said McCalla. Witness our hands & seals Dec 14, 1892.

Executed Before us }
J. B. Janes, J^r }
Elisha + McCalla, his mark }
Gilbert + Gray, his mark }

Languire + Verdel, her mark
Jn° W. McCalla

Georgia }
Elbert County } Personally comes before me J. B. Janes, J^r who on oath says that he saw Languire Verdel and Jn° W. McCalla sign the within for the purposes therein stated, and that he, together with Elisha McCalla and Gilbert Gray, Signed as witnesses.

Sworn to and Subscribed }
before me 17th Dec 1892 }
Ge° L. Almond, Ordiny }

J. B. Janes, J^r

Filed in office & Recorded Dec 17, 1892.

Ge° L. Almond, Ordiny

Duplicate [195]

Georgia }
Elbert County } This Indenture made and entered into between Jn° W. McCalla and Sidney Alexander, both of the County and State Above written, and witnesseth: that the said Alexander this day binds and Apprentices to the said McCalla his six minor children, viz, Laura Alexander now 12 years old, Alice

141

Alexander now 10 years old, Essie Alexander now 6 years old, Isaac Alexander now 4 years old, Luma Alexander now 12 years old, Lonnie Alexander now 3 years old. The first named three being girls, the last named three being boys. All of said named Children the said Alexander apprentices to the said McCalla until they arrive at the age of Twenty one years. Now the said McCalla is to take said children, treat them humanely and Kindly, furnish proper food and clothing, all necessary medical attention, give them such education as can be had at the Common Schools of the County, and cause them to be instructed in the art or Craft of husbandry or farming. And as they arrive at the age of Twenty one years, the said McCalla is to give to each such as he may deem a suitable reward for fidelity and faithfulnes services.

Signed, seald, & delivered
in Presence of }
Z. B. Taylor }
J. B. Janes, J^r }

Sid + Alexander, his mark
Jn° W. McCalla

Georgia }
Elbert County } Personally comes before me J. B. Janes, J^r who on oath says that he saw Jn° W. McCalla and Sidney Alexander sign the within for the purposes therein stated, and that he, together with Z. B. Taylor, signed as witnesses.

Sworn to and Subscribed }
before me Dec 17, 1892 }
Ge° L. Almond, Ordy }

J. B. Janes, J^r

Filed in Office and Recorded Dec 17, 1892.

Ge° L. Almond, Ordiny

Duplicate [196]

Heardmont 17 Dec 1892

Georgia }
Elbert County } This Indenture made between Amanda Mattox & John W. McCalla, all of Elbert County, Georgia. witnesseth, that the said Amanda has this day Apprenticed herself to John W. McCalla as a farm hand for the term of Five years from the 1st of January 1893, and is to demean herself properly under the employ of said McCalla, doing All things well and faithfully as may be directed by McCalla or his agents, and to be received as wages for her said services on the 30th December 1893 $40.00, 30 Dec 1894 $40.00, 30th Decr 1895 $40.00, 30 Dec

1896 $40.00, 30th Dec 1897 $40.00, which is the last payment on this contract, accounting for all lost time during said services. McCalla agrees to give in addition to the above 3# meat & 10# Flour or 12# meal per week as rations.

Witness }
Ezra + Allen, his mark }
J. B. Janes. J^r }

Amanda + Mattox, her mark
Jn° W. McCalla

Georgia }
Elbert County } Personally comes before me J. B. Janes, J^r who on oath says that he saw Jn° W. McCalla and Amanda Mattox sign the within for the purposes therein stated, and that he, together with Ezra Allen, sign as witnesses.

Sworn to & Subscribed }
before me Dec 17, 1892 }
Ge° L. Almond, Ordy }

J. B. Janes, J^r

Filed in office and Recorded 17 Dec 1892.

Ge° L. Almond, Ordiny

Duplicate [197]

Georgia }
Elbert County } This Indenture this day made and entered into between Jn° W. McCalla and Sid Alexander, both of the County and State above written, and witnesseth: That the said Sid Alexander this day binds and Apprentices himself to the said Jn° W. McCalla for a term of four years.

The said Sid Alexander is to work whenever and wherever the said McCalla may direct, and at any and all times to be subject to the Commands and requirements of the said McCalla, and at all times and in all things to deport himself in a way that Justice and right will dictate, always guarding the interests of said McCalla with care. Now the said McCalla is to treat said Sid Alexander humanely and Kindly, and require of him such work as he may perform without detriment to his health or constitution, and pay the said Sidney for the year 1893 the sum of $75.00, for the year 1894 $75.00, for the year 1895 the sum of $75.00, for the year 1896 the sum of $75.00. And in Addition to the Above money consideration, the said

McCalla is to furnish the said Sid Alexander 1 Bu meal & 12# meat per month during the full term of four (4) years.

Signed, sealed, & delivered
in presence of }
Z. B. Taylor }
J. B. Janes, J^r }

Sid + Alexander, his mark
John W. McCalla

Georgia }
Elbert County } Personally comes before me J. B. Janes, J^r who on oath says that he saw Jn° W. McCalla and Sidney Alexander sign the within for the purposes therein Stated, and that he, together with Z. B. Taylor, signed as witnesses.

Sworn to & Subscribed }
before me De 17, 1892 }
Ge° L. Almond, Ordny }

J. B. Janes, J^r

Filed and Recorded Dec 17, 1892.

Ge° L. Almond, Ordiny

Duplicate [198]

Georgia }
Elbert County } This Indenture this day made and entered into between Jn° W. McCalla and Charlotte Fleming, both of the County and State above written, and witnesseth: That the said Charlotte this day binds & apprentices herself to the said McCalla for a term of five (5) years. The said Charlotte is to work at such time and place as the said McCalla may direct and be subject at any and all times to the reasonable demands of said McCalla. Now in consideration of the above services, the said McCalla is to pay said Charlotte for the year 1893 $35.00, for the year 1894 $35.00, for the year 1895 $35.00, for the year 1896 $35.00, for the year 1897 $35.00. And in addition to the above money Considerations, the said McCalla is to furnish the said Charlotte ¼ Bu meal & 3# Meat per week during the full term of service.

Made & Signed in Duplicate in presence of said & delivd.

Witnessed by }
J. B. Janes, J^r }
Robt + Mattox, J^r, his mark }

Charlotte + Fleming, her mark
Jn° W. McCalla

Personally comes before me J. B. Janes, J^r who on oath says that he saw Jn° W. McCalla and Charlotte Fleming sign the within for the purposes therein stated, and that he, together with Robt Mattox, J^r, Signed as witnesses.

Sworn to & Subscribed }
before me Dec 21, 1892 }   J. B. Janes, J^r
Ge° L. Almond, Ordinary }

Filed in office and Recorded 21 Dec 1892.

Ge° L. Almond, Ordiny

Duplicate   [199]

Georgia }
Elbert County } This Indenture this day made and entered into between Jn° W. McCalla and Chanie Morrison, both of the County and State above written, and witnesseth: that the said Chanie Morrison this day binds and Apprentices himself to the said Jn° W. McCalla for a term of five (5) years. The said Chanie is to work at such time and place as the said McCalla may direct, Deporting herself properly at all times, and at no time neglecting the work or business of said McCalla. Now as a remuneration for the above stated service, the said McCalla agrees to treat said Chanie humanely and Kindly and to pay her for the year 1893 $35.00, for the year 1894 $35.00, for the year 1895 $35.00, for the year 1896 $35.00, for the year 1897 $35.00. and in addition to the above money consideration, the said McCalla is to furnish her ¼ Bu Meal and 3# Meat per week during the full term of service. Made and signed in duplicate.

Signed, sealed, & delivered
in presence of   }   Chanie + Morrison, her mark
J. B. Janes, J^r }   Jn° W. McCalla
Robt + Mattox, J^r, his mark }

Georgia }
Elbert County } Personally Comes before me J. B. Janes, J^r who on oath says that he saw Chanie Morrison and Jn° W. McCalla sign the within for the purposes therein Stated, and that he, together with Robt Mattox, J^r, Signed as witnesses.

Sworn to & Subscribed }
before me Dec 21, 1892 }   J. B. Janes, J^r
Ge° L. Almond, Ordny }

Filed in office & Recorded Dec 21, 1892.

Ge⁰ L. Almond, Ordny

Duplicate [200]

Georgia }
Elbert County } This Indenture, made this the 24th day of Dec 1892, between Winnie Almond, of said County, for and in behalf of Oscar Downer, being of the age of 13 years, on the one part, and Alex Downer, of the County aforesaid, of the other part. Witnesseth: that the said Winnie Almond does by these presents bind out Oscar Downer, of said County, as apprentice to said Alex Downer in the trade or craft of house servant or as Laborer upon the plantation of the said Alex Downer, to be taught the said Craft or trade of house servant or laborer, and to live with, continue, & serve the said Alex Downer as an apprentice from the date hereof for and during the term of Eight years.

During all of which time, said Winnie Almond doth covenant with the said Alex Downer that the said Oscar Downer shall well and faithfully demean himself as such faithful apprentice, observing fully the commands of the said Alex Downer, and in all things deporting and behaving himself as a faithful apprentice to the said Alex Downer, neither revealing his secrets, nor at any time neglecting or leaving the business of the said Alex Downer.

And for and in consideration of the service well & faithfully rendered by said Oscar Downer, of the first part, said Alex Downer, of the second part, doth covenant, promise, & agree to instruct his said apprentice, or otherwise cause him to be well and faithfully instructed, in the said trade or craft of house servant or laborer, and also to read the English language, and shall also allow, furnish, and provide said apprentice, with meat & drink & clothing during the said term, and all other necessaries meet and proper, in sickness and in health, and shall also, at the expiration of said term, allow & pay the said Apprentice what is now allowed by the statute in such case made and provided. Witness our hands and seals the day & year first before written.

Executed before us }
A. F. Adams } Winnie + Almond, her mark
Ge⁰ L. Almond, Ordny } Alex Downer

Filed in office and recorded Dec 24, 1892.

Ge⁰ L. Almond, Ordinary

Duplicate [201]

Georgia }
Elbert County } This Indenture, made this the 25 day of January 1893, between Hayes Ellis (father), of said County, for and in behalf of his minor child Charles Ellis, being of the age of four and one half years, on the one part, and Jo^s N. Worly, of the County aforesaid, of the other part. Witnesseth: that the said Hayes Ellis (father) does by these presents bind out his minor son Charles, of said County, as apprentice to said Jo^s N. Worly in the trade or craft of farm or house servant upon the plantation of the said Jo^s N. Worly, to be taught the said Craft or trade of house servant or farm laborer, and to live with, continue, and serve the said Jo^s N. Worly as an apprentice from the date hereof for and during the term of Seventeen years.

During all of which time, said Hayes Ellis, father as aforesaid, doth covenant with the said Jo^s N. Worly that the said Charles Ellis shall well & faithfully demean himself as such faithful apprentice, observing fully the commands of the said Jo^s N. Worly, and in all things deporting and behaving himself as a faithful Apprentice to the said Jo^s N. Worly, neither revealing his secrets, nor at any time neglecting or leaving the business of the said Jo^s N. Worly. And for and in consideration of the service well & faithfully rendered by said Hayes Ellis through his son Charles Ellis, of the first part, said Jo^s N. Worly, of the second part, doth covenant, promise, and agree to instruct his said apprentice, or otherwise cause him to be well and faithfully instructed, in the said trade or craft of house servant and farm laborer, and also to read the English language. And Shall Also allow, furnish, and provide him, said apprentice, with meat and drink and clothing during the said term, and all other necessaries meet and proper, in sickness and in health, and shall also, at the expiration of said term, allow & pay the said apprentice what is now allowed by the statute in such case made and provided.

Witness our hands & seals the day & year first before written.

Executed before us }
Executed in duplicate } Hase + Ellis, his mark
J. J. Chandler } Jo^s N. Worly
Ge^o L. Almond, Ordiny }

Filed in office and recorded Jany 25, 1892.

Ge^o L. Almond, Ordinary

Duplicate [202]

Georgia }
Elbert County } This Indenture, made this 25 day of January 1893, between Hayes Ellis, father, of said County, for and in behalf of his minor child Adaline Ellis, being of the age of three & one half years, on the one part, and James McIntosh, of the County aforesaid, of the other part. Witnesseth: that the said Hayes Ellis, father as aforesaid, does by these presents bind out his minor child Adaline Ellis, of said County, as apprentice to said James McIntosh in the trade or craft of house servant or farm laborer upon the plantation of the said James McIntosh, to be taught the said Craft or trade of house servant or farm laborer, and to live with, continue, and serve the said James McIntosh as an apprentice from the date hereof for and during the term of Eighteen years.

During all of which time, said Hayes Ellis, father as aforesaid, doth covenant with the said James McIntosh that the said Adaline Ellis shall well and faithfully demean herself as such faithful Apprentice, observing fully the Commands of the said James McIntosh, and in all things deporting and behaving herself as a faithful Apprentice to the said James McIntosh, neither revealing his secrets, nor at any time neglecting or leaving the business of the said James McIntosh.

And for and in consideration of the service well & faithfully rendered by said Hayes Ellis through said Adaline Ellis, of the first part, said James McIntosh, of the second part, doth covenant, promise, & agree to instruct his said apprentice, or otherwise cause her to be well and faithfully instructed, in the said trade or craft of house servant & farm laborer, & also to read the English language, and shall also allow, furnish, & provide his said apprentice with meat and drink & clothing during the said term, and all other necessaries meet & proper, in sickness and in health, & shall also, at the expiration of said term, allow & pay the said apprentice what is now allowed by the Statute in such case made & provided.

Witness our hands & seals the day & year first before written.

Executed before us }
Executed in duplicate }
J. J. Chandler }   Hayes + Ellis, his mark
Geº L. Almond, Ordiny }   James McIntosh

Filed in office and recorded Jany 25, 1892.

Geº L. Almond, Ordinary

Duplicate [203]

Georgia }
Elbert County } This Indenture, this day made and entered into between York Banks and Jn° W. McCalla, both of the County and State above written, and witnesseth: That the said York Banks this day binds and Apprentices to the said Jn° W. McCalla his two (2) grand children, 1 girl named Eunice Banks twelve (12) years old and a boy named Abraham Banks fourteen (14) years old. Both the above named children the said York this day binds and apprentices to the said Jn° W. McCalla until they arrive at the age of Twenty one years. The said McCalla is to treat said children humanely and kindly, furnish proper food and clothing, all necessary medical attention, Such education as can be had at the Common Schools of the County, and cause them to be instructed in the art or craft of husbandry or farming, and when they shall arrive at the age of Twenty one years, the said McCalla is to give them such amounts as he may deem a suitable reward for fidelity and faithful service. It is further agreed that from and after this date the relation of Master and Apprentice shall exist between said parties.

Made and Signed in duplicate. Sealed & delivered in presence of

Attest.   Jany 24, 1893
J. B. Janes, J^r York + Banks, his mark
Z. B. Taylor   Jn° W. McCalla

Personally comes before me J. B. Janes, J^r who on oath says that he saw York Banks & Jn° W. McCalla sign the within for the purposes therein stated, and that he, together with Z. B. Taylor, signed as witnesses.

Sworn to & Subscribed }
before me Jany 25, 1893 }   J. B. Janes, J^r
Ge° L. Almond, Ordny }

Filed in office and Recorded Jany 25, 1893.

Ge° L. Almond, Ordinary

Duplicate [204]

Georgia }
Elbert County } This Indenture, made this the 26 day of Jany 1893, between Mid Brawner, father, of said County, for and in behalf of John and Joe Brawner, being of the age of 12 and 7 years, on the one part, and John C. Hudgens, of the County aforesaid, of the other part. Witnesseth: that the said Mid Brawner does by these

presents bind out John and Joe Brawner, of said County, as apprentices to said John C. Hudgens in the trade or craft of house servants or as Laborers upon the plantation of the said J. C. Hudgens, to be taught the said craft or trade of house servants or laborers, and to live with, continue, and serve the said John C. Hudgens as apprentices from the date hereof for and during the term of John 6 and Joe 8 years [blurred].

During all of which time, said Mid Brawner doth covenant with the said John C. Hudgens that the said John & Joe shall well and faithfully demean themselves as such faithful apprentices, observing fully the commands of the said John C. Hudgens, and in all things deporting & behaving themselves as faithful apprentices to the said John C. Hudgens, neither revealing his secrets, nor at any time neglecting or leaving the business of the said John C. Hudgens. And for and in consideration of the service well & faithfully rendered by the said John and Joe, of the first part, said John C. Hudgens, of the second part, doth covenant, promise, & agree to instruct his said apprentices, or otherwise cause them to be well and faithfully instructed, in the said trade or craft of house servants or laborers, & also to read the English language. And shall also allow, furnish, & provide them, said apprentices, with meat & drink and clothing during the said term, and all other necessaries meet and proper, in sickness and in health.

Witness our hands and seals the day and year first before written.

Executed before us in duplicate.

J. J. Chandler }	Mid + Brawner, his mark
Ge⁰ L. Almond, Ordiny }	J. C. Hudgens

Filed in office and recorded Jany 26, 1892.

Ge⁰ L. Almond, Ordinary

Duplicate [205]

Georgia }
Elbert County } This Indenture, made this the 4th day of Feby 1893, between Allen Eberhart, father, of said County, for and in behalf of Biggs and Freeman Eberhart, being of the age of 16 and 14 years, on the one part, and P. M. Hawes, of the County aforesaid, of the other part. Witnesseth: that the said Allen Eberhart does by these presents bind out Biggs and Freeman, of said County, as apprentices to said P. M. Hawes in the trade or craft of house servants or laborers upon the plantation of the said P. M. Hawes, to be taught the said craft or trade of house

servants or laborers, and to live with, continue, and serve the said P. M. Hawes as apprentices from the date hereof for and during the term of Two years from Jany 1, 1874.

During all of which time, said Allen Eberhart doth covenant with the said P. M. Hawes that the said Biggs and Freeman shall well and faithfully demean themselves as such faithful apprentices, observing fully the Commands of the said P. M. Hawes, and in all things deporting and behaving themselves as faithful apprentices to the said P. M. Hawes, neither revealing his secrets, nor at any time neglecting or leaving the business of the said P. M. Hawes. And for and in consideration of the service well & faithfully rendered by the said Biggs and Freeman, of the first part, said P. M. Hawes, of the second part, doth covenant, promise, and agree to instruct Them, said apprentices, or otherwise cause them to be well and faithfully instructed, in the said trade or craft of house servants or laborers, and shall also allow, furnish, and provide them, said apprentices, with meat and drink and clothing during the said term, and all other necessaries meet and proper, in sickness and in health. However, to have the right to Sub hire.

Executed before us } Allen + Eberhart, his mark
L. C. Edwards } P. M. Hawes
Ge^o L. Almond, Ordiny }

This Duplicate filed in office and Recorded Feby 4, 1893.

Ge^o L. Almond, Ordinary

Duplicate [206]

Georgia }
Elbert County } This Indenture, made this the 7th day of February 1893, between Oliver Mattox, of said County, for and in behalf of himself, being of the age of 26 years, on the one part, and J. W. Rucker, of the County aforesaid, of the other part. Witnesseth: that the said Oliver Mattox does by these presents bind out himself, of said County, as apprentice to said J. W. Rucker in the trade or craft of house servant or as laborer upon the plantation of the said J. W. Rucker, to be taught the said Craft or trade of house servant or farm laborer, and to live with, continue, and serve the said J. W. Rucker as an apprentice from the date hereof for and during the term of two years.

During all of which time, said Oliver Mattox doth covenant with the said J. W. Rucker that said Oliver Mattox shall well and faithfully demean himself as such faithful Apprentice, observing fully the Commands of the said J. W. Rucker, and in all things deporting & behaving himself as a faithful Apprentice to the said J. W. Rucker, neither revealing his secrets, nor at any time neglecting or leaving the business of the said J. W. Rucker.

And for and in consideration of the service well & faithfully rendered by said Oliver Mattox, of the first part, said J. W. Rucker, of the second part, doth covenant, promise, and agree to instruct him, said Apprentice, or otherwise cause him to be well and faithfully instructed, in the said trade or craft of house servant or laborer, and shall also allow, furnish, & provide him, said Apprentice, with meat and drink and clothing during the said term.

Witness our hands & seals the day and year first before written.

Executed before us   }   Oliver + Mattox, his mark
J. J. Chandler   }   J. W. Rucker
Ge⁰ L. Almond, Ordiny }

This Duplicate filed in Office and recorded 7th Feby 1893.

Ge⁰ L. Almond, Ordinary

Duplicate   [207]

Georgia   }
Elbert County } This Indenture, made this the 21st day of February 1893, between William Blackwell, of said County, for and in behalf of himself, being of the age of 26 years, on the one part, and J. W. Rucker, of the County aforesaid, of the other part. Witnesseth: that the said William Blackwell does by these presents bind out himself, of said County, as apprentice to said J. W. Rucker in the trade or craft of house servant or as laborer upon the plantation of the said J. W. Rucker, to be taught the said Craft or trade of house servant or farm laborer, and to live with, continue, and serve the said J. W. Rucker as an apprentice from 1st Jany 1894 for and during the term of one years.

During all of which time, said William Blackwell doth covenant with the said J. W. Rucker that he will and shall well and faithfully demean himself as such faithful Apprentice, observing fully the Commands of the said J. W. Rucker, and in all things deporting and behaving himself as a faithful Apprentice to the said J. W. Rucker, neither revealing his secrets, nor at any time neglecting or leaving the business of the said J. W. Rucker.

And for and in consideration of the service well and faithfully rendered by said William Blackwell, of the first part, said J. W. Rucker, of the second part, doth covenant, promise, and agree to instruct him, said apprentice, or otherwise cause him to be well and faithfully instructed, in the said trade or craft of house servant or laborer, and shall also allow, furnish, and provide him, said apprentice, with meat and drink and clothing during the said term, and all other necessaries meet and proper, in sickness and in health, and pay him $100.00.

Witness our hands and seals the day and year first before written.

Executed before us }
in duplicate } William Blackwell
T. J. Campbell } J. W. Rucker
Ge° L. Almond, Ordiny }

Filed in Office and Recorded Feby 21, 1893.

Ge° L. Almond, Ordinary

Duplicate [208]

Georgia }
Elbert County } This Indenture, made this the 21st day of February 1893, between Jim Bowman, of said County, for and in behalf of himself, being of the age of 50 years, on the one part, and J. W. Rucker, of the County aforesaid, of the other part. Witnesseth: that the said Jim Bowman does by these presents bind out himself, of said County, as apprentice to said J. W. Rucker in the trade or craft of house servant or as laborer upon the plantation of the said J. W. Rucker, to be taught the said Craft or trade of house servant or farm laborer, and to live with, continue, and serve the said J. W. Rucker as an Apprentice from Jany 1, 1894 for and during the term of one years.

During all of which time, said Jim Bowman doth Covenant with the said J. W. Rucker that he will and shall well and faithfully demean himself as such faithful Apprentice, observing fully the Commands of the said J. W. Rucker, and in all things deporting & behaving himself as a faithful apprentice to the said J. W. Rucker, neither revealing his secrets, nor at any time neglecting or leaving the business of the said J. W. Rucker.

And for and in consideration of the service well and faithfully rendered by the said Jim Bowman, of the first part, said J. W. Rucker, of the second part, doth Covenant, promise, and agree to instruct him, said apprentice, or otherwise cause him to be well and faithfully instructed, in the said trade or craft of house servant or laborer, and shall also allow, furnish, and provide him, said apprentice, with meat and drink & clothing during the said term, and all other necessaries meet and proper, in sickness and in health, and pay him $100.00.

Witness our hands and Seals the day and year first before written.

Executed before us }
in duplicate }   Jim + Bowman, his mark
T. J. Camphell }   J. W. Rucker
Geº L. Almond, Ordiny }

Filed in Office and Recorded Feby 21st 1893.

Geº L. Almond, Ordiny

Duplicate   [209]

Georgia }
Elbert County }   This Indenture, made this the 21st day of February 1893, between Eugene Bowman, of said County, for and in behalf of himself, being of the age of 28 years, on the one part, and J. W. Rucker, of the County aforesaid, of the other part. Witnesseth: that the said Eugene Bowman does by these presents bind out himself, of said County, as Apprentice to said J. W. Rucker in the trade or craft of house servant or as laborer upon the plantation of the said J. W. Rucker, to be taught the said Craft or trade of house Servant or farm laborer, and to live with, continue, and serve the said J. W. Rucker as an Apprentice from 1st Jany 1894 during the term of one years.

During all of which time, said Eugene Blackwell doth Covenant with the said J. W. Rucker that he will and shall well and faithfully demean himself as such faithful apprentice, observing fully the Commands of the said J. W. Rucker, and in all things deporting and behaving himself as a faithful apprentice to the said J. W. Rucker, neither revealing his secrets, nor at any time neglecting or leaving the business of the said J. W. Rucker.

And for and in consideration of the service well and faithfully rendered by said Eugene Bowman, of the first part, said J. W. Rucker, of the second part, doth covenant, promise, and agree to instruct his said apprentice, or otherwise cause him to be well and faithfully instructed, in the said trade or craft of house servant or laborer, and shall also allow, furnish, and provide him, said Apprentice, with meat and drink and clothing during the said term, and all other necessaries meet and proper, in sickness and in health.

Witness our hands and seals the day and year first before written.

Executed before us }
in Duplicate } Eugene Bowman
T. J. Campbell } J. W. Rucker
Geº L. Almond, Ordiny }

Filed in Office and Recorded Feby 21, 1893.

Geº L. Almond, Ordy

Georgia } [210]
Elbert County } This Indenture, this day made and entered into between Jnº W. McCalla and Oliver Mattox, both of the County and State Above written, and witnesseth: That the said Oliver this day binds and apprentices himself to the said McCalla for a term of five (5) years. The said Oliver is to work whenever and wherever the said McCalla may direct, at all times rendering good and faithful service.

In consideration of the above service, the said McCalla is to pay Oliver for the year 1894 $75.00, for the year 1895 $75.00, for the year 1896 $75.00, for the year 1897 $75.00, for the year 1898 $75.00, and in addition to the above money consideration, the said McCalla is to furnish said Oliver 12# meat and 1 Bu meal per month during the full term of said service.

Made and Signed in duplicate. Sealed and delivered in presence of

King + Mattox, his mark } Oliver + Mattox, his mark
J. B. Janes, J^r } J. W. McCalla

Personally comes before me J. B. Janes, J^r who on oath says that he saw Jnº W. McCalla and Oliver Mattox sign the within for the purposes therein stated, and that he, together with King Mattox, signed as witnesses.

Sworn to & Subscribed }
before me 24 Feb^y, 1893 } J. B. Janes, J^r
Geº L. Almond, Ordiny }

This duplicate filed in office and Recorded Feby 25, 1893.

Geº L. Almond, Ordinary

Duplicate [211]

Georgia }
Elbert County } This Indenture, made this the 1st day of March 1893, between Ann Adams, of said County, for and in behalf of Jep Lofton, being of the age of Ten years, on the one part, and E. J. Bell, of the County aforesaid, of the other part. Witnesseth: that the said Ann Adams does by these presents bind out Jep Lofton, of said County, as Apprentice to said E. J. Bell in the trade or craft of house servant or laborer upon the plantation of the said E. J. Bell, to be taught the said Craft or trade of house servant or laborer, and to live with, continue, and serve the said E. J. Bell as an Apprentice from the date hereof during the term of ten years.

During all of which time, said Ann Adams doth Covenant with the said E. J. Bell that the said Jep Lofton shall well and faithfully demean himself as such faithful Apprentice, observing fully the Commands of the said E. J. Bell, and in all things deporting and behaving himself as a faithful apprentice to the said E. J. Bell, neither revealing his secrets, nor at any time neglecting or leaving the business of the said E. J. Bell.

And for and in consideration of the service well and faithfully rendered by said Jep Lofton, of the first part, said E. J. Bell, of the second part, doth covenant, promise, and agree to instruct him, said apprentice, or otherwise cause him to be well and faithfully instructed, in the said trade or craft of house servant or laborer, and also to read the English language, And shall also allow, furnish, and provide him, said Apprentice, with meat and drink and clothing during the said term, And All other necessaries meet and proper, in sickness and in health.

Witness our hands and seals the day and year first before written.

Executed before us }
in Duplicate } Ann + Adams, her mark
W. B. Henry } E. J. Bell
Geo L. Almond, Ordiny }

Filed in Office and Recorded 1st March 1893.

Geo L. Almond, Ordinary

Duplicate [212]

Georgia }
Elbert County } This Indenture, this day made and entered into, between Jno

W. McCalla, of the first part, and Lindsey Gray and Saul Gray, of the second part, all of the County and State above written, and witnesseth: That the parties of the second part this day binds and apprentices themselves to the said McCalla for and during the first term of five years, Commencing on the 1st day of April 1893 and ending the 31st day of March 1898. The said parties is to labor for the said McCalla as he may direct, and at all times demean themselves in a becoming and proper manner, and at any and all times subject to the Commands of said McCalla.

The party of the first part, Jnº W. McCalla, is to pay the parties of the second part on the 31st day of March 1894 $100.00, and 31 day of March 1895 $100.00, on the 31st day of March 1896 $100.00, on 31st day of March 1897 $100.00, on the 31st day of March 1898 $100.00, and in addition to the above money consideration the said McCalla is to furnish said Lindsey and Saul two Bushels of meal and twenty pounds of Meat per month during the full term of said service.

Made and Signed in duplicate. Sealed and delivered in presence of

Witnessed by }
J. B. Janes, Jr }
John H. McCalla }

Jnº W. McCalla
Lindsey + Gray, his mark
Saul + Gray, his mark

Georgia }
Elbert County } Personally comes before me J. B. Janes, Jr who on oath says that he saw the parties sign the within for the purposes therein stated, and that he, together with Jnº H. McCalla, signed as witnesses.

Sworn to & Subscribed }
before March 22, 1893 }   J. B. Janes, Jr
Geº L. Almond, Ordy }

Filed in office and Recorded 22 March 1893.

Geº L. Almond, Ordiny

Duplicate   [213]

Georgia }
Elbert County } This Indenture, this day made and entered into, his between Jnº W. McCalla, of the first part, and Lindsey Gray and Sarah Gray, of the second part, all of the County and State Above written, and witnesseth: That the said parties of the second part this day binds and apprentices to the said McCalla their two minor children named and ages respectfully, Elie Gray aged five years, Price Gray a boy one year old. All of said minor children of the said Sarah and Lindsey

they this day bind and apprentice to the said McCalla until they arrive at the age of twenty one years.

The said McCalla is to treat said Children humanely and Kindly, furnish proper food and Clothing, all necessary medical attention, such education as can be had at the Common Schools of the County, and Cause them to be instructed in the art or craft of husbandry or farming, and when each shall arrive at the age of Twenty (21) one years the said McCalla is to give to each such Amounts as he may deem a suitable reward for fidelity and faithfulness service. Made and signed in duplicate this 24 day of March 1893.

Signed, sealed, and delivered in presence of

	Jnº W. McCalla
J. B. Janes, Jr }	Lindsy + Gray, his mark
John H. McCalla }	Sarah + Gray, her mark

Georgia }
Elbert County } Personally comes before me J. B. Janes, Jʳ who on oath says that he saw the parties signed the within, and he, together with John H. McCalla, signed as witnesses.

Sworn to & Subscribed }
before me 22 March 1893 }   J. B. Janes, Jʳ
Geº L. Almond, Ordiny }

Filed in office and Recorded 22 March 1893.

Geº L. Almond, Ordy

Duplicate   [214]

Georgia }
Elbert County } This Indenture, made this the 1ˢᵗ day of May 1893, between Ransom Oglesby, of said County, for and in behalf of Sarah Oglesby, his daughter, being of the age of nine years, of the one part, and H. J. Brewer, of the County aforesaid, of the other part. Witnesseth: that the said Ransom Oglesby, as aforesaid, does by these presents bind out his said daughter Sarah, of said County, as Apprentice to said H. J. Brewer in the trade or craft of house servant upon the place of the said H. J. Brewer, to be taught the said craft or trade of house servant,

and to live with, continue, and serve the said Brewer as an apprentice from the date hereof for and during the term of Two years and two months.

During all of which time, said Ransom Oglesby, as aforesaid, doth Covenant with the said H. J. Brewer that the said Sarah shall well and faithfully demean herself as such faithful Apprentice, observing fully the Commands of the said Brewer, and in all things deporting & behaving herself as a faithful apprentice to the said Brewer, neither revealing his secrets, nor at any time neglecting or leaving the business of the said Brewer. And for and in consideration of the service well & faithfully rendered by the said Sarah, of the first part, said Brewer, of the Second part, doth covenant, promise, & agree to instruct his said apprentice, or otherwise cause her to be well & faithfully instructed, in the said trade or craft of house servant, and also to study the English language, and shall also furnish and provide his said apprentice with meat & drink & clothing during the said term, and all other necessaries meet and proper, in sickness and in health, and shall also at the expiration of the said term allow & pay said Apprentice the sum of Ten dollars.

Witness our hands and seals the day & year first before written.

Executed before us }
in Duplicate } Ransom + Oglesby, his mark
L. C. Edwards } H. J. Brewer
Geº L. Almond, Ordiny }

Filed in office and Recorded May 1, 1893.

Geº L. Almond, Ordy

Duplicate [215]

Georgia }
Elbert County } This Indenture, this day made and entered into, between Jnº W. McCalla, of the first part, and Oliver Blackwell, both of the County and State above written, & witnesseth: That the said Oliver Blackwell this day binds and apprentices to the said McCalla his son Ephram, Seventeen years old, and his grand son William, ten years old, until they arrive at the age of twenty one years. The said McCalla is to treat said humanely and Kindly, furnish proper food & clothing, all necessary medical attention, such education as can be had at the Common Schools of the County, and cause them to be instructed in the art or craft of husbandry or farming, and when they arrive at the age of twenty one years the

said McCalla is to give them such amount as he may deem a suitable reward for fidelity and faithful service. Made and signed in Duplicate the Dec 12, 1892.

Sealed and delivered in
presence of   }   Oliver + Blackwell, his mark
B. H. Heard   }   Jn° W. McCalla
J. B. Janes, J^r }

Georgia   }
Elbert County } Personally comes before me J. B. Janes, J^r who on oath says that he saw Oliver Blackwell and Jn° W. McCalla sign the within, for the purposes therein stated, and he, together with B. H. Heard, signed as witnesses.

Ge° L. Almond, Ordiny }   J. B. Janes, J^r

Filed in office and Recorded 19 May 1893.

Ge° L. Almond, Ordiny

Duplicate   [216]

Georgia   }
Elbert County } This Indenture, made this the 22nd day of May 1893, between Daniel Thornton, of said County, for and in behalf of his daughter Lula Thornton, being of the age of seven years, of the one part, and S. S. Brewer, of the County aforesaid, of the other part. Witnesseth: that the said Daniel Thornton, as aforesaid, does by these presents bind out Lula Thornton, his daughter, of said county, as Apprentice to said S. S. Brewer in the trade or craft of house girl or servant upon the place of the said S. S. Brewer, to be taught the said Craft or trade of house girl or servant, and to live with, continue, and serve the said Brewer as an Apprentice from the date hereof during the term of Six years.

During all of which time, said Daniel Thornton, as Aforesaid, doth covenant with the said Brewer that the said Lula shall well & faithfully demean herself as such faithful apprentice, observing fully the commands of the said Brewer, and in all things deporting & behaving herself to the said Brewer, neither revealing his secrets, nor at any time neglecting or leaving the business of the said Brewer.

And for and in consideration of the service well and faithfully rendered by said Lula, of the first part, said Brewer, of the Second part, doth covenant, promise, & agree to instruct her, said apprentice, or otherwise cause her to be well and faithfully instructed, in the said trade or craft of house girl, servant, or laborer, and also to read the English language, and shall also allow, furnish, & provide his said

Apprentice, with meat & drink & clothing during the said term, And All other necessaries meet & proper, in sickness and in health, and shall also at the expiration of the said term allow & pay the said Apprentice the sum of ten Dollars.

Witness our hands & Seals the day & year first before written.

Executed before us   }
in Duplicate   }   Daniel + Thornton, his mark
S. L. Carter   }   S. S. Brewer
Geº L. Almond, Ordy   }

Recorded May 23, 1893.

Geº L. Almond, Ordy

Duplicate   [217]

Georgia   }
Elbert County } This Indenture, made this 31st day of August 1893, between Henry Blackwell, of said County, for and in behalf of Dunstan Blackwell, being of the age of 16 years, on the one part, and Geº H. McClanahan, of the County aforesaid, of the other part, witnesseth: That the said Henry Blackwell does by these presents bind out Dunstan Blackwell, of said County, as apprentice to said Geº H. McClanahan in the trade or craft of house servant or Laborer upon the plantation of the said Geº H. McClanahan, to be taught the said Craft or trade of house servant or laborer, and to live with, continue, and serve the said Geº H. McClanahan as an apprentice from the date hereof during the term of five years.

During all of which time, said Henry Blackwell doth Covenant with the said Geº H. McClanahan that the said Dunstan Blackwell shall well & truly demean himself as such faithful Apprentice, observing fully the Commands of the said Geº H. McClanahan, and in all things deporting and behaving himself as a faithful apprentice to the said Geº H. McClanahan, neither revealing his secrets, nor at any time neglecting or leaving the business of the said Geº H. McClanahan.

And for and in consideration of the service well and faithfully rendered by said Dunstan Blackwell, of the first part, said Geº H. McClanahan, of the second part, doth covenant, promise, & agree to instruct him, said apprentice, or otherwise cause him to be well and faithfully instructed, in the said trade or craft of house servant or laborer, and also to read the English language, and shall also allow, furnish, and provide him, said apprentice, with meat & drink and clothing during the said term, and all other necessaries meet & proper, in sickness and in health, and shall also pay Henry Blackwell $25.00 per year.

Witness our hands & Seals the day & year first before written.

Executed before us }
in Duplicate   } Henry Blackwell
II. A. Roebuck   } G. H. McClanahan
Geº L. Almond, Ordny }

Filed in Office and Recorded March 31, 1893.

           Geº L. Almond, Ordinary

        Duplicate   [218]

Georgia   }
Elbert County } This Indenture, made this 27th day of Sep^t 1893, between Ryley Wilkins, of said County, for and in behalf of Jack Wilkins, being of the age of Sixteen years, on the one part, and Clark Mattox, of the County aforesaid, of the other part. Witnesseth: That the said Ryley Wilkins does by these presents bind out Jack Wilkins, of said County, as apprentice to said Clark Mattox in the trade or craft of house servant or as laborer upon the plantation of the said Clark Mattox, to be taught the said Craft or trade of house Servant or laborer, and to live with, continue, and serve the said Clark Mattox as an apprentice from the date hereof during the term of 15 months. During all of which time, said Ryley Wilkins doth Covenant with the said Clark Mattox that the said Jack Wilkins shall well & faithfully demean himself as such faithful Apprentice, observing fully the Commands of the said Clark Mattox, and in all things deporting and behaving himself as a faithful apprentice to the said Clark Mattox, neither revealing his secrets, nor at any time neglecting or leaving the business of the said Clark Mattox.

And for and in consideration of the service well & faithfully rendered by said Jack Wilkins, of the first part, said Clark Mattox, of the second part, doth Covenant, promise, and agree to instruct him, said apprentice, or otherwise cause him to be well & faithfully instructed, in the said trade or craft of house servant or laborer, and shall also allow, furnish, & provide him, said apprentice, with meat & drink during the said term, and all other necessaries meet & proper, & shall also at the expiration of the said term allow & pay the said Ryley Wilkins fifty Dollars.

Witness our hands & Seals the day & year first before written.

Executed before us }
in Duplicate } Ryley + Wilkins, his mark
R. M. Willis } Clark Mattox
Ge° L. Almond, Ordiny }

Filed in office & recorded Sep^t 27, 1893.

Ge° L. Almond, Ordinary

Duplicate [219]

Georgia }
Elbert County } This Indenture, made this the 12th day of October 1893, between Mandy McIntosh, of said County, for and in behalf of Mary, Hannah, William, George Thomas, Lace, and Peter, her seven minor children, being of the age of 20, 15, 13, 11, 9, 7, & 5 years, on the one part, and John W. McCalla, of the County aforesaid, of the other part, witnesseth: That the said Mandy McIntosh, as aforesaid, does by these presents bind out all of her said minor children, of said County, as apprentices to said John W. McCalla in the trade or craft of house servants or as laborers upon the plantation of the said McCalla, to be taught the said craft or trade of house servants or laborers, and to live with, continue, and serve the said McCalla as an apprentices from the date hereof during the term of their minority, to wit, until each is 21 years of age.

During all of which time, said Mandy McIntosh, as aforesaid, doth Covenant with the said John W. McCalla that the said above named minors shall well & truly demean themselves as such faithful Apprentices, observing fully the Commands of the said McCalla, and in all things deporting and behaving themselves as a faithful apprentice to the said McCalla, neither revealing his secrets, nor at any time neglecting or leaving the business of the said McCalla.

And for and in consideration of the service well and faithfully rendered by said Apprentices and Mandy McIntosh, of the first part, said McCalla, of the second part, doth covenant, promise, & agree to instruct his said Apprentices, or otherwise cause them to be well & faithfully instructed, in the said trade or craft of house Servant or laborer, and also to read the English language, and shall also allow, furnish, and provide his said apprentices, with meat and drink and Clothing during the said term, and all other necessaries meet and proper, in sickness and in health, and shall also at the expiration of said term allow and pay the said apprentices what is now allowed by the Statute in such case made and provided.

Witness our hands & seals the day & year first before written.

Executed & delivered }
before us in Duplicate } Mandy + McIntosh, her mark
H. J. Brewer, J. B. Janes, NP & JP } Jnº W. McCalla
N. L. Baity }

Filed in office & recorded Oct 18, 1893.

Geº L. Almond, Ordy

Duplicate [220]

Georgia }
Elbert County } This Indenture, made this the 19th day of October 1893, between Dora Bowman, of said County, for and in behalf of Willie Collins, being of the age of five years, on the one part, and Jane Maxwell, of the County aforesaid, of the other part. Witnesseth: That the said Dora Bowman does by these presents bind out Willie Collins, of said County, as apprentice to said Jane Maxwell in the trade or Craft of house servant or as laborer upon the plantation of the said Jane Maxwell, to be taught the said craft or trade of house servant or laborer, and to live with, continue, and serve the said Jane Maxwell as an Apprentice from the date hereof during the term of his minority.

During all of which time, said Dora Bowman doth Covenant with the said Jane Maxwell that the said Willie Collins shall well & faithfully demean himself as such faithful Apprentice, observing fully the Commands of the said Jane Maxwell, and in all things deporting and behaving himself as a faithful apprentice to the said Jane Maxwell, neither revealing his secrets, nor at any time neglecting or leaving the business of the said Jane Maxwell.

And for and in consideration of the service well and faithfully rendered by said Willie Collins, of the first part, said Jane Maxwell, of the second part, doth Covenant, promise, & agree to instruct his said Apprentice, or otherwise cause him to be well & faithfully instructed, in the said trade of house servant or laborer, and also to read the English language, and shall also allow, furnish, & provide his said apprentice with meat & drink & clothing during the said term, and all other necessaries meet and proper, in sickness and in health, and shall also, at the expiration of the said term, allow & pay the said apprentice what is now allowed by the Statute in such case made & provided.

Witness our hands & Seals the day & year first before written.

Executed before us }
in Duplicate } Dora X Bowman, her mark
S. L. Carter } Jane + Maxwell, her mark
Ge° L. Almond, Ordiny }

Filed in office and recorded Oc^t 19, 1893.

Ge° L. Almond, Ordinary

Duplicate [221]

Georgia }
Elbert County } This Indenture, made this the 30th day of Oc^t 1893, between Neal Upson for himself and for his son Joe, of said County, for and in behalf of Neal Upson for himself and for his son Joe, being of the ages of 34 and 15 years, on the one part, and Clark Mattox, of the County aforesaid, of the other part. Witnesseth: That the said Neal Upson for himself & son does by these presents bind out himself [smudge] and son, of said County, as Apprentices to said Clark Mattox in the trade or Craft of house servants or as laborers upon the plantation of the said Clark Mattox, to be taught the said Craft or trade of house servants or laborers, and to live with, continue, and serve the said Clark Mattox as Apprentices from the date hereof during the term of two years each.

During all of which time, said Upson for himself and his son doth Covenant with the said Clark Mattox that himself and his son shall well and faithfully demean themselves as such faithful Apprentices, observing fully the Commands of the said Clark Mattox, and in all things deporting and behaving themselves as faithful Apprentices to the said Clark Mattox, neither revealing his secrets, nor at any time neglecting or leaving the business of the said Clark Mattox.

And for and in Consideration of the service well and faithfully rendered by the said Upson and his said son, of the first part, said Clark Mattox, of the second part, doth Covenant, promise, and agree to instruct them, said apprentices, or otherwise Cause them to be well and faithfully instructed, in the said trade or craft of house servants or laborers, and shall also allow, furnish, and provide them, said Apprentices, with meat and drink & clothing during the said term.

Witness our hands and Seals the day and year first before written.

Executed before us }
in Duplicate } Neal + Upson, his mark
R. M. Willis } Clark Mattox
Geº L. Almond, Ordny }

Filed in Office and recorded Oct 30th 1893.

Geº L. Almond, Ordy

Duplicate [222]

Georgia }
Elbert County } This Indenture, made and entered into this the 9th day of October 1893, between Jincy Mattox, of the one part, and Dora Richardson of the other part, both of the State and County aforesaid. Witnesseth: That the said Dora Richardson, for and in consideration of the love and affection she has for her Aunt, the said Jincy Mattox, binds out herself and her to said Jincy Mattox her little daughter Gertrude, now in her tenth year, to her and Control her, the said Gertrude, in all of the actings and doings, and also to have the proceeds of her labor until she, said Gertrude, arrives at the age of Majority. The said Jincy Mattox on her part, agrees to feed, clothe, educate, and give all necessary medical Attention unto the said Gertrude, also to treat her with Kindness and humanity, and learn her to sew and do such other work as will best suit her for an occupation through life, and when she, the said Gertrude, arrives at the age of 21, if still living with her Aunt, the said Jincy Mattox, she the said Jincy Mattox is to give her, the said Gertrude, a good comfortable bed, bed cloak, and bed clothing sufficient for it and the articles of furniture as are necessary for Keeping House.

In Witness whereof, the said Dora Richardson and Jincy Mattox hereto set their hands and seals Day and date above written.

Signed, sealed, and }
delivered in presence of }
Clark Mattox, N. P. ex of J. P. } Dora + Richardson, her mark
R. M. Willis } Jincy + Mattox, her mark

Filed in office and recorded Nov 4, 1893.

Geº L. Almond, Ordinary

[Written vertically across the above is the following notation.]

We hereby agree and Covenant and do declare that the Indenture of Apprenticeship is found this date Null & void on this July 1st 1895.

          Jincy + Mattox, her mark
          Dora + Richardson, her mark

Attest.   Ge° L. Almond, Ordinary

        Duplicate   [223]

Georgia   }
Elbert County } This Indenture, made this the 5th day of Dec 1893, between Dick Thompson, of said County, for and in behalf of Esquire and Julius Thompson, being of the age of 20 and 17 years, on the one part, and Clark Mattox, of the County aforesaid, of the other part, witnesseth: that the said Dick Thompson does by these presents bind out Esquire and Julius Thompson, of said County, as apprentices to said Clark Mattox in the trade or craft of house servants or as laborers upon the plantation of the said Clark Mattox, to be taught the said Craft or trade of house servants or laborers, and to live with, continue, and serve the said Clark Mattox as apprentices from Jany 1, 1894 for and during the term of one year.

During all of which time, said Dick Thompson doth Covenant with the said Clark Mattox that the said Esquire and Julius Thompson shall well and faithfully demean themselves as such faithful Apprentices, ~~fully~~ observing fully the Commands of the said Clark Mattox, and in all things deporting and behaving themselves as faithful Apprentices to the said Clark Mattox, neither revealing his secrets, nor at any time neglecting or leaving the business of the said Clark Mattox. And for and in Consideration of the service well and faithfully rendered by the said Esquire and Julius Thompson, of the first part, said Clark Mattox, of the second part, doth Covenant, promise, and agree to instruct said Apprentices, or otherwise cause them to be well and faithfully instructed, in the said trade or craft of house servants, and shall also allow, furnish, and provide them, said Apprentices, with meat and drink during the said term, and shall also at the expiration of said term allow and pay the said Dick Thompson $95.00

Witness our hands and seals the day & year first before written.

Executed Before us }
in Duplicate } Dick + Thompson, his mark
J. J. Chandler } Clark Mattox
Geº L. Almond, Ordinary }

Filed in office and recorded Dec 5th 1893.

Geº L. Almond, Ordy

Duplicate [224]

Georgia }
Elbert County } This Indenture, made this the 8 day of Dec 1893, between Lizzie Fortson, of said County, for and in behalf of Mary Fortson, being of the age of five months, on the one part, and Dillie Burton, of the County aforesaid, of the other part. witnesseth: That the said Lizzie Fortson does by these presents bind out Mary Fortson, of said County, as apprentice to said Dillie Burton in the trade or craft of house servant or as laborer upon the plantation of the said Dillie Burton, to be taught the said Craft or trade of house servant or laborer, and to live with, continue, and serve the said Dillie Burton as an apprentice from the date hereof during the term of 18 years.

During all of which time, said Lizzie Fortson doth covenant with the said Dillie Burton that the said Mary Fortson shall well and faithfully demean herself as such faithful apprentice, observing fully the Commands of the said Dillie Burton, and in all things deporting & behaving herself as a faithful apprentice to the said Dillie Burton, neither revealing her secrets, nor at any time neglecting or leaving the business of the said Dillie Burton. And for and in consideration of the service well and faithfully rendered by the said Mary Fortson, of the first part, said Dillie Burton, of the second part, doth covenant, promise, & agree to instruct her said apprentice, or otherwise Cause her to be well & faithfully instructed, in the said trade or craft of house servant or laborer, and also to read the English language, and shall also allow, furnish, and provide her said apprentice with meat and drink and clothing during the said term, and all other necessaries meet & proper, in sickness and in health, and shall alow, at the expiration of the said term, allow &

pay the said apprentice what is now allowed by the statute in such case made and provided. Witness our hands and seals the day and year first above written.

Executed before us }
in Duplicate } Lizzie + Fortson, his mark
G. H. McLanahan } Dillie + Burton, her mark
Ge° L. Almond, Ordiny }

Filed in office and recorded Dec 8, 1893.

Ge° L. Almond, Ord

Duplicate [225]

Georgia }
Elbert County } This Indenture, made this the first day of February 1894, between Douglass, father, and Savannah Gray, mother, of said County, for and in behalf of their minor children, to wit, Richmond Gray being of the age of seventeen years, and Sam Gray being of the age of Sixteen years, and William Gray being of the age of twelve years, and John Gray being of the age of fourteen years, and James Gray being of the age of thirteen years, and Violet Gray being of the age of Fifteen years, and Mary Gray being of the age of Six years, and Julia A. Gray being of the age of two years, and Douglass Gray, J^r being of the age of five years, on the one part, and John W. McCalla, of the County Aforesaid, of the other part. Witnesseth: That the said Douglass Gray, father, and Savannah Gray, mother, as aforesaid, does by these presents bind out their minor children aforesaid, of said County, as apprentices to said John W. McCalla in the trade or Craft of farm hands & house servants or laborers upon the plantation of the said John W. McCalla, to be taught the said Craft or trade of farm & house servants or laborers upon farm, and to live with, Continue, and serve the said John W. McCalla as Apprentices from the date hereof for and during the term of their minority or until they shall each attain the age of twenty one years respectfully. During all of which time, said Douglass Gray, father, and Savannah Gray, mother, as aforesaid, doth Covenant with the said John W. McCalla that the said minor children aforesaid shall well & faithfully demean themselves each and all of them as such faithful Apprentices, observing fully the Commands of the said Clark Mattox, and in all things deporting and behaving themselves as faithful Apprentices to the said John W. McCalla, neither revealing his secrets, nor at any time neglecting or leaving the business of the said John W. McCalla. And for and in Consideration of the service well and faithfully rendered by the said Douglass Gray & Savannah Gray through their minor children, of the first part, said John

W. McCalla, of the second part, doth Covenant, promise, and agree to instruct his said apprentices, or otherwise cause them to be well and faithfully instructed, in the said trade or craft of house servants and farm hands or laborers, and shall also furnish & provide, allow and furnish the said

apprentices, with meat and drink and clothing during the said term, and [226] all other necessaries meet and proper, in sickness and in health, and shall also at the expiration of said term, as aforesaid, allow and pay the said apprentices each and all of them what is now allowed by the Statute in such cases made and provided.

Witness our hands and Seals the day and year first before written.

Executed in duplicate }
in our presence } Jn° W. McCalla
J. J. Chandler } Douglass Gray
Ge° L. Almond, Ordiny } Savannah + Gray, her mark

Filed in office and Recorded Feb[y] 1st 1894.

                                          Ge° L. Almond, Ordinary

                     Duplicate   [227]

Georgia }
Elbert County } This Indenture, made this the 2nd day of April 1894, between Russel Christian, of said County, for and in behalf of James Christian, his minor son, being of the age of 12 years, on the one part, and M[rs] E. A. Tate, of the County Aforesaid, of the other part. Witnesseth: That the said Russel Christian, father of James Christian Aforesaid, does by these presents bind out James Christian, his son, of said County, as apprentice to said M[rs] E. A. Tate in the trade or Craft of house servant or as laborer upon the plantation of the said M[rs] E. A. Tate, to be taught the said Craft or trade of house servant or laborer, and to live with, continue, and serve the said M[rs] E. A. Tate as an apprentice from the date hereof during the term of his minority years.

During all of which ~~your~~ time, said Russel Christian, father as aforesaid, doth Covenant with the said M[rs] E. A. Tate that the said James Christian shall well and faithfully demean himself as such faithful Apprentice, observing fully the Commands of the said M[rs] E. A. Tate, and in all things deporting and behaving himself as a faithful apprentice to the said M[rs] E. A. Tate, neither revealing her secrets, nor at any time neglecting or leaving the business of the said M[rs] E. A.

Tate. And for and in Consideration of the service well and faithfully rendered by the said James Christian, of the first part, said Mrs E. A. Tate, of the second part, doth Covenant, promise, & agree to instruct him, said apprentice, or otherwise Cause him to be well and faithfully instructed, in the said trade or craft of house servant or laborer, also to read the English language, And shall also allow, furnish, & provide him, said Apprentice, with meat & drink & clothing during the said term, and all other necessaries meet & proper, in sickness and in health, and shall also, at the expiration of said term, allow and pay to said apprentice what is now allowed by statute in such case made & provided.

Witness our hands and Seals the day & year above written.

Executed Before us   }   Russel + Christian, his mark
James P. Chandler, J. P. }   E. A. Tate
J. R. Mattox   }

Duplicate. Filed in office and recorded April 2, 1894.

                          Ge° L. Almond, Ordinary

               Duplicate

Georgia   }
Elbert County   } This Indenture, made this the Second day of June 1894, between Claiborn & Jane Rucker, of said County, for and in behalf of Ed, Ben, & Robert Rucker, being of the ages of 16, 15, & 13 years, on the one part, and Peyton M. Hawes, of the County aforesaid, of the other part. Witnesseth: That the said Claiborn and Jane Rucker, does by these presents bind out Ed, Ben, & Robert Rucker, of said County, as apprentice to said Peyton M. Hawse in the trade or Craft of house servant or as laborer upon the plantation of the said Peyton M. Hawse, to be taught the said Craft or trade of house servant or laborer, and to live with, continue, and serve the Said Peyton M. Hawse as an apprentice from the date hereof for & during the term of their minority.

During all of which time, said Claiborn & Jane Rucker doth Covenant with the said Peyton M. Hawse that the said Ed, Ben, & Robert Rucker shall well & faithfully demean themselves as such faithful apprentices, observing fully the Commands of the said Peyton M. Hawse, and in all things deporting & behaving themselves as faithful Apprentices to the said Peyton M. Hawse, neither revealing his secrets, nor at any time neglecting or leaving the business of the said Peyton M. Hawse. And for and in Consideration of the service well & faithfully rendered by the said Ed, Ben, & Robert, of the first part, said Peyton M. Hawse, of the second part, doth Covenant, promise, & agree to instruct them, said apprentices, or otherwise cause them to be well & faithfully instructed, in the said trade or craft of house servant or laborer, also to read the English language, And shall also allow, furnish, & provide them, said Apprentices, with meat & drink & clothing However, to subline if he chose.

Witness our hands & seals the day & year first before written.

Executed Before us }
in Duplicate. } Claiborn + Rucker, his mark
J. J. J. Chandler } Jane + Rucker, her mark
Geº L. Almond, Ordiny } P. M. Hawse

Filed in office & recorded June 2, 1894.

Geº L. Almond, Ordy

Duplicate [229]

Georgia }
Elbert County } This Indenture this day made and entered into between George Gray and Mary Jane Martin, both of the County and State Above written, and witnesseth: That the said Mary Jane Martin this day binds and Apprentices to the said George Gray her daughter, Lilla Martin, one year old, until she arrives at the age of twenty one years.

The said George is to treat said child humanely and Kindly, furnish proper food and clothing, all necessary medical attention, such education as can be had at the common schools of the County, and when said child arrives at the age of twenty one the said George is to pay it such Amount as he may deem a suitable reward for fidelity and faithful service. The said child to also be instructed in the art or craft of husbandry or farming, and the relation of Master and apprentice shall exist from and after the recording of this writing. Made and signed in duplicate, sealed and delivered in presence of this Aug 20, 1894.

J. B. Janes, Jr, N. P. } George + Gray, his mark
Z. B. Taylor } Mary Jane + Martin, her mark

Filed in office and recorded this August 23, 1894.

Geº L. Almond, Ordinary

Duplicate [230]

Georgia }
Elbert County } This Indenture, made this second day of June 1894, between Aggie Turner, of said County, for and in behalf of Jack Turner, being of the age of six years, on the one part, and Rebecca J. Dickerson, of the County Aforesaid, of the other part. Witnesseth: That the said Aggie Turner does by these presents bind out Jack Turner, her son, of said County, as Apprentice to said Rebecca J. Dickerson in the trade or Craft of house servant or as laborer upon the plantation of the said Rebecca J. Dickerson, to be taught the said craft or trade of house servant or laborer, and to live with, continue, & serve the said Rebecca J. Dickerson as an apprentice from the date hereof for and during the term of fifteen years.

During all of which time, said Aggie Turner doth Covenant with the said Rebecca J. Dickerson that the said Jack Turner shall well and faithfully demean himself as such faithful Apprentice, observing fully the Commands of the said Rebecca J. Dickerson, and in all things deporting & behaving himself as a faithful apprentice to the said Rebecca J. Dickerson, neither revealing her secrets, nor at any time neglecting or leaving the business of the said Rebecca J. Dickerson. And for and in consideration of the service well and faithfully rendered by the said Jack Turner, of the first part, said Rebecca J. Dickerson, of the second part, doth Covenant, promise, & agree to instruct him, said apprentice, or otherwise cause him to be well & faithfully instructed, in the said trade or craft of house servant or laborer, & also to read the English language, and shall also allow, furnish, & provide him, said apprentice, with meat & drink & clothing during the said term, and all other necessaries meet & proper, in sickness & in health, and shall also at the expiration of said term allow & pay to said apprentice what is now allowed by statute in such case made & provided.

Witness our hands and seal the day & year first before written.

Executed before us }
in duplicate } Rebecca J. + Dickerson, her mark
J. M. Dickerson } Aggie + Turner, her mark
Ge⁰ L. Almond, Ordinary }

Filed in office and recorded Nov 2, 1894.

Ge⁰ L. Almond, Ordinary

Duplicate [231]

Georgia }
Elbert County } This Indenture, made this 9th day of November 1894, between Bunk Eberhart, of said County, for and in behalf of himself, being of the age of 22 years, of the one part, and Ada L. Oglesby, of the County aforesaid, of the other part. Witnesseth: That the said Bunk Eberhart does by these presents bind out himself, of said County, as apprentice to said Ada L. Oglesby in the trade or craft of house servant or as laborer upon the plantation of the said Ada L. Oglesby, to be taught the said craft or trade of house servant or laborer, and to live with, continue, and serve the said Ada L. Oglesby as an apprentice from the 1st Jany 1895 for and during the term of three years.

During all of which time, said Bunk Eberhart doth Covenant with the said Ada L. Oglesby that he will well and faithfully demean himself as such faithful apprentice, observing fully the Commands of the said Ada L. Oglesby, and in all things deporting and behaving himself as a faithful Apprentice to the said Ada L. Oglesby, neither revealing her secrets, nor at any time neglecting or leaving the business of the said Ada L. Oglesby.

And for and in Consideration of the service well and faithfully rendered by the said Bunk Eberhart, of the first part, said Ada L. Oglesby, of the second part, doth covenant, promise, & agree to instruct him, said apprentice, or otherwise cause him to be well and faithfully instructed, in the said trade or craft of house servant or laborer, and shall also allow, furnish, & provide him, said apprentice, with meat & drink & clothing during the said term, and all other necessaries meet and proper, in sickness and in health.

Witness our hands and seals the day & year first before written.

Executed Before us }
in duplicate } Bunk + Eberhart, his mark
J. J. Chandler } Ada L. Oglesby, by
Geo L. Almond, Ordiny } Geo B. Lumpkin

Filed in office and recorded Nov 9, 1894.

Geo L. Almond, Ordy

Duplicate [232]

Georgia }
Elbert County } This Indenture, made this the 5th February 1894, between Wm

174

Blackwell, of Elbert County said State, and Jo^s W. Rucker, of Elbert County said State, witnesseth: that the said Wm Rucker, in cause of certain of the promises & undertakings of the said Jo^s W. Rucker hereinafter set forth, does hereby bind himself to the said Jo^s W. Rucker for the first term of three years from Jany 1, 1895, and he hereby agrees to contract with said Jo^s W. Rucker to work faithfully under his direction at such place and at such labor as Jo^s W. Rucker may desire and direct, and to respect and obey all orders & commands of the said Jo^s W. Rucker, and at all times to demean himself orderly and soberly. And the said Wm Blackwell further agrees to account to the said Jo^s W. Rucker for all lost time except in case of temporary sickness not exceeding three days, the same to be deducted from the wages hereinafter set forth and at the same rate.

And the said Jo^s W. Rucker, in consideration of the promises & undertakings of the said Wm Blackwell, agrees & contracts with the said Wm Rucker to furnish him with board, lodging, & wages as follows: He further agrees to pay said Wm Blackwell wages by the year as follows: On Jany 1, 1896 Eighty Dollars, on Jany 1, 1897 Eighty Dollars, on Jany 1, 1898 Eighty dollars. It is further agreed that should this Contract be terminated by the death of either party during either of said years, said Wm Blackwell shall be paid pro rata for the time he served during said year at the price fixed for said year. Said Jo^s W. Rucker further agrees to teach said Wm Blackwell the trade of Agriculture in all its details.

In witness whereof, the said Wm Blackwell & Jo^s W. Rucker have hereunto set their hands & seals the day & year first above written.

Signed, sealed, delivered, & executed }
in duplicate in presence of } J. W. Rucker
S. O. Hawes, N. P. } William Blackwell
I. C. Vanduzen }

Duplicate. Filed in office & Recorded Dec 5, 1894.

        Ge° L. Almond, Ordinary

    Duplicate   [233]

Georgia }
Elbert County } This Indenture, made this February 5th 1894, between Eugene Bowman, of Elbert County said state, and Jo^s W. Rucker, of Elbert County, Ga., witnesseth: that the said Eugene Bowman, in consideration of the promises and undertakings of the said Jo^s W. Rucker hereinafter set forth, does hereby bind himself to the said Jo^s W. Rucker for the full term of three years from Jany 1, 1895,

and he hereby agrees and contracts with said Jo^s W. Rucker to work faithfully under his direction at such place and at such labor as Jo^s W. Rucker, and at all times to demean himself orderly and soberly. And the said Eugene Bowman further agrees to account to said Jo^s W. Rucker for all lost time except in case of temporary sickness not exceeding three days, the same to be deducted from the wages hereinafter set forth and at the same rate.

And the said Jo^s W. Rucker, in consideration of the promises and undertakings of the said Eugene Bowman, agrees and contracts with the said Eugene Bowman to furnish him with board, lodging, and wages as follows: He further agrees to pay said Eugene Bowman wages by the year as follows: On Jany 1, 1896 Eighty Dollars, on Jany 1, 1897 Eighty Dollars, on Jany 1, 1898 Eighty Dollars. It is further agreed that should this contract be terminated by the death of either party during either of said years, said Eugene Bowman shall be paid prorata for the time he served during said year at the price fixed for said year. Said Jo^s W. Rucker further agrees to teach said Eugene Bowman the trade of Agriculture in all its details.

In witness whereof, the said Eugene Bowman and Jo^s W. Rucker have hereunto set their hands and seals the day and year first above written.

Signed, sealed, delivered, and executed }
in duplicate in presence of } J. W. Rucker
S. O. Hawes, N. P. } Eugene Bowman
I. C. Vanduzen }

Filed in office and Recorded Dec 5th 1894.

Ge^o L. Almond, Ord^y

Duplicate [234]

Georgia }
Elbert County } This Indenture, made this the 22 day of December 1894, between William Washington, of said County, for and in behalf of George Washington, being of the age of 11 years, of the one part, and J. B. Janes, S^r, of the County aforesaid, of the other part. Witnesseth: That the said William Washington does by these presents bind out Ge^o Washington, of said County, as apprentice to said J. B. Janes, S^r in the trade or craft of house servant or as laborer upon the plantation of the said J. B. Janes, S^r, to be taught the said Craft or trade of house servant or laborer, and to live with, continue, & serve the said J. B. Janes, S^r as an apprentice from the date hereof for and during the term of three years.

During all of which time, said William Washington doth covenant with the said J. B. Janes, S^r that the said Ge^o Washington will well and faithfully demean himself as such faithful apprentice, observing fully the Commands of the said J. B. Janes, S^r, and in all things deporting and behaving himself as a faithful apprentice to the said J. B. Janes, S^r, neither revealing his secrets, nor at any time neglecting or leaving the business of the said J. B. Janes, S^r. And for and in consideration of the service well & faithfully rendered by the said George Washington, of the first part, said J. B. Janes, S^r, of the second part, doth Covenant, promise, & agree to instruct him, said apprentice, or otherwise cause him to be well & faithfully instructed, in the said trade or craft of house servant or laborer, and shall also allow, furnish, & provide him, said apprentice, with meat & drink during the said term, and to pay William Washington $20.00 per year.

Witness our hands and seals the day & year first before written.

Executed Before us   }
in duplicate   }   J. B. Janes, S^r
T. J. Wall   }   William + Washington, his mark
Ge^o L. Almond, Ordinary }

Filed in office and recorded Dec 22, 1894.

                            Ge^o L. Almond, Ordinary

              Duplicate   [235]

Georgia   }
Elbert County }   This Indenture, made this 6th Jany 1894, between William Fortson, of said County, for and in behalf of Robert Fortson, being of the age of Fifteen years, of the one part, and John C. Hudgens, of the County aforesaid, of the other part. Witnesseth: That the said William Fortson does by these presents bind out Robert Fortson, of said County, as apprentice to said J. C. Hudgens in the trade or craft of house servant or as laborer upon the plantation of the said J. C. Hudgens, to be taught the said craft or trade of house servant or laborer, and to live with, continue, & serve the said J. C. Hudgens as an apprentice from the date hereof for and during the term of two years.

During all of which time, said W. Fortson doth covenant with the said J. C. Hudgens that the said Robert Fortson will well & faithfully demean himself as such faithful apprentice, observing fully the commands of the said J. C. Fortson, and in all things deporting & behaving himself as a faithful apprentice to the said J. C. Fortson, neither revealing his secrets, nor at any time neglecting or leaving the business of the said J. C. Hudgens. And for and in consideration of the service well & faithfully rendered by the said Robert Fortson, of the first part, said J. C. Hudgens, of the second part, doth covenant, promise, & agree to instruct him, said apprentice, or otherwise cause him to be well & faithfully instructed, in the said trade or craft of house servant or laborer, and shall also allow, furnish, & provide him, said apprentice, with meat & drink during the said term, and to pay said William Fortson $60.00 for 1894 and $65.00 for 1895 and Fortson to make good last term.

Witness our hands & seals the day & year first before written.

Executed before us }
in duplicate } William + Fortson, his mark
A. J. Hudgens } J. C. Hudgens
Clark Mattox, N. P. & J. P. }

Filed in office & Recorded Jany 31, 1895.

Ge^o L. Almond, Ordiny

Duplicate [236]

Georgia }
Elbert County } This Indenture, made this the 7 Jany 1895, between John Verdel, of said County, for and in behalf of himself, being of the age of 20 years, of the one part, and James H. Rucker, of the County aforesaid, of the other part. Witnesseth: That the said John Verdel does by these presents bind out himself, of said County, as apprentice to said James H. Rucker in the trade or craft of house servant or as laborer upon the plantation of the said Ja^s H. Rucker, to be taught the said craft or trade of house servant or laborer, and to live with, continue, and serve the said James H. Rucker as an apprentice from the date hereof for & during the term of Five years. During all of which time, said John Verdel doth covenant with the said James H. Rucker that he will well & faithfully demean himself as such faithful apprentice, observing fully the commands of the said James H. Rucker, and in all things deporting and behaving himself as a faithful apprentice to the said James H. Rucker, neither revealing his secrets, nor at any time neglecting or leaving the business of the said James H. Rucker. And for and in consideration of the service well & faithfully rendered by the said John Verdel, of the first part, said James H. Rucker, of the second part, doth covenant, promise, & agree to instruct him, said apprentice, or otherwise cause him to be well & faithfully instructed, in the said trade or craft of house servant or laborer, and shall also

allow, furnish, & provide him, said apprentice, with meat & drink & clothing during the said term, and its wages to be paid are already paid this day.

Witness our hands & Seals the day & year first before written.

Executed before us }
in Duplicate }   John Verdel
J. W. Stovall }   J. H. Rucker
Ge° L. Almond, Ordy }

Filed in office Jany 7th 1895.

Ge° L. Almond, Ordiny

Recorded Jany 31st 1895.

Ge° L. Almond, Ordy

Duplicate   [237]

Georgia }
Elbert County } This Indenture, made this the 12th day of March 1895, between Dora Morrison (mother), of said County, for and in behalf of her minor children, to wit, James Morrison age Eight years, Jessie Morrison aged 13, Eliza Morrison age 16, on the one part, and John W. McCalla, of the County Aforesaid, of the other part. Witnesseth: That the said Dora Morrison (mother), as aforesaid, does by these presents bind out her minor children aforesaid as apprentices to said John W. McCalla in the trade or craft of farm hands or house servants or as laborers upon the plantation of the said Jn° W. McCalla, to be taught the said craft or trade of farm laborers and house servants, and to live with and serve the said Jn° W. McCalla as apprentices from the date hereof for and during the term of their minority. During all of which time, said Dora Morrison, mother as aforesaid, doth Covenant with the said Jn° W. McCalla that the said minor children Shall will well and faithfully demean themselves each and all of them as such faithful apprentices, observing fully the Commands of the said Jn° W. McCalla, and in all things deporting and behaving themselves each and all of them as faithful apprentices to the said John W. McCalla.

And for and in consideration of the service well & faithfully rendered by the said Dora Morrison through her minor children, of the first part, said Jn° W. McCalla, of the second part, doth Covenant, promise, and agree to instruct his said apprentices, or cause them to be well & faithfully instructed, in the said trade or craft of farm hands or house servants, and also shall furnish and provide the said apprentices with meat & drink & clothing during the said term, and All necessaries in sickness and in health, and at the expiration of said term pay the said apprentices what is now allowed by law in such cases made and provided. Witness our hands and seals the day & year above written.

Executed in duplicate }
and in presence of }   Jnº W. McCalla
John H. Craig }   Dora + Morrison, her mark
Geº L. Almond, Ordny }

Filed in office and recorded March 13, 1895.

Geº L. Almond, Ordy

Duplicate [238]

Georgia }
Elbert County } This Indenture, made this 18 day March 1895, between Willis Fortson, father, of said County, for and in behalf of Hughy Fortson, being of the age of 14 years, of the one part, and P. M. Hawes, of the County aforesaid, of the other part. witnesseth: That the said Willis Fortson does by these presents bind out Hughy Fortson, of said County, as apprentice to said P. M. Hawes in the trade or craft of house servant or as laborer upon the plantation of the said P. M. Hawes, to be taught the said Craft or trade of house servant or laborer, and to live with, continue, and serve the said P. M. Hawes as an apprentice from the date hereof for & during the term of seven years.

During all of which time, said Willis Fortson doth covenant with the said P. M. Hawes that the said Hughy Fortson shall well & faithfully demean himself as such faithful apprentice, observing fully the Commands of the said P. M. Hawes, and in all things deporting & behaving himself as a faithful apprentice to the said P. M. Hawes, neither revealing his secrets, nor at any time neglecting or leaving the business of the said P. M. Hawes. And for and in consideration of the service well & faithfully rendered by the said Henly Forly, of the first part, said P. M. Hawes, of the second part, doth covenant, promise, & agree to instruct him, said apprentice, or otherwise cause him to be well and faithfully instructed, in the said trade or craft of house servant or laborer, and shall also allow, furnish, & provide him, said apprentice, with meat & drink & clothing during the said term, and all other necessaries meet and proper, in sickness and in health.

Witness our hands & Seals the day and year first Above written.

Executed before us }
in Duplicate } Willis + Fortson, his mark
L. M. Kend } P. M. Hawes
Ge° L. Almond, Ordiny }

Filed in office & Recorded March 18, 1895.

Ge° L. Almond, Ordy

Duplicate [239]

Georgia }
Elbert County } This Indenture, made this the 19 March 1895, between Ida Ozley, Mother, of said County, for and in behalf of Tom Allen, being of the age of 4½ years, of the one part, and Thomas Allen, of the County aforesaid, of the other part. Witnesseth: That the said Ida Ozley does by these presents bind out Tom Allen, of said County, as Apprentice to said Thomas Allen in the trade or craft of house servant or as laborer upon the plantation of the said Thomas Allen, to be taught the said craft or trade of house servant or laborer, and to live with, continue, and serve the said Thomas Allen as an apprentice from the date hereof for and during the term of his minority. During all of which time, said Ida Ozley doth Covenant with the said Thoˢ Allen that the said Tom Allen shall well and faithfully demean himself as such faithful Apprentice, observing fully the Commands of the said Thomas Allen, and in all things deporting & behaving himself as a faithful apprentice to the said Thomas Allen, neither revealing his secrets, nor at any time neglecting or leaving the business of the said Thomas Allen.

And for and in consideration of the service well and faithfully rendered by the said Tom Allen, of the first part, said Thomas Allen, of the second part, doth covenant, promise, and agree to instruct him, said apprentice, or otherwise cause him to be well & faithfully instructed, in the said trade or craft of house servant or laborer, and also to read the English language, and shall also allow, furnish, & provide him, said apprentice, with meat and drink & clothing during the said term, and all other necessaries meet and proper, in sickness and in health, and shall also, at the expiration of the said term, Allow and pay the said Apprentice what is now allowed by the Statute in such case made and provided. Witness our hands & Seals the day and year first before written.

Executed before us }
in Duplicate } Ida + Ozley, her mark
Geº H. McLanahan } Thoˢ + Allen, his mark
Geº L. Almond, Ordiny }

Filed in office and recorded 19 March 1895.

Geº L. Almond, Ordiny

Duplicate [240]

Georgia }
Elbert County } This Indenture, made this 25 April 1895, between Mid Brawner (father), of said County, for and in behalf of Lela, Lula, & Frances Brawner, being of the age of 13, 12, & 8 years, of the one part, and H. C. Rousey, of said County, of the other part. Witnesseth: That the said Mid Brawner does by these presents bind out Lela, Lula, & Frances Brawner, of said County, as apprentices to said H. C. Rousey in the trade or craft of house servants or as Laborers upon the plantation of the said H. C. Rousey, to be taught the said craft or trade of house servants or laborers, & to live with, Continue, & serve the said H. C. Rousey as Apprentice from the date hereof for & during the term of their minority.

During all of which time, said Mid Brawner doth Covenant with the said H. C. Rousey that the said Lela, Lula, & Frances Brawner shall well & faithfully demean themselves as such faithful apprentices, Observing fully the commands of the said H. C. Rousey, and in all things deporting and behaving themselves as faithful apprentices to the said H. C. Rousey, neither revealing his secrets, nor at any time neglecting or leaving the business of the said H. C. Rousey.

And for and in consideration of the service well & faithfully rendered by the said Lela, Lula, & Frances Brawner, of the first part, said H. C. Rousey, of the second part, doth Covenant, promise, & agree to instruct them, said apprentices, or otherwise cause them to be well & faithfully instructed, in the said trade or craft of house servants, and shall also allow, furnish, & provide said apprentices with meat & drink & clothing during the said term, & all other necessaries meet & proper, in sickness & in health.

Witness our hands & Seal the day & year first before written.

Executed before us }
in Duplicate   }   H. C. Rousey
D. B. Alexander   }   Mid + Brawner, his mark
L. M. Heard, Not Pub }

Filed in office & recorded 4 May 1895.

                                    Ge⁰ L. Almond, Ordiny

                     Duplicate   [241]

Georgia   }
Elbert County }   This Indenture, made this the 3rd day of July 1895, between Martha Harris, col, of said County, for and in behalf of Rosa Lee Harris, col, being of the age of two years, of the one part, and Rebecca C. Upshaw, col, of the County aforesaid, of the other part. Witnesseth: That the said Martha Harris does by these presents bind out Rosa Lee Harris, of said County, as apprentice to said Rebecca C. Upshaw in the trade or craft of house servant or as laborer upon the plantation of the said Upshaw, to be taught the said craft or trade of house servant or laborer, and to live with, continue, and serve the said Rebecca C. Upshaw as an Apprentice from the date hereof for & during the term of her minority.

During all of which time, said Martha Harris doth Covenant with the said Rebecca C. Upshaw that the said Rosa Lee Harris shall well & faithfully demean herself as such faithful apprentice, observing fully the commands of the said Rebecca C. Upshaw, and in all things deporting & behaving herself as a faithful apprentice to the said Rebecca C. Upshaw, neither revealing her secrets, nor at any time neglecting or leaving the business of the said Rebecca C. Upshaw.

And for and in consideration of the service well & faithfully rendered by the said Rosa Lee Harris, of the first part, said Rebecca C. Upshaw, of the second part, doth covenant, promise, and agree to instruct her said apprentice, or otherwise cause her to be well & faithfully instructed, in the said trade or craft of house servant or laborer, and also to read the English language, and shall also allow, furnish, & provide her said apprentice, with meat & drink & clothing during the said term, and all other necessaries meet & proper, in sickness and in health, and shall also, at the expiration of said term, allow & pay the said Apprentice what is now allowed by the statute in such case made & provided. Witness our hands & seal the day & year first before written.

Executed before us }
in duplicate } Rebecca C. Upshaw
H. J. Brewer } Martha + Harris, her mark
Geº L. Almond, Ordy }

Filed in office & recorded July 3, 1895.

Geº L. Almond, Ordiny

Duplicate [242]

Georgia }
Elbert County } This Indenture, made this Second day of July 1895, between Dora Richardson, of said County, for and in behalf of Gertrude Richardson, being of the age of 11 years, of the one part, and W. H. M. Webb, of the County aforesaid, of the other part. Witnesseth: That the said Dora Richardson does by these presents bind out Gertrude Richardson, of said County, as apprentice to said W. H. M. Webb in the trade or craft of house servant or as laborer upon the plantation of the said Webb, to be taught the said craft or trade of house servant or laborer, & to live with, continue, & serve the said Webb as an apprentice from the date hereof for and during the term of her minority.

During all of which time, said Dora Richardson doth covenant with the said Webb that the said Gertrude Richardson shall well & faithfully demean herself as such faithful apprentice, observing fully the commands of the said Webb, and in all things deporting & behaving herself as a faithful apprentice to the said Webb, neither revealing his secrets, nor at any time neglecting or leaving the business of the said Webb.

And for and in consideration of the service well & faithfully rendered by the said Gertrude Richardson, of the first part, said Webb, of the second part, doth covenant, promise, & agree to instruct her, said apprentice, or otherwise cause her to be well & faithfully instructed, in the said trade or craft of house servant or laborer, and to read the English language, and shall also allow, furnish, & provide her, said apprentice, with meat & drink & clothing during the said term, & all other necessaries meet and proper, in sickness & in health.

Witness our hands & seals the day & year first before written.

Executed before us }
in duplicate }   Dora + Richardson, her mark
J. J. Chandler }   W. H. M. + Webb, his mark
Geº L. Almond, Ordny }

Filed in office July 2 & Recorded July 3, 1895.

        Geº L. Almond, Ordy

We hereby annul this Indenture Nov 5, 1895.

Witness   Dora + Richardson, her mark
Geº L. Almond, Ordy   W. H. M. + Webb, his mark

      Duplicate   [243]

Georgia }
Elbert County } This Indenture, made this 17th day of September 1895, between Martha Blackwell, of said County, for and in behalf of Albert Rucker, her guardian, being of the age of 15 years, of the one part, and W. H. Mattox & Son, of the County aforesaid, of the other part. Witnesseth: That the said Martha Blackwell, as aforesaid does by these presents bind out Albert Rucker, of said County, as apprentice to said W. H. Mattox & Son in the trade or craft of house servant or as laborer upon the plantation of the said Mattox's, to be taught the said craft or trade of house servant or laborer, and to live with, continue, & serve the said W. H. Mattox & Son as an apprentice from the date hereof for & during the term from now until Jany 1, 1898.

During all of which time, said Martha Blackwell doth covenant with the said W. H. Mattox & Son that the said Albert Rucker shall well & faithfully demean himself as such faithful apprentice, observing fully the Commands of the said W. H. Mattox & Son, and in all things deporting & behaving himself as a faithful apprentice to the said W. H. Mattox & Son, neither revealing their secrets, nor at any time neglecting or leaving the business of the said W. H. Mattox & Son.

And for & in consideration of the service well & faithfully rendered by the said Albert Rucker, of the first part, said W. H. Mattox & Son, of the second part, doth covenant, promise, & agree to instruct his said apprentice, or otherwise cause him to be well & faithfully instructed, in the said trade or craft of house servant or laborer, and shall also allow, furnish, & provide him, said apprentice, with meat

& drink & clothing during the said term, and all other necessaries meet & proper, in sickness & in health, & to pay said Blackwell $5.00 every two months.

Witness our hands & seals the day & year first before written.

Executed before us }
in duplicate } Martha + Blackwell, her mark
W. W. Adams } W. H. Mattox & Son
Ge° L. Almond, Ordny }

Filed in office & recorded Sep^t 17th 1895.

Ge° L. Almond, Ordinary

Duplicate [244]

Georgia }
Elbert County } This Indenture, made this 19th day of November 1895, between Mary Jane Morrison and Llewellyn Bowman, both of the County and State above written, and Witnesseth: that the said Mary Jane Morrison this day binds and apprentices to the Said Llewellyn Bowman until they arrive at their majority her two minor boys, one Frank Morrison nine years old and Porter Morrison Six years old.

The Said Mary Jane Covenants on her part that the Said Children shall after this writing be Subject to the sole Control and Management of the Said Lewellyn and shall at all times deport themselves as is becoming said Apprentices. The Said Bowman is to treat Said children humanely and Kindly, furnish proper food and clothing, all necessary Medical attention, and cause them to be instructed and to receive such education as may be had at the Common Schools of the County, and instruct or learn them the art or business of husbandry or farming, and at all times and in all things to treat them as his own children, also in addition to the above the Said Llewellyn Bowman is to give to each child on arrival at their majority such amts as he may deem a Sufficient reward for their fidelity & faithful Service.

Made in Duplicate. Signed, Sealed, and delivered in these presence.

W. T. Brownlee   Mary Jane X Morrison, her mark
J. B. Janes, J^r, N. P. & ex off J. P.   Llewellyn Bowman

Filed in office & Recorded Nov 20th 1895.

Ge° L. Almond, Ordinary

Duplicate [245]

~~Georgia }~~
~~Elbert County } This Agreement, made this the 1tth day of Dec 1895, by and between Bob and Martha Carter, aged seven and four years, of the first part, and John W. McCalla, of said State & County, party of the second part, witnesseth: that~~

Duplicate

Georgia }
Elbert County } This agreement, made this 11 day Dec 1895, by and between Robert Carter, father of Thos Parks Carter and Martha Carter, aged seven and four years, of the first part, and John W. McCalla, of said State and County, party of the second part. Witnesseth: that the said Robert Carter hereby binds and apprentices to the said John W. McCalla the said Thos Parks Carter and Martha Carter until they are each Twenty one years old, upon the following terms. Said John W. McCalla agrees to take said Thos Parks and Martha Carter into his Custody and to teach them business of husbandry, furnish them with protection, food, suitable clothing, and necessary medicine and medical attention, teach them habits of industry, honesty, and morality, Cause them to be taught the elementary elements principals of Mathematics and to read English, and Shall govern them with humanity, using only the same degree of force to compel their obedience as a father may use with his minor child. And when the said apprentices shall arrive at the age of twenty one years, they are to receive from the said John W. McCalla Two hundred dollars in cash. In consideration of all of which, said John W. McCalla is to be entitled to the services of the said Apprentices & their earnings until they are twenty one years old each. Witness our hands & seals this Dec 11, 1895. Read over in the presence of the parties hereto before signing & executed in Duplicate.

Signed, seal, & delivered }
in presence of }   Robert + Carter, his mark
Ja^s McIntosh }   Jn° W. McCalla
Abda Oglesby, J. P. }

Filed in office & recorded Dec 11, 1895.

Ge⁰ L. Almond, Ordinary

Duplicate [246]

Georgia }
Elbert County } This Indenture, made this 8th day of Jany 1895, between Willis Fortson, of said County, for and in behalf of Belian, Hughy, & Willis Fortson, being of the ages of 16, 14, & 10 years, of the one part, and Jn⁰ C. Brown, of the County aforesaid, of the other part. Witnesseth: That the said Willis Fortson, as aforesaid does by these, presents bind out Belian, Hughy, & Willis Fortson, of said County, as apprentices to said Jn⁰ C. Brown in the trade or craft of house servants or as laborers upon the plantation of the said Jn⁰ C. Brown, to be taught the said craft or trade of house servant or laborers, and to live with, continue, and serve the said John C. Brown as apprentices from the 1st of Jany 1897 during the term of three years.

During all of which time, said Willis Fortson doth covenant with the said Jn⁰ C. Brown that the said Belian, Hughy, & Willis Fortson shall well and faithfully demean themselves as such faithful apprentices, observing fully the commands of the said Jn⁰ C. Brown, and in all things deporting and behaving themselves as faithful apprentices to the said Jn⁰ C. Brown, neither revealing his secrets, nor at any time neglecting or leaving the business of the said Jn⁰ C. Brwn. And for and in consideration of the services well & faithfully rendered by the said Belian, Hughy, & Willis Fortson, of the first part, said Jn⁰ C. Brown, of the second part, doth Covenant, promise, & agree to instruct them, said apprentices, or otherwise cause them to be well & faithfully instructed, in the said trade or craft of house servants or laborers, and shall also allow, furnish, & provide them, said Apprentices, with meat & drink & clothing during the said term, and all other necessaries meet & proper, in sickness & in health.

Witness our hands & seals the day & year first above written.

Executed before us }
in duplicate }   Willis + Fortson, his mark
J. C. Swearengine }   Jn⁰ C. Brown
Ge⁰ L. Almond, Ordiny }

Filed in office & recorded Jany 8, 1896.

Ge⁰ L. Almond, Ordy

Duplicate [247]

Georgia }
Elbert County } This Indenture, made this the 9th Jany 1896, between Arda Wilhite (Mother), of said County, for and in behalf of Frank Wilhite, being of the age of 16 years, of the one part, and Charles H. Allen, of the County aforesaid, of the other part. Witnesseth: that the said Arda Wilhite, as aforesaid, does by these presents bind out Frank Wilhite, of said County, as apprentice to said Chas H. Allen in the trade or craft of house servant or as laborer upon the plantation of the said Chas H. Allen, to be taught the said craft or trade of house Servant or laborer, and to live with, continue, & serve the said Chas H. Allen as an apprentice from the date hereof for and during the term of Five years.

During all of which time, said Ardra Wilhite, as aforesaid, doth Covenant with the said Chas H. Allen that the said Frank Wilhite shall well & faithfully demean himself as such faithful apprentice, observing fully the commands of the said C. H. Allen, and in all things deporting & behaving himself as a faithful apprentice to the said Chas H. Allen, neither revealing his secrets, nor at any time neglecting or leaving the business of the said Chas H. Allen. And for and in consideration of the service well & faithfully rendered by the said Frank Wilhite, of the first part, said Charles H. Allen, of the second part, doth covenant, promise, & agree to instruct his said apprentice, or otherwise cause him to be well & faithfully instructed, in the said trade or craft of house servant or laborer, and shall also allow, furnish, & provide him, said apprentice, with meat & drink & clothing during the said term, & other necessaries meet & proper, in sickness and in health, all shall also pay to said Ardra $52.00 per annum.

Witness our hands & seals the day & year first before written.

Executed before us }
in duplicate } Ardra + Wilhite, her mark
W. H. Irvin } C. H. Allen
Geo L. Almond, Ordy }

Filed in office & recorded Jany 9, 1896.

Geo L. Almond, Ordy

Duplicate [248]

Georgia }
Elbert County } This Indenture, made this 3rd day of Jany 1896, between Sarah

Mattox, of said County, for and in behalf of Willie Wootten, being of the age of 13 years, of the one part, and S. S. Brewer, of the County aforesaid, of the other part. Witnesseth: that the said Sarah Mattox, as aforesaid, does by these presents bind out Willie Wootten, of said County, as apprentice to said S. S. Brewer in the trade or craft of house servant or as laborer upon the plantation of the said S. S. Brewer, to be taught the said craft or trade of house servant or laborer, & to live with, continue, & serve the said S. S. Brewer as an apprentice from the date hereof for and during the term of five years. During all of which time, said Sarah Mattox, as aforesaid, doth covenant with the said S. S. Brewer that the said Willie Wootten shall well & faithfully demean himself as such faithful apprentice, observing fully the Commands of the said S. S. Brewer, and in all things deporting & behaving himself as a faithful apprentice to the said S. S. Brewer, neither revealing his secrets, nor at any time neglecting or leaving the business of the said S. S. Brewer.

And for and in consideration of the service well & faithfully rendered by the said Willie Wootten, of the first part, said S. S. Brewer, of the second part, doth covenant, promise, & agree to instruct him, said apprentice, or otherwise cause him to be well & faithfully instructed, in the said trade or craft of house servant, and shall also allow, furnish, & provide him, said apprentice, with meat & drink & clothing during the said term, and all other necessaries meet & proper, in sickness & in health.

Witness our hands and seals the day & year first before written.

Executed before us }
in duplicate } Sarah + Mattox, her mark
J. J. Smith } S. S. Brewer
Ge° L. Almond, Ordny }

Filed in office & recorded Jan[y] 13, 1896.

Ge° L. Almond, Ordy

Duplicate [249]

Georgia }
Elbert County } This Indenture, made this 19th day of March 1896, between Robert Morrison, of said County, for and in behalf of Georgeann, Joe, Janie, Grady, & Gordon, being of the age of 14, 13, 10, 6, & 3 years, of the one part, and M[rs] M. C. Barkesdale, of the County aforesaid, of the other part. Witnesseth: That the said Robert Morrison does by these presents bind out Georgeann, Joe, Janie, Grady, & Gordon, of said County, as apprentices to said M[rs] M. C. Barkesdale in

the trade or craft of house servant or as laborer upon the plantation of the said Mrs M. C. Barkesdale, to be taught the said craft or trade of house servants or laborers, and to live with, continue, and serve the said Mrs M. C. Barkesdale as apprentices from the date hereof for and during the term of their minority. During all of which time, said Robert Morrison doth Covenant with the said Mrs M. C. Barkesdale that the said Georgeann, Joe, Janie, Grady, & Gordon shall well & faithfully Demean themselves as such faithful Apprentices, observing fully the commands of the said Mrs M. C. Barkesdale, and in all things deporting themselves as such faithful apprentices to the said Mrs M. C. Barkesdale, neither revealing her secrets, nor at any time neglecting or leaving the business of the said Mrs M. C. Barkesdale.

And for and in consideration of the service well & faithfully rendered by the said Georgeann, Joe, Janie, Grady, & Gordon, of the first part, said Mrs M. C. Barkesdale, of the second part, doth Covenant, promise, & agree to instruct them, said apprentices, or otherwise cause them to be well & faithfully instructed, in the said trade or craft of house servants or laborers, and shall also allow, furnish, & provide said apprentices with meat & drink & clothing during the said term, and all other necessaries meet & proper, in sickness & in health.

Witness our hand & seal the day & year first before written.

Executed before us }
in duplicate } Mary C. Barkesdale
Jo^s N. Worly } Robt + Morrison, his mark
Ge^o L. Almond, Ordy }

Filed in Office & recorded March 19, 1896.

        Ge^o L. Almond, Ordy

     Duplicate   [250]

Georgia }
Elbert County } This Indenture, made and entered into this 28th day of May 1896, between Fannie Tate and Charlotte Tate, the mother of Eula Jones, now aged five years and three months, all of said County. witnesseth: That the said Charlotte hereby binds to the said Fannie Tate the said Eula Jones, until the said Eula Jones is twenty one years old, or married, upon the following terms. The said Fannie Tate agrees to take into her custody said Eula Jones, to furnish her with protection, wholesome food, suitable clothing, necessary medicine and medical attention, teach her habits of industry, honesty, and morality, using only the same degree of force to compel her obedience as a mother may use with her

minor child, and is to give said Eula Jones such education as she, the said Fannie Tate, would give to her own child.

In consideration of all of which, said Fannie Tate is to be entitled to the services and earnings of said Eula Jones until she is twenty one years old or married.

Witness our hands and seals the 28th day of May 1896.

Signed, sealed, & delivered }
in duplicate } Charlotte + Tate, her mark
Bessie Bell DuBose } Fannie + Tate, her mark
J. D. DuBose, J. P. }

Filed in office and recorded June 5, 1896.

Ge° L. Almond, Ordy

Duplicate [251]

Georgia }
Elbert County } This Indenture, made this First July 1896, between Dave Roebuck, of said County, for and in behalf of Edward and George Roebuck, being of the ages of 16 & 13 years, of the one part, and E. J. Bell, of the County Aforesaid, of the other part. Witnesseth: That the said Roebuck does by these presents bind out Edward & George Roebuck, of said County, as apprentices to said E. J. Bell in the trade or craft of house servants or as laborers upon the plantation of the said E. J. Bell, to be taught the said craft or trade of house servants or laborers, and to live with, continue, and serve the said E. J. Bell as apprentices from the date hereof for & during the term of twelve months.

During all of which time, said Dave Roebuck, as Aforesaid, doth Covenant with the said E. J. Bell that the said Edward & George Roebuck shall well & faithfully demean themselves as such faithful Apprentices, observing fully the Commands of the said E. J. Bell, and in all things Deporting themselves as such faithful Apprentices to the said E. J. Bell, neither revealing his secrets, nor at any time neglecting or leaving the business of the said E. J. Bell. And for & in consideration of the service well & faithfully rendered by the said Edward & George Roebuck, of the first part, said E. J. Bell, of the second part, doth Covenant, promise, & agree to instruct them, said Apprentices, or otherwise cause them to be well & faithfully instructed, in the said trade or craft of house servants or laborers, and shall also allow, furnish, & provide said apprentices with meat &

drink & clothing during the said term, and all other necessaries meet & proper, in sickness & in health.

Witness our hands & Seals the day & year first before written.

Executed before us }
in duplicate } Dave + Roebuck, his mark
Abda Oglesby } E. J. Bell
Geº L. Almond, Ordny }

Filed in Office & recorded July 1, 1896.

Geº L. Almond, Ordy

Duplicate [252]

Georgia }
Elbert County } This Indenture, made this the 17th day of July 1896, between W. J. Gaines, father, of said County, for and in behalf of Marian L. Gaines, being of the age of five years, of the one part, and B. B. Broadwell & wife, of the County aforesaid, of the other part. Witnesseth: That the said W. J. Gaines does by these presents bind out Marian L. Gaines, of said County, as apprentice to said B. B. Broadwell & wife in the trade or craft of house servant or as laborer upon the plantation of the said B. B. Broadwell & wife, to be taught the said craft or trade of house servant or laborer, & to live with, continue, & serve the said B. B. Broadwell & wife as apprentices from the date hereof for and during the term of sixteen years.

During all of which time, said [blot] W. J. Gaines doth Covenant with the said B. B. Broadwell & wife that the said Marian L. Gaines shall well & faithfully Demean himself as such faithful apprentice, observing fully the commands of the said B. B. Broadwell & wife, and in all things deporting & behaving himself as such faithful apprentice to the said B. B. Broadwell & wife, neither revealing his secrets, nor at any time neglecting or leaving the business of the said B. B. Broadwell & wife.

And for and in consideration of the service well & faithfully rendered by the said Marian L. Gaines, of the first part, said B. B. Broadwell & wife, of the second part, doth covenant, promise, & agree to instruct his said apprentice, or otherwise cause him to be well & faithfully instructed, in the said trade or craft of house servant or laborer, and shall also allow, furnish, & provide him, said apprentice, with meat & drink & clothing during the said term, and all other necessaries meet & proper, in sickness and in health.

Witness our hands & seals the day & year first before written.

Executed before us }   W. J. Gaines
in duplicate   }   B. B. Broadwell
J. T. Taylor   }   E. E. Broadwell
J. M. Taylor, J. P. }

Filed in Office & recorded July 21, 1896.

Ge° L. Almond, Ordy

Duplicate [253]

Georgia   }
Elbert County } This Indenture, made and entered into this 12th day of June 1896, between Ja^s B. Thornton, of Hart County, and William J. Gaines of Elbert County, the father of Benjamin Franklin Gaines, now aged 2 years & 6 months, all of said County. Witnesseth: that the said W. J. Gaines hereby binds and apprentices to the said J. B. Thornton the said B. F. Gaines until the said B. F. Gaines is twenty one years old, under the following terms. Said Ja^s B. Thornton Agrees to take into his custody said B. F. Gaines, teach him the business of husbandry, furnish him with protection, wholesome food, suitable clothing, necessary medicine and medical attention, teach him the habits of industry, honesty, and morality, cause him to be taught the elementary principles of mathematics and to read English, and shall govern him with humanity, using only the same degree of force to compel his obedience as a father may use with his minor child. and when the said B. F. Gaines shall arrive at the age of twenty one, he is to receive from the said Ja^s B. Thornton one hundred dollars cash. In consideration of all of which, said Ja^s B. Thornton is to be entitled to the services and earning of said B. F. Gaines until he is twenty one years old.

Witness our hands and seals this June the 12th 1896.

Signed, sealed, & delivered }
in presence of   }
B. L. Adams   }   J. B. Thornton
W. A. Craft, J. P.   }   W. J. Gaines

Filed in office and recorded Sep^t 21, 1896.

Ge° L. Almond, Ordiny

Duplicate [254]

Georgia }
Elbert County } This Indenture, made the 28th 1896, between Joe Holly, father, of said County, for and in behalf of Early Holly, being of the age of 15 years, of the one part, and E. J. Bell, of the County aforesaid, of the other part. witnesseth: That the said Joe Holly does by these presents bind out Early Holly, of said County, as apprentice to said E. J. Bell in the trade or craft of house servant or as laborer upon the plantation of the said E. J. Bell, to be taught the said craft or trade of house servant or laborer, and to live with, continue, & serve the said E. J. Bell as apprentice from the date hereof for and during the term of two years.

During all of which time, said Joe Holly doth covenant with the said E. J. Bell that the said Early Holly shall well & faithfully demean himself as such faithful Apprentice, observing fully the commands of the said E. J. Bell, and in all things deporting and behaving himself as such faithful apprentice to the said E. J. Bell, neither revealing his secrets, nor at any time neglecting or leaving the business of the said E. J. Bell.

And for and in consideration of the service well & faithfully rendered by the said Early Holly, of the first part, said E. J. Bell, of the second part, doth covenant, promise, & agree to instruct him, said apprentice, or otherwise cause him to be well & faithfully instructed, in the said trade or craft of house servant or laborer, and shall also allow, furnish, & provide him, said apprentice, with meat & drink & clothing during the said term, and all other necessaries meet & proper, in sickness & in health.

Witness our hands & seals the day & year first before written.

Executed before us }
in duplicate }
B. B. Broadwell }
Ge° L. Almond, Ord }

Joe + Holly, his mark
E. J. Bell

Filed in Office & recorded Sept 29, 1896.

Ge° L. Almond, Ordy

Duplicate [255]

Georgia }
Elbert County } This Indenture, made this the 2nd day of January 1897, between Sarah Mattox, Mother, of said County, for and in behalf of her Minor son Reuben Toliver, being of the age of 17 years, on the one part, and L. H. A. Bell, of the County aforesaid, of the other part. Witnesseth: that the said Sarah Mattox, Mother as aforesaid, does by these presents bind out her minor son Reuben Toliver, of said County, as apprentice to said L. H. A. Bell in the trade or craft of Husbandry or as Laborer upon the plantation of the said L. H. A. Bell, to be taught the said craft or trade of Husbandry or laborer, and to live with, continue, and serve the said L. H. A. Bell as apprentice from the date hereof for and during the term of one year.

During all of which time, said Sarah Mattox, Mother as aforesaid, doth covenant with the said L. H. A. Bell that the said Reuben Toliver shall well and faithfully demean himself as, and in all things deporting and behaving himself as such faithful Apprentice to the said L. H. A. Bell, neither revealing his secrets, nor at any time neglecting or leaving the business of the said L. H. A. Bell. And for and in consideration of the service well and faithfully rendered by the said Reuben Toliver, of the first part, said L. H. A. Bell, of the second part, doth covenant, promise, and agree to instruct him, said apprentice, or otherwise cause him to be well and faithfully instructed, in the said trade or craft of Husbandry or laborer, and provide him, said Apprentice, with meat and drink during the said term, and shall also at the expiration of said term allow and pay the said Apprentice Fifty Dollars, which Sum may be paid during the term of service from time to time. Witness our hands and seals the day and year first before written. Executed Before us. The Mother agrees that the wages, except $6.75, may be paid by said Bell to the Minor.

R. M. Willis, Clerk }   Sarah X Mattox, her mark
Superior Court }   L. H. A. Bell
Acting Ordinary }

Filed Jany 2nd 1897.

R. M. Willis, Clerk acting Ordinary

[In the left hand margin, the clerk entered the following.]

just time for sickness or otherwise to be deducted from amt to be paid.

Duplicate [256]

Georgia }
Elbert County } This Indenture, made this the 27th day of January 1897, between Hal Mattox and E. J. Bell, both citizens of said County, witnesseth: that the said Hal Mattox, in consideration of promises and undertakings of the said E. J. Bell hereinafter set fourth, does hereby bind himself to the said E. J. Bell for the term of eleven months, commencing on the first day of February 1897 and ending the thirty first day of December 1897, and he hereby contracts and agrees with the said E. J. Bell to work faithfully under his directions, respect and obey all orders and commands of the said Bell with reference to the business hereinafter set forth at all times, & to demand himself orderly and soberly. And the said Hal Mattox further agrees to account to the said Bell for all lost time, except in cases of temporary sickness. And should this contract be terminated by the death of either of the parties to this indenture, then the compensation of the said Hal Mattox for the time of actual service. And the said E. J. Bell, in consideration of the promises and undertakings of the said Hal Mattox, agrees and contracts with the said Mattox to furnish him with the regular quantity of provisions per week that farm hands and laborers receive. He further agrees to pay the said Mattox seventy two dollars for the term herein specified, the same to be paid monthly as follows, Eight dollars per month for the months of February, March, and April, and six dollars per month for the remaining months. And he further agrees to teach the said Mattox the trade of a farmer in all its details. In witness whereof, the said Hal Mattox and the said E. J. Bell have hereunto respectively set their hands and affixed their seals the day and year first above written. Executed in duplicate in the presence of

J. Ben Almond
R. M. Willis, Clerk
Superior Court
acting Ordinary

Ed Bell
Hal X Mattox, his mark

Recorded Feby 27th 1897.

R. M. Willis, Clk
Acting Ordinary

Duplicate [257]

Georgia }
Elbert County } This Indenture, made this the 23rd day of November 1896, between Delia Ann Pass, said County, for and in behalf of Fannie Hughes, being

of the age of nine years, on the one part, and P. B. Butler, of the County aforesaid, of the other part. Witnesseth: that the said Delia Ann Pass, as aforesaid, does by these presents bind out Fannie Hughes, of said County, as Apprentice to said P. B. Butler in the trade or craft of house servant or as Laborer upon the plantation of the said P. B. Butler, to be taught the said craft or trade of house servant or laborer, and to live with, continue, and serve the said P. B. Butler as apprentice from the date hereof for and during the term of twelve years. During all of which time, said Delia Ann Pass, as aforesaid, doth covenant with the said P. B. Butler that the said Fannie Hughes shall well and faithfully demean herself as such faithful apprentice, observing fully the commands of the said P. B. Butler, and in all things deporting and behaving herself as a faithful apprentice to the said P. B. Butler, neither revealing his secrets, nor at any time neglecting or leaving the business of the said P. B. Butler.

And for and in consideration of the service well and faithfully rendered by the said Fannie Hughes, of the first part, said P. B. Butler, of the second part, doth covenant, promise, and agree to instruct her, the said apprentice, or otherwise cause her to be well and faithfully instructed, in the said trade or craft of house servant or laborer, and also to read the English language, and shall also allow, furnish, and provide her, the said apprentice, with meat and drink and clothing during the said term, and all other necessaries meet and proper, in sickness and in health. Witness our hands and seals the day and year first before written.

Executed before us. signed in duplicate.

Z. B. Rogers	}	Delia Ann X Pass, her mark
R. M. Willis, Clerk	}	P. B. Butler
Elbert Sup[r] Court	}	

Recorded Feb[y] 27th 1897.

R. M. Willis, CSC. acting Ordinary

Duplicate [258]

Georgia }
Elbert County } This Indenture, made this the 29th day of January 1897, between P. P. Proffitt, Judge City Court of Elberton, said County, for and in behalf of Charles Christly, being of the age of 5 years, of the one part, and H. M. Seymore, of the County aforesaid, of the other part. Witnesseth: that the said P. P. Proffitt, Judge as aforesaid, does by these presents bind out Charles Chrisly, of said County, as apprentice to said H. M. Seymore in the trade or craft of or as Laborer

upon the plantation of the said H. M. Seymore, to be taught the said craft or trade of laborer, and to live with, continue, and serve the said H. M. Seymore as apprentice from the date hereof for and during the term of minority. During all of which time, said P. P. Proffitt, Judge as aforesaid, doth covenant with the said H. M. Seymore that the said Charles Chrisly shall well and faithfully demean himself as such faithful Apprentice, observing fully the commands of the said H. M. Seymore, and in all things deporting and behaving himself as a faithful Apprentice to the said H. M. Seymore, neither revealing his secrets, nor at any time neglecting or leaving the business of the said H. M. Seymore.

And for and in consideration of the service well and faithfully rendered by the said Charles Chrisly, of the first part, said H. M. Seymore, of the second part, doth covenant, promise, and agree to instruct his said apprentice, or otherwise cause him to be well and faithfully instructed, in the said trade or craft of labor, and also to read the English language, and shall also allow, furnish, and provide his said Apprentice with meat and drink and clothing during the said term, and all other necessaries meet and proper, in sickness and in health, and shall also at the expiration of said term allow and pay the said Apprentice what is now allowed by the statute in such case made and provided.

Witness our hands and seals the day and year first before written.

Executed before us.

H. J. Brewer	}	P. P. Proffitt
R. M. Willis, Clerk	}	Judge C. C. C. Elberton
Sup^r Court E. C.	}	H. M. Seymore

Filed in office January 29, 1897. Recorded Feby 27th 1897.

R. M. Willis, CSC. acting Ordinary

Duplicate [259]

Georgia }
Elbert County } This Indenture, made this the 27th day of February 1897, between Mandy Wilhite, of said County, for and in behalf of Mid Brown, her Son, being of the age of 16 years, of the one part, and J. E. Herndon, of the County aforesaid, of the other part. Witnesseth: that the said Mandy Wilhite, as aforesaid, does by these presents bind out Mid Brown, of said County, as Apprentice to said J. E. Herndon in the trade or craft of Servant as a Laborer upon the plantation of the said J. E. Herndon, to be taught the said craft or trade of Servant or laborer,

and to live with, continue, and serve the said J. E. Herndon as apprentice from the date hereof for and during the term of five years. During all of which time, said Mandy Wilhite, as aforesaid, doth covenant with the said J. E. Herndon that the said Mid Brown shall well and faithfully demean himself as such faithful apprentice, observing fully the commands of the said J. E. Herndon, and in all things deporting and behaving himself as a faithful apprentice to the said J. E. Herndon, neither revealing his secrets, nor at any time neglecting or leaving the business of the said J. E. Herndon. And for and in consideration of the service well and faithfully rendered by the said Mid Brown, of the first part, said J. E. Herndon, of the second part, doth covenant, promise, and agree to instruct his said apprentice, or otherwise cause him to be well and faithfully instructed, in the said trade or craft of Servant or laborer, and also to read the English language, and shall also allow, furnish, and provide his said Apprentice, with meat and drink and clothing during the said term, and all other necessaries meet and proper, in sickness and in health, and shall also at the expiration of the said term allow and pay the said Apprentice what is now allowed by the statute in such case made and provided.

Witness our hands and seals the day and year first before written.

Executed before us.

H. J. Brewer	}	Mandy X Wilhite, her mark
R. M. Willis, Clerk	}	J. E. Herndon
Superior Court	}	

Filed in office February 27, 1897.

R. M. Willis, Clerk

This is unsworn.

Filed in office March 2, 1897.

Ja^s J. Burch, Ordinary

Duplicate [260]

Georgia }
Elbert County } This Indenture, made this them third day of March in the year of Our Lord 1897, between Alford Smith and J. Bowshoff, both od Said County. Witnesseth: That the Said Alford Smith, for and in consideration of promises and undertakings of the Said J. Bowshoff hereinafter set forth, does hereby bind

himself to the said J. Bowshoff [illegible] working faithfully under his direction, respect and obey all orders and commands of the said Bowshoff with reference to the business hereinafter set forth, and at all times demean himself orderly and soberly. And the said Alford Smith further agrees to account to the said Bowshoff for all lost time, except in cases of temporary sickness. If such sickness should be of longer duration at any one time that six days, then such lost time is to be accounted for at the same rate per day as he is then receiving pay under this contract. And should this Contract be terminated by the death of either party to this indenture, then the Compensation of the said Alford Smith shall be pro rata for the time completed in the year in which the death may occur. And the said J. Bowshoff, in consideration of the promises and undertakings of the said Alford Smith, agrees and contracts with the said Smith to furnish him with board, lodging, and every day necessary apparel and washing. He further agrees to pay the Said Smith the sum of fifty dollars, which sum shall be paid over to the said Smith upon the termination of this contract. An any amount of money that the said Smith may be owing the said Bowshoff when double payment is to be made. And he further agrees to teach, or cause to be taught, the Said Smith the trade of a tailor.

In witness whereof, both the parties hereto have hereunto set their hands and affixed their Seals. Executed in duplicate in the presence of

H. J. Brewer   }   Alford Smith
Abda Oglesby, J. P. }   J. Bowshoff

Received in office March 3rd 1897.

Ja^s J. Burch, Ord

Duplicate   [261]

Georgia   }
Elbert County } This Indenture, made this the 2nd day of March 1897, between Jake Almond, of said County, for and in behalf of his minor sons Tom and Alfred, being of the age of Tom 19 & Alfred 17 years, of the one part, and John C. Hudgens, of the County aforesaid, of the other part. Witnesseth: that the said Jake Almond, as aforesaid, does by these presents bind out his said sons Tom & Alfred, of Said County, as Apprentice to Said John C. Hudgens in the trade or craft of Servants as Laborers upon the plantation of the said John C. Hudgens, to be taught the said craft or trade of Servant or laborer, and to live with, continue, and serve the said John C. Hudgens as an Apprentice from the date hereof for and during the term of their Minority. During all of which time, said Jake Almond, aforesaid,

doth covenant with the said John C. Hudgens that the said Tom & Alfred shall well and faithfully demean themselves as such faithful Apprentices, observing fully the commands of the said John C. Hudgens, and in all things deporting and behaving Themselves as a faithful Apprentices to the said John C. Hudgens, neither revealing his secrets, nor at any time neglecting or leaving the business of the said John C. Hudgens.

And for and in consideration of the service well and faithfully rendered by the said Tom and Alfred, of the first part, said John C. Hudgens, of the second part, doth covenant, promise, and agree to instruct his said Apprentices, or otherwise cause them to be well and faithfully instructed, in the said trade or craft of Servant or laborer, and also to read the English language, and shall also allow, furnish, and provide his said Apprentices with meat and drink and clothing during the said term, and all other necessaries meet and proper, in sickness and in health, and shall also at the expiration of the Said term allow and pay the said Apprentices what is now allowed by the statute in such cases made and provided.

Witness our hands and seals the day and year first before written.

Executed before us.

| H. J. Brewer } | Jake + Almond, his mark |
| Ja^s J. Burch, ordinary } | John C. Hudgens |

Recorded in Office March 2nd 1897.

Ja^s J. Burch, Ordinary

Duplicate [262]

Georgia }
Elbert County } This Indenture, made and entered into this 10th day of March in the year of our Lord eighteen hundred and ninety seven, between James Y. Swift and Elijah McIntosh, the father of Robert McIntosh, aged fifteen years, all of said County. Witnesseth: That the said Elijah hereby binds and apprentices to the said James Y. Swift the said Robert from this date to the 25th day of December 1898 upon the following terms. Said Swift agrees to take into his custody the said Robert, to furnish him with protection, wholesome food, suitable clothing, necessary medicine and medical attention, & to teach him the business of husbandry, teach him habits of industry, morality, and honesty, and shall govern him with humanity, using only the Same degree of force to compel his obedience as a father may use with his minor Child. and when said term of service shall

have ended, to pay the father of said Robert the sum of one hundred and seven and $^{50}/_{100}$ dollars in money or its equivalent. In Consideration of all of which, the said James Y. Swift is to be entitled to the services of the said Robert for the period of time herein specified. Witness our hands and seals This 10th day of March 1897.

Sealed, signed, and delivered in the presence of

C. P. Harris   Elijah + McIntosh, his mark
Ja^s J. Burch, Ordinary   James Y. Swift

Recorded in office in March 11th 1897.

Ja^s J. Burch, Ordinary

Duplicate   [263]

Georgia }
Elbert County } This Indenture, made this the 12th day of March 1897, between Joe Carter, Father, of said County, for and in behalf of his minor children, Mat Carter, ham Carter, and Rosa Lee Carter, being of the age of 12, 14, and 8 years, of the one part, and George H. McLanahan, of the County aforesaid, of the other part. Witnesseth: that the said Joe Carter, Father as aforesaid, does by these presents bind out said minor children, of Said County, as Apprentices to Said George H. McLanahan in the trade or craft of Husbandry or as laborers upon the plantation of the said George H. McLanahan, to be taught the said craft or trade of Husbandry or laborer, and to live with, continue, and serve the said George H. McLanahan as an Apprentice from the date hereof for and until their Majority.

During all of which time, Said Joe Carter, Father as aforesaid, doth covenant with the said George H. McLanahan that the said minor children shall well and faithfully demean their selfs as such faithful Apprentices, observing fully the commands of the said George H. McLanahan, And in all things deporting and behaving their self as a faithful Apprentice to the said George H. McLanahan, neither revealing his secrets, nor at any time neglecting or leaving the business of the said George H. McLanahan. And for and in Consideration of the services well and faithfully rendered by the said Minor Children and Joe Carter, of the first part, said George H. McLanahan, of the second part, doth covenant, promise, and agree to instruct his said Apprentices, or otherwise cause them to be well and faithfully instructed, in the said trade or craft of Husbandry or laborer, and also to read the English language, and shall also allow, furnish, and provide his said Apprentices with meat & drink and clothing during the said term, and all other necessaries meet and proper, in sickness and in health, and shall also at the expiration of the Said term allow and pay the said Apprentices what is now allowed by the statute in such cases made & provided. Witness our hands & seals the day & year first before written.

Executed before us March 12, 1897.

over

Ja^s J. Burch, ordinary	Joe + Carter, his mark	[264]
Thos B. Smith	George H. McLanahan	

Recorded in office March 12, 1897.

Ja^s J. Burch, Ordinary

Georgia }
Elbert County } This Indenture, made this the 13th day of January 1897, between P. P. Proffitt, Judge of City Court Elberton, of said County, for and in behalf of Asa B. Chrisly, being of the age of 10 years, of the one part, and D. G. Seymore, of the County aforesaid, of the other part. Witnesseth: That the said P. P. Proffitt, Judge aforesaid, does by these presents bind out Asa B. Chrisly, of said County, as Apprentice to Said D. G. Seymore in the trade or craft of Labor upon the plantation of the said D. G. Seymore, to be taught the said craft or trade of labor, and to live with, continue, and serve the said D. G. Seymore as an Apprentice from the date hereof for and during the term of his Minority. During all of which time, said P. P. Proffitt, Judge as aforesaid, doth covenant with the said D. G. Seymore that the said Asa B. Chrisly shall well and faithfully demean himself as such faithfully Apprentice, observing fully the commands of the said D. G. Seymore, and in all things deporting and behaving himself as a faithful Apprentice to the said D. G. Seymore, neither revealing his secrets, nor at any time neglecting or leaving the business of the said D. G. Seymore.

And for and in consideration of the service well and faithfully rendered by the said Asa B. Chrisly, of the first part, said D. G. Seymore, of the second part, doth covenant, promise, and agree to instruct his said Apprentice, or otherwise cause him to be well and faithfully instructed, in the said trade or craft of labor, and also to read the English language, and shall also allow, furnish, and provide his said Apprentice with meat and drink and clothing during the said term, and all other necessaries meet and proper, in sickness and in health, and shall also at the expiration of the Said term

allow and pay the said Apprentice what is now allowed by the statute in   [265]
such case made and provided.

Witness our hands and seals the day and year first before written.

Executed before us   }
H. J. Brewer   }   P. P. Proffitt
R. M. Willis, Clerk   }   Judge City Court Elberton
Sup^t Court   }   D. G. Seymore

Filed in office Jany 13, 1897.

R. M. Willis, Clerk

Georgia   }   [266]
Elbert County   } This Indenture, made and entered into this the 17th day of May in the year of our Lord eighteen hundred and ninety Seven, between J. H. Jones & Company, a partnership composed of J. H. Jones and W. O. Jones, of the one part, and George Biggs, col, the father of Stephen Biggs aged 19 years, William Biggs aged 18 years, and James Biggs aged 17 years, and George Biggs, jr aged 15 years, of the other part. Witnesseth: That the said George Biggs hereby binds and apprentices to the said J. H. Jones & Co the said Stephen Biggs, William Biggs, and James Biggs, and George Biggs, jr until they each shall become twenty one years of age, upon the following terms. Said J. H. Jones & Co agrees to take into their Custody Said Stephen Biggs, William Biggs, and James Biggs, and George Biggs, jr to teach them the business of husbandry, furnish them with protection, wholesome food, Suitable clothing, necessary medicine and medical attention, teach them habits of industry, honesty, and morality, Cause them to be taught the elementary principles of Mathematics and to read English, and shall govern them with humanity, using only the Same degree of force to compel their obedience as a father may use with his minor children, and when Said Stephen, William, and James arrive at the age of twenty years each Respectively, they are to be rewarded for as by law in such case provided. In Consideration of all of which, the said J. H. Jones & Co are to be entitled to the services of the Said Stephen, William, and James until they each Shall become twenty one years of age. Witness our hands and seals the day and year above written.

Signed, sealed, and delivered in the presence of

H. F. Snelling   J. H. Jones & Co
Ben^j H. Kay   George + Biggs, his mark
Executed in Duplicate

Index

—
Alice, 114
Annie, 106
Fannie, 106
Gertrude, 166
Gordon, 58
Marshall, 47
Mary, 4
Mary Margaret, 99
Mary Margret, 99
Rachel, 106
Sarah, 106
Tom Joe, 113
Adams, 44, 45
  A. F., 146
  Ann, 156
  B. L., 194
  E. S., 44, 45
  W. B., 77, 129, 130, 133, 134
  W. W., 186
Alexander, 141, 142
  Alice, 142
  D. B., 32, 55, 80, 92, 183
  Essie, 142
  Isaac, 142
  J. L., 76
  John, 76
  Laura, 141
  Lonnie, 142
  Luma, 142
  Mary L., 76
  Roda, 76
  Sid, 142, 143, 144
  Sidney, 141, 142, 144
  Ticorn, 98
  William, 76

Allen
  C. H., 189
  Charles H., 189
  Chas. H., 189
  Ezra, 143
  Moriah, 72, 73
  Thomas, 181
  Thos., 181, 182
  Tom, 181
Almond, 46
  Alfred, 119, 120, 201, 202
  Berry, 69, 70
  Cosby, 69
  Elbert, 119, 120
  Geo. L., 37, 38, 39, 40, 41, 42, 43,
    44, 45, 46, 47, 48, 49, 50, 51,
    52, 53, 54, 55, 56, 57, 58, 59,
    60, 61, 62, 63, 64, 65, 66, 67,
    68, 69, 70, 71, 72, 73, 74, 75,
    76, 77, 78, 79, 80, 81, 82, 83,
    84, 85, 86, 87, 88, 89, 90, 91,
    92, 93, 94, 96, 97, 99, 100, 101,
    102, 103, 104, 105, 106, 107,
    108, 109, 110, 112, 113, 114,
    115, 116, 117, 118, 119, 120,
    121, 122, 123, 124, 125, 126,
    127, 128, 129, 130, 131, 132,
    133, 134, 135, 136, 137, 138,
    139, 140, 141, 142, 143, 144,
    145, 146, 147, 148, 149, 150,
    151, 152, 153, 154, 155, 156,
    157, 158, 159, 160, 161, 162,
    163, 164, 165, 166, 167, 168,
    169, 170, 171, 172, 173, 174,
    175, 176, 177, 178, 179, 180,
    181, 182, 183, 184, 185, 186,

187, 188, 189, 190, 191, 192,
193, 194, 195
J. Ben, 197
Jacob, 119, 120
Jake, 201, 202
John, 69
Tom, 119, 120, 201, 202
Winnie, 146
Anderson
J. E., 68
Andrew, 29
Geo. L., 96
J. A., 5, 6, 7, 8, 11, 12, 13, 14, 15,
16, 17, 18, 19, 20, 21, 22, 23,
24, 25, 26, 27, 28, 29, 30, 32,
33, 34, 35, 36, 37, 96
James A., 8, 9, 10, 11, 12, 14, 15,
16, 17, 18, 19, 20, 21, 24, 25,
26, 28, 31, 32, 33, 34, 35, 36
Arnold, 79, 80
McAlpin, 79
W. T., 72, 73, 75
Ashworth
Mary A. A. E., 27
Mary A. A. E. A., 27
Sarah J., 27
Bailey
Ezekiah, 5, 34
Baily
Ezekiah, 37, 38
J. P., 75, 76
Baity
N. L., 164
Banks
Abraham, 149
Eunice, 149
York, 149
Barkesdale
M. C., 190, 191
Mary C., 191

Barnett
J. S., 40, 43
Bell, 197
Bessie, 76
Catherine, 76
E. J., 156, 192, 193, 195, 197
E. W., 8, 9
Easter, 138, 139
Ed, 197
Enoch W., 8
Henry, 76
L. H. A., 196
Lizzie, 138, 139
Lucy, 76
Mary, 138
Victor, 77
Victoria, 76, 77
Willie, 76
Zanie, 75
Biggs
George, 205
George, Jr., 205
James, 205
Stephen, 205
William, 205
Blackwell, 186
Anna, 132
Annie, 100
Calvin, 72
Chan, 125
Charity, 132, 133, 134
Charlotte, 117
Dougherty, 117
Dunstan, 161
Dunston, 63
Elijah, 132, 133, 134
Elizabeth, 113, 114
Ephram, 159
Henry, 63, 64, 161, 162
James, 63

Jesse, 132
Jessie, 100
John, 63
Judge, 124, 125
Lavinia, 117
Lena, 100
Lige, 100, 101
Lina, 100, 132
Lins, 117
Lonhannah, 117
Lucy, 126
Lula, 132
Martha, 185, 186
Mattie, 125
Mollie, 124, 125
Nathan, 117
Oliver, 159, 160
William, 152, 159, 175
Wm., 175
Bohannan
  James T., 42
  Jas. T., 43
Bond
  A. J., 22
  J. R. E., 31
  L. A., 58, 59, 71, 72, 84
Booth
  J. J., 98, 99, 111
Bourne
  George, 115
  Sam, 115, 116
  Wesley, 115
Bowman, 186
  Alice, 110
  Dora, 164, 165
  Esau, 110
  Eugene, 154, 155, 175, 176
  George, 110
  Ida, 110
  Jim, 153, 154

John, 110
Lewellen, 140
Lewellyn, 186
Llewellen, 140
Louellen, 140
Osborn, 110
Oss, 109, 110
Sam, 115
T. J., 24
Walton, 110
Bowshoff, 201
  J., 200, 201
Brawner
  Eliza, 23
  Frances, 182
  Georgia, 23
  James, 21
  Joe, 149, 150
  John, 85, 86, 90, 149, 150
  Lela, 182
  Lula, 182
  Mid, 90, 91, 149, 150, 182, 183
Brewer, 159, 160
  Fred, 129, 130
  H. J., 81, 82, 86, 94, 158, 159, 164, 184, 199, 200, 201, 202, 205
  Heilly, 129
  Hilly, 130
  John M., 69
  Katie, 129, 130
  S. S., 160, 161, 190
  Sallie, 129, 130
  Sherman, 129, 130
Broadwell
  B. B., 193, 194, 195
  E. E., 194
Brown
  A. J., 96
  Fannie Sophia, 17

George, 13, 14
H. J., 77
J. H. B., 93
Jno. C., 112, 188
John C., 188
Mid, 199, 200
N. M., 6, 7
R. J., 10
Rolan J., 9, 10
W. T. M., 93
William M., 33
Brownlee
  W. T., 186
Bryan
  Jasper, 89, 90, 98, 110, 111
  W. C., 98, 99, 111
Bullard
  Fannie, 104, 105
  Jesse, 104
Burch
  Dorcas, 38, 39
  Dorcas A., 32
  Jas. J., 200, 201, 202, 203, 204
Burton
  Dillie, 168, 169
Butler
  P. B., 198
Cade
  Mary Jane, 130, 131
  Sing, 130
Campbell, 45, 49, 50
  J. E., 39, 40
  T. J., 153, 154, 155
  Thom, 46
  Thomas, 45, 46, 49, 50
  Thomas, 46
  Thos. J., 67
Carlton
  Thos. C., 48
Carpenter

  S. N., 21, 26, 43
Carson
  Leola, 120
  Marie Lou, 120
  Pat, 120, 121
  Ruddie, 120
  Sallie, 120
  Sindy, 120
  Thos., 120
Carter
  Allen, 79, 80
  Bob, 187
  Ham, 203
  Joe, 203, 204
  Louise, 79
  Martha, 187
  Mat, 203
  Paul, 79
  Robert, 187
  Rosa Lee, 203
  S. L., 120, 161, 165
  Sarah, 28, 29
  Thos. Parks, 187
Cary
  W. H., 80, 81, 82
Chandler
  J. J., 117, 119, 123, 126, 138, 147, 148, 150, 152, 168, 170, 174, 185
  J. J. J., 172
  James P., 171
  T. A., 21
Chrisly
  Asa B., 204
  Charles, 199
Christian
  City, 7, 8
  Dick, 64, 65, 66, 87, 88
  Georgia, 36, 78
  James, 170, 171

Janie, 78, 80, 82
Jimmie, 81
Jinnie, 78
Jno., 107
John, 107
John H., 87
John Henry, 65
Leanna, 39, 40
Mary, 36
Mary, Jr., 35
Mary, Sr., 35
Russel, 170, 171
Russell, 78, 79, 80, 81, 82
S. M. F., 109
Sam, 64
Stephen, 35, 36, 109
Christly
  Charles, 198
Clark
  Elizabeth, 48
  Gabe, 85
  Lizzie, 28, 29
  Moses, 48
  Robert, 74
  Robt., 74
  Sam, 74, 75
  Wiley, 48
  Wyley, 48
  York, 85
Cleveland
  A. J., 33, 34
  Andrew J., 33
  Della, 85, 86
  F. B., 34
Collins
  Willie, 164
Cordell
  T. J., 83
Craft
  W. A., 194

Craig
  John H., 180
Daniel, 4
  A. C., 4
  Allen, 31
  Allen C., 4
  Allen, Jr., 31
  Allen, Sr., 31
  John G., 30
  Robert, 4
  Robert, 4
  Voges, 30, 31
  Vorges, 31
  W. R., 30, 31
Davis, 44
  J. W., 44
  Jefferson, 14, 15
  W. T., 19, 22
  William T., 10, 11, 19
  Wm. T., 19
Deadwyler, 44
  J. L., 78
  Madison M., 44
  Madison Marcus, 44
  Mat, 55
  Mit, 55
  Mitt, 44
Derrett
  Eliza, 56
Dickerson
  David, 7
  Fill, 6
  J. M., 173
  Rebecca J., 173
  Wade, 6, 7
Dixon
  Elizabeth, 25
Downer
  Alex, 146
  Oscar, 146

DuBose
  Bessie Bell, 192
  J. D., 192
Dunbar
  Ada, 93
  J. J., 93
Duncan
  Janes, 94
  Lony, 94
  Samantha, 94
  W. T., 127, 128
Dye
  George, 17, 18
  J. J., 89, 92
Earl
  C. E., 83
Earle
  C. E., 83
Eberhart
  Allen, 150, 151
  Biggs, 150, 151
  Bob, 16
  Bunk, 174
  Freeman, 150, 151
  Gussie, 92
  James, 88
  Jane, 88, 89, 92
  Louisa, 88
Edwards
  L. C., 151, 159
  T. C., 93
  W. H., 4
Eldridge, 52
  Frances, 52, 53
  Henry, 52, 53
Ellenburge
  John, 25
Ellis
  Adaline, 148
  Charles, 147

Hase, 147
Hayes, 147, 148
Fleming
  Charlotte, 116, 144, 145
  Josephine, 116
  May Liza, 116
  Missouri, 116
  Russel, 116
  Willis, 116
Flemming
  D. R., 97
Forly
  Henly, 180
Fortson, 22, 178
  Addie, 137, 138
  Asa C., 22
  Belian, 188
  Claudia, 131, 132
  Geo. T., 92
  Hughy, 180, 188
  Jimmie, 137
  Lizzie, 168, 169
  Mary, 168
  Robert, 177, 178
  Sam, 39
  Susan R., 32
  Thomas J., 29, 30
  Thos. J., 29
  W., 177
  William, 177, 178
  Willis, 180, 181, 188
Fuller
  James J., 15, 16
Gaines
  B. F., 194
  Jack, 10
  Marian L., 193
  W. J., 193, 194
  William J., 194
Gairdner, 79, 80

H. K., 79
Goss, 59
  H. J., 5, 27
  J. W., 31
  Junius, 59
  Pauline, 59, 60
Gray
  Alexander, 89, 90, 98, 110, 111
  Amanda, 104
  Douglass, 169, 170
  Douglass, Jr., 169
  Earnest, 89
  Elie, 157
  Geo., 104
  George, 104, 172
  Gilbert, 141
  Henry T., 22
  James, 169
  John, 169
  John Price, 104
  Lindsey, 157
  Lindsy, 158
  Louisa, 34, 35
  Mary, 104, 169
  Nancy, 98, 111
  Price, 157
  Rese, 22
  Richmond, 169
  Sam, 169
  Sarah, 103, 104, 157, 158
  Saul, 157
  Savannah, 169, 170
  Ticorn, 110, 111
  Toccoa, 34, 35
  Violet, 169
  William, 169
Greenway
  Caroline, 37, 38
  Mary Jane, 37
  Wade Hampton, 38

Griffin
  James, 96
  William, 96
  Wm., 96, 97
  Wm., Jr., 97
Grimes
  Fannie, 66, 86, 87
  Francis, 70
  Jack, 66
  Julia, 67, 70, 86, 87
  Lewis, 66, 67, 68, 70, 71, 86, 87
Grogan
  John H., 5
  Louisa, 5
  Wm. M., 65
Gunter
  Anderson, 32, 33
Ham
  Harrison, 29, 30
  John, 29, 30
  Wesley, 29, 30
Harper
  A. O., 101, 102
  Frank, 38
  Georgia, 36, 82
  J. M., 119
  Mary Alice Cornelia, 32
  Mary E. A. C., 32
Harris
  Betsey, 61
  Betsy, 61
  C. P., 203
  Felix, 61
  John Henry, 62, 63
  Martha, 183, 184
  Rosa Lee, 183
  Tom, 61, 62, 63
Harrison
  Betsy, 62
  Felix, 62

Haslett
  W. M., 11, 12, 19, 33
  William M., 32, 33
  Wm. M., 32
Hatter
  Mary, 46
Hawes, 49
  P. M., 49, 150, 151, 180, 181
  Peyton M., 171
  S. O., 175, 176
Hawse
  P. M., 172
Haygood
  George, 60
  George, Jr., 60, 61
  George, Sr., 60, 61
Heard
  B. H., 133, 134, 160
  Bedford H., 132, 133, 134
  Harriett, 83
  L. M., 183
  Levi, 123, 124
  Susie, 83
Hendricks
  W. B., 71
Henry
  Harriet, 20
  Jacob, 20
  Lucy, 7, 8
  Martha, 7, 8
  O. L., 35
  Overton L., 34
  W. B., 8, 105, 156
Herndon
  G. M., 129
  J. E., 128, 129, 199, 200
Hester
  Addie, 68, 69
  Robert, 18
  Robt., 28

  Tho. J., 102
  Thos. J., 73, 132
Hill, 135
  George, 135
  Henry, 135
  Jackson, 135
  Janie, 135
  Richard, 135
  Washington, 95
  William, 95
  Wm., 95
Holly
  Early, 195
  Joe, 195
Howard
  Jane, 63, 64
Hudgens
  A. J., 178
  J. C., 62, 63, 91, 92, 150, 177, 178
  Jno. C., 23, 61
  John C., 61, 62, 63, 90, 149, 150, 177, 201, 202
Hudgins
  J. C., 23
  John C., 23
Hudson
  Jane, 75, 76
Hughes
  Fannie, 197, 198
Hulme
  George W., 14
  John, 19
  Loucinda, 13, 14
  Oliver, 11, 12
  Wilson, 10, 11
Humble
  Edwin, 47
Humbles, 45
  City, 45, 50
  Dunston, 45

Edwin, 41, 46
Frank, 41, 42, 45, 46
Johnny, 46
Scoot, 41
Scott, 45
Hunter
  Ellen, 122, 123
Hutchison
  William, 27
  Wm., 27
Irvin
  W. H., 189
James
  John D., 20
Janes
  J. B., 164
  J. B., Jr., 95, 96, 99, 100, 103, 105, 106, 107, 108, 109, 110, 113, 114, 115, 116, 121, 122, 131, 136, 137, 139, 140, 141, 142, 143, 144, 145, 149, 155, 157, 158, 160, 172, 186
  J. B., Sr., 92, 176, 177
  T. S., 88, 89
  Thompson S., 88
Johnson, 50
  Julia, 50, 51
  William, 50, 51
  Willis, 50, 51
Jones, 51, 52, 53
  Eula, 191, 192
  Fannie, 57
  Francis, 28
  Harriett, 56, 57
  Henrietta, 51
  Henry, 49
  J. H., 205
  James, 8
  John J., 52, 53
  John Wesley, 51

John Wesly, 51
Lindsey, 49
Lindsy, 49
M. H., 30
M. R., 54
Martin R., 53
Mary, 49
Mary F., 53
Mary Frances, 53
Nathan, 28
R. H., 36
Rebecca, 49
Thomas S., 54, 55
Thos. S., 54
W. M., 124
W. O., 205
Jordan, 47
  Julia, 105, 106
  Rachel, 47
Kay
  Benj. H., 205
Kemper
  J. F., 106
Kend
  L. M., 181
Kimball
  Thomas, 47
  Thos., 46
Kimble
  Thom, 46
  Thomas, 46, 47
  Thos., 47
Land
  S. J., 88
Lewis
  D. W., 58, 59
Little
  A. J., 125
Lively
  Ida, 57, 58

Sarah C., 57, 58
Lofton
  Jep, 156
Lovinggood, 86, 87
  S. J., Jr., 86, 87
  S. J., Sr., 86, 87
Lumpkin
  Geo. B., 174
Maley, 51
  T. A. S., 51
Maly
  T. A. S., 51
Martin
  Lilla, 172
  Mary Jane, 172
Mathews, 49, 50
  W. J., 49
  Wm. J., 50
Mattox, 48, 86, 185, 197
  Amanda, 99, 142, 143
  Ammanda, 99
  Annie J., 74
  Asa, 131
  Augustus, 123
  Binx, 52
  C. M., 135, 136
  Clark, 23, 24, 26, 162, 163, 165, 166, 167, 168, 178
  Doc, 52
  Ella, 12, 13
  Georgia Ann, 114
  Guss, 122
  Hal, 197
  Harvey, 52
  Henry, 52
  J. R., 171
  Jincy, 166, 167
  King, 102, 103, 155
  Lewis, 52
  M., 23
  Oliver, 114, 115, 151, 152, 155
  Oscar, 114
  Pleasant, 18
  Robert, Jr., 139
  Robt., Jr., 139, 144, 145
  S. P., 74
  Sarah, 190, 196
  W. H., 18, 73, 74, 76, 77, 78, 79, 85, 86, 95, 185, 186
  William H., 12, 13, 18, 85
  Wilson, 122, 123, 124
  Wm. H., 13, 18, 48, 95
  Z. H. C., 24, 26
Maxwell
  J. O., 10
  James M., 14, 15
  Jane, 164, 165
  John M., 11, 12, 13
  W. P., 42
McCalla, 52, 58, 71, 84, 99, 100, 103, 105, 107, 108, 109, 110, 113, 114, 115, 116, 118, 120, 121, 135, 136, 139, 140, 141, 142, 143, 144, 145, 149, 155, 157, 158, 159, 160, 163
  Alaney, 103
  Beatrix, 103
  Elisha, 113, 141
  J. W., 58, 99, 100, 101, 103, 106, 113, 114, 115, 135, 140, 155
  Jno. H., 116, 157
  Jno. W., 47, 49, 52, 84, 85, 96, 99, 100, 103, 104, 105, 106, 107, 108, 109, 110, 113, 114, 115, 116, 118, 120, 121, 122, 124, 131, 133, 134, 135, 136, 137, 139, 140, 141, 142, 143, 144, 145, 149, 155, 157, 159, 160, 164, 170, 179, 180, 187
  John H., 116, 157, 158

John W., 58, 59, 71, 72, 84, 85,
   99, 100, 103, 107, 116, 142,
   144, 163, 169, 170, 179, 187
Peter, 113
McClanahan
   G. H., 162
   Geo. H., 161
McCraskey
   D. C., 35
McDuffee
   Arther, 33, 34
   Arthur, 33
   Larah, 34
   Larra, 33
McGehee
   Willis, 21
McIntosh, 136
   Alfred, 127, 128
   America, 43
   Anna, 127
   Ben, 136, 137
   Carry, 71
   Cornelia, 71, 72
   Elijah, 202, 203
   George, 127, 163
   Hannah, 163
   James, 148
   James M., 49
   Jas., 187
   Jno., 71
   Lace, 128, 163
   Lou, 71
   Luther, 71
   Mandy, 163, 164
   Mary, 127, 163
   May, 71
   Melis, 136
   Peter, 128, 163
   Robert, 202, 203
   Sarie, 136

Thomas, 128, 163
W. M., 14
William, 43, 127, 136, 163
McLanahan
   G. H., 169
   Geo. H., 182
   George H., 203, 204
Meriwether
   D., 95
Mewborn
   Asa J., 97
Mize
   J. L., 46
Moats
   Nevada, 42
Moore
   L. L., 57
   Mary E., 57, 58
Morrison, 58
   Addie, 68
   Anderson, 130, 131
   Andy, 85
   Ann, 44, 45, 56, 68, 69
   Chanie, 145
   Charles, 108
   Charlott, 141
   Chas., 108
   Dane, 141
   Dora, 179, 180
   Dunn, 108
   Ed, 58
   Eliza, 106, 179
   Frank, 186
   Geo., 102
   George, 102, 108
   Georgeann, 190, 191
   Gordon, 190, 191
   Grady, 190, 191
   Inda, 103
   Indiana, 102

216

James, 179
Janie, 190, 191
Jessie, 179
Jno. Henry, 108
Joe, 102, 190, 191
Julia, 58, 59
King, 102
Lem, 58, 59
Louie, 108
Mary Jane, 186
Mary Lou, 108
Mc, 103
Porter, 186
Robert, 190, 191
Robt., 191
Moss, 47
  John, 47
Nancy
  Nancy, 110
Oglesby
  Abda, 40, 187, 193, 201
  Ada L., 174
  D. P., 16, 17
  Drury P., 16
  Laura, 56, 57
  Laurah, 56
  Ransom, 158, 159
  Sarah, 158, 159
  Walton, 56, 57
Oliver
  A. S., 119, 120, 124, 125
Ozley
  Ida, 181, 182
Pass
  Carl, 128
  Delia Ann, 197, 198
  Edward, 128
  Janie, 128
  Liza, 128
  Mary, 128

  Rebecca, 128
  William, 128, 129
Penn
  N. J., 42
  Nary J., 41
  Nery J., 41
Proffitt
  P. P., 198, 199, 204, 205
Ray
  Dillard, 94
Reynolds
  J. M., 25
Richardson
  Dora, 131, 132, 166, 167, 184, 185
  Gertrude, 184
Robuck
  H. A., 28
Roebuck, 192
  Dave, 192, 193
  David, 6, 7
  Edward, 192
  George, 192
  H. A., 11, 12, 16, 17, 18, 19, 20, 33, 54, 55, 62, 63, 70, 162
  Henry A., 29
  Mit, 55
Rogers
  Z. B., 198
Rousey
  H. C., 182, 183
Rucker
  A. R., 37, 38
  Albert, 185
  Ben, 171
  Claiborn, 171, 172
  Ed, 171
  J. H., 179

J. W., 37, 38, 117, 126, 133, 134,
   151, 152, 153, 154, 155, 175,
   176
James H., 178
Jane, 171, 172
Jas. H., 178
Jos. W., 175, 176
Julian, 40
Robert, 171
Wm., 175
Sanders
   J. A., 9
Seymore
   D. G., 204, 205
   H. M., 198, 199
Shannan
   Jno. P., 107, 109
   John P., 107, 109
Shannon
   J. P., 17
   John P., 40
Shumate
   A. M., 133, 134
Smith, 137, 201
   Alford, 200, 201
   Henrietta, 137, 138
   J. J., 190
   Thos. B., 204
   Thos. M., 42
Snelling
   H. F., 205
Speed
   J. T., 100, 101
Stark
   Carrie, 101
   Martha J., 101
   Martha Jane, 101, 102
Starke
   E. B., 104, 105
Stovall

J. W., 179
Swearengine
   J. C., 188
Swift, 202
   James Y., 202, 203
   Thos. M., 6, 7
Tate, 44
   Charlotte, 191, 192
   E. A., 170, 171
   E. B., 139
   E. B., Jr., 5, 6, 7, 8, 13, 15, 17, 18
   Fannie, 191, 192
   John, 45, 56
   Josie, 91, 92
   Lula, 91
   Lulah, 91
   R. F., 81
Taylor
   J. F., 194
   J. M., 194
   Z. B., 84, 85, 99, 100, 101, 103,
      104, 105, 106, 108, 110, 113,
      114, 115, 116, 118, 121, 122,
      135, 136, 137, 139, 140, 142,
      144, 149, 172
Teasly
   Georgia A., 38, 39
Tenant
   Henraetta, 9
   Jane, 9, 10
Thompson
   Dick, 167, 168
   Esquire, 167
   Julius, 167
Thornton, 59
   Clark, 112
   D. W., 64, 65, 66, 69, 70
   Dan, 112
   Daniel, 160, 161
   Henry, 55, 59, 60

218

Ida, 112
J. B., 194
Jas. B., 194
Lula, 160
Melie, 112
Rona, 112
Toliver
  Reuben, 196
Trensard
  J. A., 4
Turman
  Reubin, 15, 16
Turner
  Aggie, 173
  Jack, 173
  John W., 16, 27
  R. A., 47
Upshaw, 183
  Rebecca C., 183, 184
  W. H., 112
Upson
  Joe, 165
  Neal, 165, 166
Vail
  Amos L., 4
Vanduzen
  I. C., 175, 176
Vanduzer
  William T., 29
  Wm. T., 9, 13, 14, 15, 18, 24, 25
Verdel
  Addie, 73, 118
  Ala, 118
  Albert, 118
  Charity, 121, 122
  Cleveland, 118
  Dock, 84
  Etta, 121
  Fannie, 118
  Geo., 73

George, 73, 118
Gip, 131
Gipson, 73, 74, 118, 131
Hugh, 84
Jane Ann, 84
John, 178, 179
Languire, 141
Lucy, 118
Mary Frances, 84
Willie, 121
Verdell
  Gipson, 118
Wall
  T. J., 177
Walton
  Fannie, 26
  Laura, 26
  Lena, 24
  Luther, 24
Warren
  D. H., 91
Washington
  Geo., 176, 177
  George, 176, 177
  John, 54
  William, 176, 177
Webb, 184
  A. G., 66, 67, 68, 70, 71, 87
  W. H. M., 184, 185
White, 50
  Anna, 119
  Henry, 119
  Ida, 119
  J. S., 127, 128
  Lula, 119
  M. E., 60, 61
  Sam, 119
  Steve, 130
  T. R., 50, 51, 60, 61, 75, 76
  Tinsley R., 50

Tinsly R., 76
Wm. J., 26
Wilhite
  Arda, 189
  Ardra, 189
  Frank, 189
  J. L., 65, 66, 87, 88
  Jno. L., 65
  John L., 65, 87
  Mandy, 199, 200
Wilkins
  Jack, 162
  Ryley, 162, 163

Williams, 72
  Henry, 71, 72
Willis
  R. M., 43, 55, 59, 90, 92, 99, 111, 130, 163, 166, 196, 197, 198, 199, 200, 205
Wootten
  Willie, 190
Worly
  Jas. L., 64
  Jos. N., 47, 74, 90, 147, 191
  Joseph N., 74

www.ingramcontent.com/pod-product-compliance
Lightning Source LLC
Chambersburg PA
CBHW020648300426
44112CB00007B/291